International Project Finance

A Legal and Financial Guide to Bankable Proposals

JOSEPH TANEGA, MPhil (Oxon)

PAWAN SHARMA
Associate, Debevoise and Plimpton

Tottel publishing

Published by
Tottel Publishing Ltd
Maxwelton House
41-43 Boltro Road
Haywards Heath
West Sussex
RH16 1BJ

ISBN: 978-1-84592-446-1

© Joseph Tanega and Pawan Sharma 2000
Formerly published by LexisNexis Butterworths

This edition reprinted by Tottel Publishing Ltd 2006

British Library Cataloguing-in-Publication Data.
A catalogue record for this book is available from the British Library.

Typeset by Doyle & Co, Colchester
Printed and bound in Great Britain by
Marston Book Services, Abingdon, Oxfordshire

Contents

Contents

Contents

8 Negotiating deal terms for transaction efficiency   156

Table of legislation and cases

1

Introduction

LEARNING OBJECTIVES

After reading this chapter you will be able to:

- *Explain what project finance is*
- *Distinguish between recourse and non-recourse financing*
- *Describe the various parties to a project finance transaction*

1.1 INTRODUCTION TO INTERNATIONAL PROJECT FINANCE

Project finance is not new. *Non-recourse* financing of commercial properties is a form of project finance. Toll roads and toll bridges involve a form of project finance that has been in existence for centuries. Many of the more commonly understood examples of project finance involve municipal utility projects such as turnpikes, water systems, sewer systems and electric utilities. In the 1980s, independent power projects and waste-to-energy projects were popular in the US. Power is still a major source of project finance projects, but the arena has moved primarily to Asia where the demands for new power capacity are tremendous. Similarly, proposed toll roads alone, worldwide, could generate more than $120 billion of financing within the next ten years, with the bulk of this divided among the US, Western Europe and Asia. In addition, numerous private ventures will be financed on a project finance basis. This is fast becoming a typical way of financing investments in the emerging and developing countries. However, while the growth in new public and private financing is expected to reach into hundreds of billions of dollars per year over the course of the next ten years, it is not without risk.

Project finance in emerging market countries

Asian Crisis 1997 With the collapse of the Thai Bhat in the summer of 1997 and the consequent falling domino effect across the South East Asian region, many large project finance deals were put on hold.

Russian Crisis 1998 In the summer of 1998, the Russian rouble collapsed and the Government unofficially 'defaulted' on its debts. Hundreds of projects were put on hold until the debts could be restructured. Western banks exposed to this whirlwind of change saw billions of US dollar assets collapse.

'Restructuring risk' is not the same as country risk, but recent experience means that project financiers need to take into account the real possibility that governments may default and that the actual cost of funding may need to be reassessed. This puts pressure on all parties to the transaction to come up with a co-ordinated solution that fairly apportions the risk.

1.2   WHAT IS PROJECT FINANCE?

The term 'project finance' is now being used in almost every language in every part of the world. It is the hoped for solution to infrastructure, public and private venture capital needs. It has been successfully used in the past to raise trillions of dollars of capital and promises to continue to be one of the major financing techniques for capital projects in both developed and developing countries.

Understanding the nature of project finance and how it differs from other financing techniques is critical to all the major players in large capital projects, such as commercial bankers, investment bankers, general contractors, sub-contractors, insurance companies, suppliers and customers. All these participants will become part of one seamless web of financing with mutual and multiple dependencies on each other's performance. Their contractual obligations become part of a network of obligations that supports the financing and each shares a different aspect of the risk and reward of the entire project. The result is ideally a financing that is supported by the project itself, together with numerous limited obligations of the participants. It is important to realise from the outset that there should not be a single 'deep pocket' for the creditors to look to for payment, otherwise this would be simply another form of loan based upon the security on non-project assets.

Project finance is the financing of a capital project *primarily* on the basis of its own revenues. It is emphasised 'primarily' because there will be limited guarantees or obligations from others, including project sponsors, contractors, customers or suppliers to cover certain financing risks. However, except for these specific, written guarantees or obligations, the financing will be *non-recourse*, which means that creditors can look only to the project and its revenues for payments.

The project financing, together with the equity from the project sponsors, must be sufficient in amount to pay all the design, construction, equipment and site costs and all other costs to bring the project to a stage of full operation, plus providing working capital for the project. The project financing may include equity investments from passive investors and, in practically all cases, will include substantial debt from passive investors. The equity provided by the project sponsors may be cash or may be in contributions of property, services or rights such as preliminary engineering, site improvements, site acquisition, technology transfers or limited guarantees to cover one or more identified project risks. Although every project financing will involve a project capable of generating revenues, the actual details and structures of project financing are as uniquely different and numerous as there are different types of projects.

A technical definition of project finance

Project finance borrowing means any borrowing to finance a project:

- ■ Which is made by a single-purpose entity whose principal assets and core businesses are made of that project and whose liabilities in respect of any such borrowing concerned are not directly or indirectly the subject of a guarantee, indemnity or any other form of assurance, undertaking, or support from any affiliate, associate, holding or subsidiary company;

- ■ In respect of which the individual or individuals making such borrowing available to the relevant borrower have no recourse whatsoever to any member of that entity for repayment or payment of any sum relating to such borrowing other than:
  - recourse to the borrower for amounts limited to aggregate cash flow or net cash flow from such project; and/or
  - recourse to the borrower for the purpose only of enabling amounts to be claimed in respect of that borrowing in an enforcement of any security interest given by the borrower over the assets comprised in the project to secure that borrowing, provided that:
  - the extent of such recourse to the borrower is limited to the amount of any recoveries made on any such enforcement, and
  - such individual or individuals are not entitled, by virtue of any right or claim arising out of or in connection with such borrowing, to commence proceedings for the winding-up or dissolution of the borrower or to appoint a receiver in respect of the borrower or any of its assets; and/or
  - recourse to such borrower generally under any form of completion assurance, guarantee, or undertaking which recourse is limited to a claim for damages for breach of such obligation by the person against whom such recourse is available;

- ■ And which the lender shall have agreed in writing to treat as a project finance borrowing.

1.3 DEGREE OF RECOURSE IS KEY DISTINCTION

One of the key differences between a project financing and a corporate financing lies in the extent of recourse to the borrower. In a project financing the extent of recourse is usually limited to a pool of project assets. In a corporate financing the lender will have recourse to all the assets to the extent that the same have been charged, assigned, pledged or hypothecated. In the event that the borrower fails to pay a debt when due, then subject to terms of the security interest created pursuant to the loan and/or security agreements, the lender is able to petition the court to wind up the borrower. The lender is also entitled under law to recover the value of the assets on a pari passu basis with all the other secured creditors, up to the full amount of the secured debt.

1.4   THE MYTH OF NON-RECOURSE

Strictly speaking non-recourse finance is extremely rare. In most project financing there is some, albeit limited, recourse beyond the assets that are being financed. For example, security may be in the amount to a full or partial completion guarantee, undertakings to cover cost overruns, comfort letters, or any other contractual agreement that explicitly covers a specific contingency during the life of the project.

Sometimes the only form of tangible support that a lender may receive over and above the project assets is a right to rescind the project loan agreement with the borrower. This leads to a claim of damages for breach of any of the undertakings, covenants, representations or warranties given by the borrower. Where the borrower is a specifically formed entity, such as a bankruptcy remote special purpose vehicle with no other assets other than the project assets, a right to claim for damages from the borrower is likely to add nothing to a claim under the project loan agreement. Where a borrower does have other assets, a lender may be afforded additional recourse through contractual claims for damages under the project loan agreement.

It must be remembered that from a lender's perspective a claim for damages under English law, and under most common law jurisdictions, is not the same as a claim for recovery of debt under, for example, a financial guarantee, warranty or undertaking. At a simple level a claim for damages is an unliquidated claim whereas recovery of a debt is liquidated. A claim for damages is subject to certain common law rules. Under *Hedley Byrne & Co Ltd v Heller & Partners Ltd*[1] the lender must show that the loss was caused by the breach in question and that the loss must have been reasonably foreseeable at the time the undertaking or warranty was given. In any case, the lender is under a duty to mitigate his loss. In the case of recovering a debt, the lender needs only to show that a loan was incurred or assumed by the borrower and that such is now due. Lenders therefore seek wherever possible to structure arrangements with the view of obtaining liquidated claims against borrowers.

The principle of limited recourse financing has been recognised under English law. Jessel MR in *Williams v Hathaway*[2] held that it was permissible to pay under a proviso to a covenant to limit the personal liability under the covenant without destroying it.

When choosing the method of financing a project there are always compelling reasons for selecting one method over another. Typically in a project financing the project sponsors seek to reduce and if possible eliminate any exposure to project debt (from a balance sheet perspective) and the risk of project failure. The opportunity to avoid project debt on the balance sheets is a strong driver for choosing project finance, especially in countries where accounting standards require accounting for 'substance' as in the UK pursuant to FRS5. Project sponsors may, on the other hand, wish to share in the risks of the project. This occurs in the case of multi-sponsor project risk sharing agreements which obviates contentious claims by apportioning an appropriate amount of risk to each party. Current loans and/or contractual commitments may restrict borrowers from borrowing funds in a conventional manner. Particular projects and jurisdictions may offer tax incentives such as tax holidays as well as concessions and therefore be a source of potentially high profits.

Concessionary agreements and licences enable host governments to promote project finance. Even in the best of economic climates, it is not easy for any government to attract foreign investment. However, project finance offers the opportunity to do this as well as to attract foreign skills and know-how, reduce public sector borrowing and enable the development of necessary infrastructure including health, education and welfare.

1   [1964] AC 465.
2   (1877) 6 Ch D 544.

1.5 PARTIES TO A PROJECT FINANCING

It would be useful to list and define the principal players in the typical project financing at the outset, as follows.

1.5.1 Project owner

The project owner is generally a corporation or limited partnership created for the sole purpose of owning the project. The particular legal form of this project entity (whether limited liability company, joint venture, partnership, or other legal form), is usually created under the laws of the country in which the project is located and is determined on the basis of the legal and regulatory framework of the host country, the tax situation and the tax planning of the project sponsors. The project owner will be at the centre of all contracts, borrowings and construction and operation of the project. Its only activity will be to own and operate the project. It will be controlled by its equity owners and how this control works may be set forth in its charter, a joint venture agreement or partnership agreement and may also be subject to local law governing the establishment of the particular kind of entity used.

The project company is frequently established in the form of a special purpose vehicle (SPV), in which case the lenders will expect a newly incorporated entity in the relevant jurisdiction and will seek to have restrictive covenants on the ability of the borrower to undertake any non-project activities. The purpose of this is to ensure that the lenders are not exposed to any existing or additional risks unrelated to the project. The typical types of covenants that a lender would undertake include the following provisions: dealing with further financial indebtedness (a negative pledge), creating or permitting additional security interests, entering into arrangements or other agreements unconnected with the project, lending money to third parties, altering accounting policies and periods, declaring or paying dividends, altering constitutional documents or the constitution and dissolving or establishing subsidiaries. Any of these acts would substantially increase the risk of non-repayment by the borrowers to the lenders.

1.5.2 Project sponsor

The project sponsor(s) is the person who expects to take the active role in managing the project. They generally become equity owners and will receive the upside profit either through their equity ownership or management contracts if the project succeeds. In most cases, the project sponsor brings operational and management resources to the project. However, a project sponsor could be a contractor, equipment supplier, local partner or a combination thereof. The project sponsor is often required to cover certain liabilities or risks of the project through limited guarantees or management or service agreements.

The involvement of strong or influential sponsors is crucial for most projects to succeed. The extent to which sponsors are involved differs for each project. For example, support may be given in the form of equity injections, comfort letters, technological support, pre- and post completion commitments or managerial support. Sponsors may include the host government, which may have a social and economic interest in the project. However, the normal case is that the host government will not participate directly in a project but rather through an agency or other vehicle in which it has an interest.

1.5.3 Lenders

These are the commercial banks, investment bankers or other institutional investors that provide the debt portion of the financing. In the case of international projects, major lenders include multinational organisations, such as the World Bank, the International Finance Corporation (the World Bank affiliate that finances private projects), the European Bank for Reconstruction and Development, the Asian Development Bank and similar organisations, and may also include export lenders or guarantors (such as the US Ex-Im Bank). Most nations have programmes to assist exporting equipment to foreign projects or to encourage project investments locally. These programmes need to be explored on a case-by-case basis, but will almost inevitably impact the make-up of the lender group and the financing. In some jurisdictions, such as the US, there are state and municipal-level programmes to encourage capital investments.

The sheer scale of a typical project financing means that the financing cannot be undertaken by one single financial institution. Rather in most cases syndicates of lenders are formed, which will include a number of domestic lenders. In a typical syndication, a number of banks will be parties to the loan agreement and will act as the arranging banks. By doing so they take the risk of underwriting the loan, ie being able to down sell the loan to a number of other participators in the syndicate.

1.5.4 Facility agent

One of the lenders will be appointed as the facility agent for the purpose of administrating the loan on behalf of the syndicate. The role tends to be more than it seems in that project financings are inevitably complex. However, the facility agent is very unlikely to assume legal liability of the other lenders in connection with the project since their role will be limited to administrative and mechanical matters.

1.5.5 Technical bank

Unlike the facility agent, a technical bank will usually have the responsibility of calculating and assessing the coverage ratios, monitoring the general progress of the project, liaising with technical advisers to the project and being responsible for technical monitoring and identifying events of default.

1.5.6 Insurance bank

The insurance bank undertakes negotiations in connection with project insurances. Acting for itself and as agent for the syndicate members, it will liaise with the insurance adviser and ensure that the lender's position is fully covered in terms of project insurance.

1.5.7 Account bank

The account bank will be the bank through which all project cash flows pass and are recorded, ie for purposes of collection and disbursements.

1.5.8   Equity investors

These may be any of the lenders mentioned above or any of the candidates for project sponsor who do not expect to have an active management role as the project goes forward and becomes an operating business. In effect, in the case of lenders, they are putting equity alongside their debt as a way to obtain an enhanced return if the project is successful. In most cases, the equity investment is combined with agreements that allow the equity investor to sell its equity to the project owner if the equity investor wishes to get out. There also may be options on behalf of the project owner to repurchase the equity if the owner wishes to do so.

Third party investors normally look to invest in a project on a much longer time scale than a contractor who in most cases will want to sell out once the construction has reached completion. Many third party investors are development or equity funds, which diversify their portfolios by investing in a number of projects. These entities take an active role in the management of a project by appointing members of their own organisations to the board of the project company.

1.5.9   Customers, suppliers and contractors

These include the major customer or customers of the project, the engineers and contractors responsible for designing and building the project and the suppliers of raw materials involved in producing the product, such as fuel, and power. Any or all of these parties may be contractually part of the financing. For example, in a power project the power purchase agreement with the utility customer will be crucial to the financing. Long-term fuel or other supply contracts may be critical as well. As discussed below, the contractors in most projects will be asked to take on special obligations.

1.5.10   Construction company

In the case of an infrastructure project the contractor will be one of the key project parties during the construction period. Typically a constructor's remit will be based either on the 'turnkey model' – to design, engineer, procure and construct the project facility assuming all responsibility for on-time completion – or the 'EPC model' – to engineer, procure, and construct but not design the project facility.

In either case the contractor will invariably be a company well known in its field and with a track record for constructing similar facilities, ideally with a well-regarded profile and in the same part of the world. In large infrastructure projects, consortia of contractors may become involved in the project, which will either take jointly and severally or severally all the liability as if one contractor were involved. Lenders in this case prefer consortiums of contractors to undertake joint and several liability since the risk of failure of performance is the total responsibility of each member of the consortium.

Most projects are structured on the basis that only one turnkey or EPC contractor will be employed. Although there will be a number of subordinated designers, contractors, and sub-contractors, they will all be guided by one project manager. This hierarchical structure simplifies reporting lines and helps focus the allocation of resources and co-ordinate control.

1.5.11   Regulatory agencies

Project finance projects are subject to all the regulations of the local jurisdiction, such as environmental, zoning, permits and taxes, to name but a few. Publicly owned projects also will be subject to various procurement and public contract laws. In the US, tax exempt financing may be available but will subject the project to additional approvals and restrictions. International projects present equal or greater levels of required approvals, such as investment approvals by central government, the relevant ministries and licensing authorities. In developing countries there may also be required currency exchange and supplier, offtake and concession approvals and agreements.

1.5.12   Multilateral and export credit agencies

Numerous projects are co-financed by the World Bank or its investment banking arm, the International Finance Corporation (IFC), and regional development banks such as the European Bank for Reconstruction and Development, the Asian Development Bank (ADB) and the African Development Bank. These multilateral agencies are able to ensure the bankability of a project financing by providing international commercial banks with a degree of protection against a variety of political risks, including the failure of a host government to make agreed payments or to provide necessary regulatory approvals.

Multilateral agencies may also put political pressure on host governments, since no host government wants to be seen by other governments as failing to make payments.

Export credit agencies play important roles in infrastructure and other projects in emerging markets by stimulating international trade. These agencies normally provide low cost financing arrangements to local manufacturers who wish to transport their technology to foreign lands.

1.5.13   Host governments

At a minimum the host government is likely to be involved through the issuance of consents and permits both at the outset of the project and on a periodic basis throughout the duration of the project. They may also be offering preferential rights to access of local infrastructure or suppliers and help set the floor level prices of offtake agreements for the purchase of the project's products over a term of years.

1.5.14   Purchasers

In infrastructure projects the project company will normally contract in advance with an identified purchaser to purchase the project's output on a long-term basis. For example, in a gas project there may be a long-term gas offtake agreement with a gas purchaser. Similarly, in a power project the purchaser/offtaker may be the regional or domestic energy authority which through the use of a power purchase agreement may contract to purchase the output of the project on a long-term basis.

In some projects essential supplies to the project are purchased by the project company and sold on a 'take-or-pay' basis, where the purchaser assumes the risks of the goods even though they may have not or will not be delivered at some future date.

1.5.15 Insurers

Insurers play a crucial role in most projects. If there is a major catastrophe or casualty affecting the project then the sponsor and the lenders will look to the insurers to cover them against loss.

Checklist: Practical Tips

This checklist is intended to highlight the various issues and steps involved in a project financing. It is not, however, a substitute for professional representation in any specific situation.

- Assemble your own team of experienced advisers to assist you in project financing. Don't depend on the other players to tell you how the structure will or should work – their own self-interest will be reflected in their suggestions!

- Evaluate the strength and weaknesses of the proposed participants. Strong well-known participants will be better able to withstand additional costs when the going gets tough. Their actions will be more predictable and the team efforts required are more likely to succeed.

- Evaluate the project technology. Does it have a properly evaluated track record? In general, unproven technology needs deep pockets.

- Review the financial projections to satisfy yourself that the financing will be viable. Chapter 3 and the Business Plan Form in Chapter 7 are devoted to these issues.

- Review all the special risks, such as country risk, currency exchange, currency valuations and other risks which could severely impact the project.

- Work with US agencies (AID, Ex-Im Bank, UNCTAD, Commerce Department), the World Bank and other government sponsored agencies to evaluate international projects and identify special funding sources.

- For US projects, contact state and local agencies to help evaluate the prospects of the project and to discover other funding sources. This guidance applies to other jurisdictions which are currently promoting project finance schemes, such as the UK, Germany, France and Italy.

- Ensure that you understand not only your own contract obligations to the project, but also to what extent and which other parties will be able to cover obligations. Mapping the various obligations on a chart visually is not only helpful but perhaps the easiest way of comprehending the network of relationships.

- Make sure the other participants have the capability and incentive to fulfil their obligations to the project.

- Consider carefully the ability of the project to receive all necessary governmental approvals (eg environmental, zoning, permits and taxes). In international projects the list of approvals is often longer and not always clearly revealed in laws and regulations.

- Finally, make sure you can deliver on each and every obligation you accept for the project.

1.6   THE UK PFI MODEL

A great many of the projects financed under the UK Government's Private Finance Initiative (PFI) have in fact been financed using the BOT model or one of its many variants. These have involved the appropriate government department (or public sector body) granting concessions to the project sponsors to undertake the project for an agreed term of years. Typical examples include roads and prisons. In the case of roads, the government department is the Highways Agency, which has granted a number of concessions to sponsors to build, upgrade or maintain roads for the agreed concession period and then to retransfer the assets at the end of the concession period back to the relevant government department. Likewise, in the case of prisons, the Secretary of State for the Home Department has granted a number of concessions to private investors to build and operate prisons on a privatised basis for the duration of the concession. At the end of the concession, the prison is transferred back to the Secretary of State.

One of the key features of a number of the large infrastructure PFI projects which have already been undertaken is the composition of the sponsor groups. These projects usually have a joint venture form, with the sponsor groups normally including a leading contractor, a leading facilities management company, often an investment bank (which may have arranged the financing) and other companies providing specialist services called for by the particular project (for example, information technology, security or equipment supply). In most other respects, these projects follow the structure adopted for other BOT concession-based projects, with the lenders looking to the terms of the concession agreement as their principal source of security but, in addition, taking security over all other available project assets.

Another feature of recent PFI projects is the UK Government's desire to attract outside equity investment into these projects (so-called third party equity). The aim of the government is that the third party investors will form a nucleus of long-term investors in the project (in contrast to, say, the contractor, who in many cases will want to dispose of all or a majority of its shares following completion of the construction phase). Specialist PFI funds and development/venture capital institutions are starting to invest in PFI projects alongside the sponsor group.

1.7   UK PRIVATE FINANCE INITIATIVE PROJECTS

1.7.1   History

The Private Finance Initiative was officially launched by the UK Conservative Government in November 1992. By 1996, more than 1,000 potential projects, with an aggregate value of more than £27bn, had been identified in the UK. The initiative grew from the idea that private contractors should not only build infrastructure (as was traditionally the case) but also be responsible for maintaining and servicing it.

The thinking was that the subsequent obligation to maintain a particular road, hospital, building or railway line would motivate the builder to build to higher standards and, conversely, the opportunity to manage the asset at a fee payable by the public sector would provide a return on the capital investment. After a period of the contractor managing the asset (so as to give the contractor a return on his capital investment), the asset is returned to the public sector. Most PFI contracts are of medium or long-term duration and signed UK projects range from 7 to 99 years.

One of the first areas in which PFI contracts were developed was roads where the contracts were structured as Design Build Finance & Operate ('DBFO') contracts. The transport sector has seen the majority of PFI projects, with the Channel Tunnel Rail Link the largest at £2.7bn. Following on from the rail and roads examples, the idea has been applied to schools, hospitals, prisons, museums and social housing.

Despite initial indications to the contrary, the new Labour Government of 1997 decided to continue the PFI programme, although on a more limited basis. It launched a review chaired by Malcolm Bates and is currently in the process of implementing all its recommendations.

Some of the planned roads projects have already been scrapped and various plans have been adopted to streamline the process so that top priority projects are implemented first.

1.7.2   Parties

The parties commonly involved in UK PFI and their roles are described below.

Treasury

The Treasury funds PFI projects and its officials are responsible for policy development. They determine the discount rate that has to be used to determine the NPV of a project and this will determine whether or not a project goes ahead.

Private Finance Panel and 4Ps

PFI for central government projects is promoted by the Private Finance Panel (PFP), a quasi-governmental body funded by the Treasury, and PFI for local authorities by the Public Private Partnership Panel (the '4Ps'). The PFP is staffed by a combination of Treasury employees and industry and the 4Ps mainly by local authority councillors. Both bodies are considered the first port of call by tenderers and are influential in recommending particular professional advisers. The Labour Government has replaced the PFP by a new central Treasury-based taskforce with effect from September 1997. The taskforce will assess each project for financial viability before it is put out to tender.

Government agency

A PFI project can fall under the auspices of either a central government department, a local government body that derives its authority from central government, or a quasi-governmental body such as the National Health Service. The relevant agency is responsible for drawing up specifications and the terms of the tender, selecting a short list from the bidders and a contractor. It will establish a project team for this task to handle the day-to-day management of the project and a project board to oversee progress. Another team will monitor the performance of the contractor and the PFI contract will entitle them to inspect and test any aspect of the project facilities, attend meetings of the contractor and audit its records and reports.

Project company or contractor

A number of private sector companies will form a consortium and set up a project company or contractor, usually a special purpose vehicle, to tender for the PFI transaction. The consortium participants are called sponsors and their respective rights and obligations as shareholders of the special purpose vehicle will be set out in a shareholders' agreement. The sponsors provide equity funding and their shareholdings will be in proportion to their involvement or commitment to the project. The sponsors will be most concerned with the risks being taken on by the contractor project company.

Funders

Most of the funding in UK PFI transactions has come from banks providing loan facilities. Banks already have the analytical and structuring skills necessary for PFI deals because of its similarity to straightforward project finance. For very long-term projects, banks will generally look for stable and predictable cash flow. This, and the fact that the market for loans exceeding 20 years in length is limited, inevitably excludes some projects and has caused some sponsors to look elsewhere for finance.

1.7.3   PFI negotiation procedure – a summary

Potential tenderers should be given a minimum of 37 days to respond to the advertisement in the Official Journal. The government agency must then select a minimum of three bidders and invite them to negotiate (the ITN stage). They should be selected on the basis of their economic or financial standing or technical capacity. A pre-qualification questionnaire may be used in this process to weed out any unqualified bidders. An Information Memorandum will outline the format in which responses would be made and the criteria that will be used to select the shortlist of at least three. These bidders will each be asked to submit a preliminary bid and these bids may then be discussed in clarifying negotiations. This may be followed by creating a further shortlist and giving each of these bidders a formal Invitation to Tender (the M stage). No more than four bidders will be invited to the FIT stage. These bids are then evaluated in accordance with published criteria and a successful bidder selected. The bidder will be selected on the basis that they presented the most economically advantageous, and not necessarily the lowest, bid.

The process has been criticised as very lengthy and costly and one of the main criticisms of the PFI programme in the UK has been the high cost of tendering. Sponsors have called for the government agency to share the costs of the tender with the tenderers after the shortlisting stage.

2

Key project risks

LEARNING OBJECTIVES

After reading this chapter you will be able to:

- *Identify major project risks*
- *Allocate project risks amongst the project participants*
- *Determine the use and significance of securities and guarantees*

2.1 INTRODUCTION TO PROJECT RISKS[1]

In writing a bankable proposal, the sponsor must address the specific risks of the project with the aim of presenting a clear plan of how to overcome them, either by mitigation or by laying them off to other parties. Before we discuss what these risks are, the rationale and methodologies for determining project risks will be examined.

2.1.1 Identification and allocation of risks

The essence of any project financing is the identification of all key risks associated with the project and the apportionment of those risks among the various parties participating in the project. Without a detailed analysis of these project risks at the outset, the parties do not have a clear understanding of what obligations and liabilities they may be assuming in connection with the project and therefore they are not in a position to consider appropriate risk-mitigation exercises at the relevant time. Should problems arise when the project is under way, it can result in considerable delays, large expenses and arguments as to who is responsible.

1 The source for the ideas on project risks is quoted with kind permission from Gregg Haddock (May 1995) 'Financing Renewable Energy Projects' in *Innovative Financing Schemes for Energy and Environmental Technology and Services*, Workshop Tuesday, 11 April 1995 Proceedings, Luxembourg-Kirchberg, Chambre des Metiers, European Commission, Directorate-General XVII – Energy.

Thus the sponsors will be particularly concerned to ensure that they have identified and understood all the risks that they will be assuming in connection with the project. They will want to be certain that they are able effectively to manage and monitor these risks in a cost-efficient manner. In situations where they are not able to do so, they may transfer these risks onto another party involved in the project, which is better able to manage any particular risks (perhaps a supplier, contractor or purchaser of products). Alternatively, where it is not possible to transfer the risk, the sponsors may find some other way of managing the risk such as by taking out insurance or, more radically, by altering the structure of the project in order to reduce or extinguish the risk.

The lenders will have similar concerns. Additionally, they will need to consider these issues:

■   when assuming any risks associated with a particular project, they will need to be satisfied that there are no regulatory constraints imposed on them by any of the authorities which regulate their activities or pursuant to laws applicable to them;

■   they may have to report non-credit risks assumed by them in connection with their activities to their regulatory authorities; and

■   generally speaking, the more risk that a lender is expected to assume in connection with a project, the greater the reward in terms of interest and fees they will expect to receive from the project.

The task of identifying and analysing risks in a project is not one that can be left to any one party or their advisers. Rather, it is likely to involve the project parties themselves, accountants, lawyers, engineers and other experts, all of whom will need to give their input and advice on the risks involved and how they might be managed. Only when the risks have been identified can the principal parties (the sponsors and the banks) decide which parties should bear which risks and on what terms and at what price.

2.1.2 Ground rules

There are some ground rules that should be observed by the parties involved in a project when determining which party should assume a particular risk:

■   a detailed risk analysis should be undertaken at an early stage;

■   risk allocation should be undertaken prior to detailed work on the project documentation.

As a general rule, a particular risk should be assumed by the party best able to manage and control that risk. For instance, the risk of cost overruns and delays in construction projects are best managed by the main contractor. In a power project, the power purchaser (if a state entity) is the best position to assume the risks associated with a grid failure and consequent electricity supply problems.

Risks should not be 'parked' with the project company, especially where the project company is a special purpose vehicle. The point here is that where there is a disagreement between, say, the fuel supplier and a power purchaser in a power project over who should assume a particular risk, there may be a temptation to park the risk in question with the project company. However, this is simply storing up problems for the future as the project company will rarely be in a position to manage or control that risk, let alone pay for it.

Due to their complexity, each project will have a different risk profile, that is, each project will have different kinds of risks and the magnitude of risks will differ from project to project. In general, however, there are some major areas of risk which every proposer should be aware of and should keep in mind when planning to write a bankable proposal.

The following is a list of some of the key project risks encountered in different types of projects. Of course, not all of these risks will necessarily be encountered in each project, but it is likely that most projects will need to consider one or more of these risks and decide by whom these risks are to be assumed and how. It has already been seen earlier in this section that, once these risks have been identified, it is through the various contractual arrangements between the parties that these risks are, for the most part, apportioned and assumed:

- sponsor risk;
- pre-completion risk;
- completion or construction risk;
- technology risk;
- input or supply risk;
- operational risk;
- approvals, regulatory and environmental risk;
- market, offtake and sales risk;
- reserve and production risk;
- counterparty risk;
- political risk;
- legal and structural risk.

The bank will expect a clear analysis of each of these risks from the sponsor and how the sponsor thinks he can mitigate them. Each of these risks is discussed in turn.

2.1.3 Sponsor risk

Sponsor risk is extremely important and recent discussions with project lending banks suggest that it is becoming more rather than less important in the current market. Sponsor risk is closely associated with completion risk. The bank's view on completion risk will be strongly influenced by their view of sponsor risk.

Sponsor risk may be broken down into two elements:

- equity commitment; and
- corporate strength and experience (so-called 'corporate substance').

Regarding equity, lenders will normally require a contribution of anything from 15 per cent to 50 per cent of the project cost to ensure the sponsor's continued commitment.

Regarding corporate substance, regardless of whether the lender is seeking pre-completion guarantees from the sponsor, the banks predictably like to work with corporate sponsors with substantial technical expertise and financial 'depth'.

The backstop value to a bank of a sponsor who can commit resources, either financial or technical, to turning around a problematic project is very great. Therefore entrepreneur sponsors of industrial projects – who will often not have the same corporate 'substance' as major companies – should anticipate and prepare for a discussion with potential lenders on this issue.

The attitude of potential lenders towards sponsor risk is a key factor in steering many sponsors towards inviting a more substantial sponsor to enter into a joint venture arrangement. This will usually have the effect of reducing sponsor risk in the eyes of a potential lender. Smaller sponsors should not assume, however, that it will be a waste of time to approach bankers before the support of a more substantial partner has been negotiated. This is especially true for smaller sized projects which are not dependent on large infrastructure development. On the contrary – if the original sponsor is aware in detail of the type and extent of support the banks will require from the equity investor(s) in a project, it will be in a much stronger position when negotiating the terms of any joint venture with a new partner. Indeed, banks may be very helpful in finding potential joint venture partners, as will a good financial adviser.

2.1.4 Pre-completion risk

Banks are willing in certain circumstances to assume pre-completion risk for projects, ie they may be prepared for their lending to be limited in recourse to the project itself before completion occurs. Acceptance of pre-completion risk is by no means the norm however. Often banks will require some kind of external recourse until completion, for example, a guarantee from third parties such as the owners of a project-owning joint venture company. Entrepreneur sponsors in particular should therefore be prepared for lender concern on the issue of pre-completion risk as they will usually not be able to offer blanket guarantees of such risks which would be acceptable to the lender. The sponsor, possibly with the help of a financial adviser, should analyse the pre-completion risk issues likely to be raised by potential debt providers and should be in a position to demonstrate that:

■ the pre-completion risks involved are modest;

■ everything possible has been done to mitigate these risks or to lay them off elsewhere.

Lenders will require adequate insurance to be in place against physical damage, consequential loss and third party and public liability. Such insurance is important during the pre-completion, completion and operation phases. A good insurance adviser will be able to assist in this area.

2.1.5 Completion risk

In any infrastructure project involving a construction element this is likely to be one of the key risks. In essence, the risk is whether or not the project can be built on time, on budget and in accordance with the applicable specifications and design criteria. In assessing these risks, the lenders will, in particular, look at the overall contract structure and the identity of the parties involved.

Lenders will focus upon the cost overrun and time delay risks of project completion in great detail. This is the period of highest risk for lenders. They may face a total write-off in respect of a project which never produces cash flow. Lenders will seek to minimise this risk by requiring fixed-price 'turnkey' contracts to be negotiated with the contractors. They will also analyse whether the various contractors are financially sound and whether their obligations are covered by performance bonds or third party sureties. It may be possible, subject to the robustness of the project economics, to pre-agree a debt-funded cost overrun contingency facility, or indeed to raise additional equity up-front to cover this risk.

The key areas likely to be of concern to the lenders are:

- **Type of contract**   Is the construction contract a turnkey contract with a prime contractor, or are the works being undertaken by a series of sub-contractors on a project management basis? Lenders have a strong preference for turnkey arrangements as this avoids gaps appearing in the contract structure and disputes between the sub-contractors as to where particular risks lie. Lenders will also prefer, where appropriate, that the contractor assume responsibility for the design element of the works (in contrast to the position taken under an EPC contract where the contractor does not undertake the design work). This means that the project company and the lenders can look to one party for all aspects of the construction works during the construction period.

- **Fixed price lump sum contracts**   Project lenders have a clear preference for fixed price lump sum contracts as this reduces the likelihood of cost overruns being the responsibility of the project company. If there are to be any changes to the contract price, the lenders will want to have a say on this, particularly if this is as a result of changes to specifications on the part of the project company.

- **Completion date**   The lenders will want to ensure that there is a fixed date for completion with minimum tolerance. If there are to be any delays, then the lenders will want to see the liquidated damages in an amount sufficient to cover the project company's costs of servicing the loans and operating costs during the period of the delay. In reality, however, it is seldom possible to obtain full coverage in terms of liquidated damages and what is generally negotiated is a fixed per diem amount for an agreed period. Under English law, a distinction is drawn between liquidated damages clauses, which amount to a genuine pre-estimate of the damage likely to result from a delay, and clauses which penalise the contractor unfairly. A clause will generally be considered to be a penalty clause if the amount specified in the contract is extravagant and unconscionable compared with the greatest loss that could be conceived to have flowed from the breach. The term used in the contract will be irrelevant-it is the substance of the clause that will be taken into consideration. In addition, a penalty may arise where compensation is by way of a single lump sum payable on the occurrence of one or more events. The lender should therefore make sure that the liquidated damages are set at a realistic rate and also that provision is made for the assignment of these rights to it. Further, the risk of any delays that are not the fault of the project company will need to be addressed in any other project contracts that the project company is a party to. For example, if there is a delay as a result of a force majeure event which delays construction, then the force majeure provisions in any offtake contract under which the project company is required to deliver products from the project must take account of such delays.

- **Force majeure**   Force majeure provisions must be reasonable and the contractor should take all steps to circumvent the problem. They must not arise as a result of an action or inaction on the part of the contractor or contracting consortium.

- **Bonding requirements**   Lenders will normally require the contractor to place a bond to the value of 20–25 per cent of the contract price in order to cover appropriate performance of defect liability.

2.1.6 Technology risk

Banks pay a great deal of attention to technology risk. Because of their risk-reward relationship with a project, bankers are keen to limit risk and, in particular, they will always seek to avoid accepting risks which should properly be taken by the equity owners of the project. Any technology which is at the leading edge of current practice will be placed in this category. As a technology becomes more established banks may become comfortable with the predictability of the processes involved and on the rare occasion begin to accept the technology risk. However, project sponsors should be prepared for a detailed examination of the technology risk issue by potential debt-providers, even for such technologies, and should seek to demonstrate in their initial paper:

■ that the technology has a satisfactory track record;

■ that the contractor building the project has experience of the technology;

■ the adequacy of the guarantees and warranties which have been negotiated;

■ the ease with which maintenance and, if necessary, component replacement can be carried out;

■ that the availability and efficiency levels predicted can be easily achieved.

Potential lenders may also require the opinion of an independent technical consultant to the project.

2.1.7 Input and supply risk

The input and supply risk is the risk relating to the provision of the relevant source of energy and raw materials to the project in question. Where there is a distinct (and finite) supply of fuel for a project, bankers will look for an independent corroboration of the sponsor's reserve figures by a reputable consultant. Given the risk-reward relationship the banker has with the project, he will typically wish to concentrate on any 'core' reserves which have the highest degree of certainty and to have his debt repaid well within the predicted economic life of these reserves. Even when there is no reserve factor to be considered project sponsors should, when approaching potential financiers, be prepared to demonstrate the security of supply arrangements, including the basis of pricing of the fuel. The sponsors' presentation should show that the assumptions made relating to the quantities and pricing of fuel are conservative and that even on this basis the proposed debt can be retired with a significant margin of safety. Lenders usually wish to take security over any fuel supply contracts and this factor should be borne in mind by sponsors when contracts are being drawn up.

2.1.8 Operational risk

Operational risk is the risk to the forecasted cash flow arising from the failure of operations of the project. Just as banks will wish to ensure that the contractor employed to construct a project is competent and financially sound, they will also wish to satisfy themselves that the operating team engaged to run the project is skilled in the employment of the relevant technology and able to deal with all foreseeable situations, whether they are routine or require additional inputs of skills and resources.

Banks are often reassured when a project sponsor employs a third party operations and maintenance ('O&M') contractor, because of the deeper reserves of skills and personnel which this can make available to a project and because O&M costs can thereby be contractually fixed. Sponsors are well advised to consider this option, even though it may involve greater expense, because of the additional comfort factor which it provides to lenders.

Sponsors should also take great care to review the efficiency levels, downtimes and outages which are predicted in the cash flows they provide to banks. It is better to predict easily achievable levels of efficiency and availability and refer to the higher levels which may be achieved than to present a base case with levels set at the high end of what can be achieved, even if the sponsor thinks that these targets can be met.

Issues of concern to the lenders are:

- Who is the operator?

- Does the project company have the necessary expertise to manage and operate the project?

- How are operating costs to be managed? Who is responsible for increases in operating costs?

- Is the operator also responsible for maintaining the facility or is there a separate maintenance contractor? As with construction contracts, the lenders will be concerned that any breach of the operating agreement by the operator will give rise to liquidated damages at an acceptable level; and

- Do the force majeure provisions in the operating agreement tie in with the other project agreements to which the project company is a party? In particular, any delays in production as a result of operating problems should not be at the risk of the project company.

Not every project will have an independent operator and sometimes the project company itself will also be the operator. While this reduces the risk of an additional party default, clearly the lenders will want to be satisfied that the project company has the experience and resources available to it to operate the project facility properly and to manage this risk.

There is a temptation to think that once the project has been completed on time and on budget the operational stage of the project should be plain sailing. There are, however, many examples to show that this is far from being the case and the recent unhappy experiences with Eurotunnel demonstrate what disasters can lie in store during this period.

2.1.9 Approvals, regulatory and environmental risk

The risk of not obtaining necessary regulatory approvals to begin a project should be considered conditions precedent to any proposal. There is also the risk that other regulatory risks, such as environmental risk, may live to haunt the lenders if the project should fail and decontamination costs have to be borne by the lender who takes possession of the security in order to satisfy the outstanding loan. The environmental and regulatory considerations should be explicitly set out in the bankable proposal and are to be found in the relevant sections of the Bankable Proposal Form in Chapter 7. In this section, we shall discuss the concerns which bankers have in regards to this risk.

Lenders are increasingly concerned to protect themselves against the consequences of a project breaching official consents and guidelines, especially in the environmental field. It is already the case in the US and the UK that lenders who take possession of their security when a project fails to perform may themselves be liable for the legal consequences of pollution caused by that project. The position is not so hard and fast in other countries, but bankers are concerned that the increasing trend towards environmental regulation at all levels of government – local, national and supranational – might increase the danger of them being forced to meet vast claims arising out of pollution caused by borrowers.

It is essential, therefore, when approaching a potential lender to prepare and present full details of all consents and approvals – planning, environmental, generating licence, etc – which are expected to be required and the status of the efforts being made to obtain such consents. Evidence should also be provided of the ability of the proposed project to meet all present and likely future constraints and limits. Foreseeing what environmental and planning agencies might impose by way of constraints in the future is clearly not an easy task. However, a banker being asked to rely on a project's cash flow for repayment over, say, a seven-year period will wish to assess and limit the risk of the project being closed down by environmental regulators when the debt raised to build it is only partly repaid.

Banks will not necessarily require all consents and approvals to be in place before they will negotiate a financing structure, but sponsors should expect the granting of all necessary consents to be a condition precedent to be fulfilled before any loan funds can be drawn.

Sponsors should expect potential lenders to take detailed legal advice on this issue.

Checklist: Environmental costs

In addition to the fines and penalties for pollution, environmental costs could include:

■ fees payable to regulatory and licensing bodies;

■ the cost of preparing environmental impact assessments to obtain planning permission for major projects;

■ the cost of taking out insurance to cover the risk of environmental damage and compliance with associated risk management techniques required by insurers;

■ the cost of compliance with new packaging and labelling requirements;

■ the implementation of strategies for good environmental management and practice, eg through environmental audit programmes;

■ the cost of using best available technology or techniques not entailing excessive cost to prevent or minimise pollution from industrial processes;

■ loss of profits arising from the forced shut-downs of plant;

■ clean-up costs of polluted sites and civil liabilities for damage to property, health or the environment;

■ loss of value due to contamination of land;

■ increased waste disposal, handling and transportation costs; and

■ the imposition of environmental taxes on the use of non-renewable resources or the production of polluting products (note, for example, the incentives created by the differential taxes imposed in the UK on leaded and unleaded petrol respectively).

2.1.10 Market, offtake and sales risk

Market risk

There are two principal elements here. First, there is the risk that there is no market for the products of the project. Second, there is the risk that the price at which the products can be sold is insufficient to service the project debt. Many projects are structured in such a way that long-term offtake contracts are entered into with third parties on terms such that this risk is wholly or partially covered. For example, in an independent power project, the project may be structured so that a power purchase contract is entered into with the local state energy authority with a pricing mechanism containing a component which covers both the operating costs of the project company as well as its debt-servicing requirements (usually called a 'capacity charge' or 'availability charge'). A properly structured contract will provide for the offtaker to assume the credit risk in these circumstances thus removing most of the market risk for the lenders.

Offtake and sales risk

The offtake and sales risk is the risk that the project may fail to generate adequate income. A lender can only be repaid when a project is generating cash and therefore banks have an acute interest in all aspects of the offtake or sales risk. Only in rare cases will project lenders accept the 'volume' risk, that is, the danger that the output from a given project will not find a purchaser at all. Whether or not they will accept the risk of an acceptable price being achieved for the project's output will depend on a number of factors including the maturity of the market for such products and the volatility of prices in such markets. Both of these factors should be stated in the bankable proposal.

For example, the availability of long-term, guaranteed-price power purchase contracts is a key element in substantially eliminating the volume and price risks from energy projects. Some contracts may offer banks an outstanding offtake agreement whereby the purchaser of the energy is of undoubted financial standing and the generator has the ability to set output pricing over the life of the contract.

Sponsors should expect lenders as a general rule to require the repayment of their loans during the life of any such preferential offtake contract or, if they are prepared to consider having a portion of the debt repaid after the volume and price risk have re-emerged, to take a very conservative view of likely price trends.

Sponsors should also take into account that lenders will almost certainly wish to take a security interest in sale contracts.

Where there are no guaranteed offtake arrangements, then the lenders will usually have the following concerns:

■ Is there a ready market for the project's products? For example, in an oil project the market risk is more a price risk than a purchaser risk as there is an international spot market for oil. Of course, there may be a problem if a field is producing low-grade hydrocarbons oil as this will not be so readily saleable. Gas, on the other hand, is traditionally not traded on a spot basis but on a long-term basis (largely because it is considerably more difficult to handle and so to transport) and therefore lenders are much more likely to be looking at long-term gas offtake contracts.

■ In power projects in emerging markets, electricity is invariably sold under long-term purchase agreements (usually entered into with the local state energy authority). A recent development has been the structuring and financing of a number of so-called merchant power plants which do not have the benefit of long-term offtake contracts, although these are likely to be restricted to projects in certain developed countries having specific (favourable) characteristics.

■ Part of the market risk will be how the products are going to be transported to the purchasers. Obviously this will depend greatly on the type of project in question. Lenders will want to see proper arrangements in place so that there is no (or little) risk of them assuming the consequences of delays in the transportation process.

Take-or-pay contracts

One of the ingenious devices created (or perhaps borrowed) by project financiers for managing market risk in some projects is the use of 'take-or-pay' contracts. This is a contract entered into between the project company and a third party whereby the third party agrees to take delivery of a minimum amount of products of the project over a period of years and to pay for those products whether or not it actually takes delivery of them. Lenders will try to ensure that these contracts contain 'hell-or-high-water' clauses so that the offtaker is obliged to pay for the products notwithstanding any default by the project company or otherwise.

The incentive for the offtaker to enter project company such contracts will be the desire to obtain certainty of supply in circumstances and at a price which otherwise might be unavailable to it. Alternatively, the offtaker may be a shareholder or otherwise related to the project company, so that it is prepared to assume certain project risks. Take-or-pay contracts can be extremely valuable and can amount, in effect, to a virtual financial guarantee of the loan during the operating period. Questions have been raised in some jurisdictions as to whether such contracts amount to a penalty and are therefore unenforceable. The better view, as a matter of English law, appears to be that they should not be struck down as penalties and that freedom of contract should prevail.

Take-or-pay contracts have been used in a great many project financings and in many different guises. Most commonly, they are used as a means of financing pipelines and other projects where the project's assets are being shared (and therefore financed) by a number of different users. Many power-purchase agreements are effectively structured on a take-or-pay basis.

2.1.11 Reserve and production risk

In some projects, such as hydrocarbons and minerals projects, one of the most important risks will be the reserves risk and, allied to that, the degree of difficulty in extracting those reserves. As part of the process of evaluating such a project, the lenders will invariably employ a reserves engineer to analyse the geology and structure of a hydrocarbons reservoir or minerals deposit, as appropriate.

As part of this process, lenders would expect to see the reserves classified by the engineer into various industry-wide categories. Thus, a lender would expect to see a classification into proven reserves (or 'P90 reserves' – the likelihood of recovery exceeding the stated figure is deemed to be 90 per cent), probable reserves (or 'P50 reserves' – there is a 50 per cent chance that ultimate recovery will be greater than the stated value) and 'possible reserves'. In calculating how much they are prepared to lend on a project, lenders will generally only take account of proven reserves and occasionally (in an otherwise robust project) a small slice of probable reserves.

Lenders will not only be concerned about the classification of reserves but also, as mentioned above, the likely degree of difficulty in extracting those reserves, particularly where new technology or drilling is involved. Thus, even in the case of proven reserves, these will be subject to the further caveat that they must be 'economically recoverable'. A typical definition of economically recoverable reserves might be:

> 'Economically recoverable reserves' means, at any time, those quantities of proven reserves of crude oil, gas and natural gas liquids which are projected and estimated in the most recent banking case as being capable of being won and saved from wells in the field under existing economic and operating conditions, that is, prices and costs prevailing at that time during the period from the effective date of such banking case until the final economic production date, being the day preceding that six-month period during which it is estimated and projected in the current banking

case that forecast net cash flow will be negative for such six-month period and will remain negative on a cumulative basis thereafter.'

Even when the lender has established to its satisfaction that it is lending against proven reserves which are economically recoverable, the prudent project lender will not lend against 100 per cent of those reserves and will exclude the 'reserve tail' (the last 25 per cent or 30 per cent) as a further comfort zone.

2.1.12   Counterparty risk

This category of risk overlaps with a number of the categories above but it is convenient to isolate it by way of example. This is the risk that any counterparty with which the project company contracts in connection with a project might default under that contract.

The types of counterparty include:

■   the contractor;

■   a bank providing performance or defects liability bonding for a contractor;

■   a supplier of goods or services to the project company;

■   a purchaser of products from the project company;

■   an insurer providing insurances in connection with the project;

■   a third party providing undertakings or support in connection with the project;

■   a host of other relevant parties.

If any of these parties defaults in the performance of their respective obligations, then the project may run into difficulties. The first difficulty may be in connection with litigation over the contract in question, which may be expensive and time-consuming to sort out. Even if the litigation is successful or an agreed settlement can be achieved avoiding litigation (whether using alternative dispute resolution procedures or otherwise), there is still the financial risk that the counterparty will have the resources available to make the payment due. In many cases, lenders (and indeed sponsors) will recognise this risk and, where the project company is contracting with companies that are perceived to be financially weak, will demand either parent company guarantees (if available) or even bank guarantees or letters of credit to support these obligations.

Finally, the breach of many of these obligations in the project contracts will give rise to damages-based claims, which are unliquidated claims. Thus, the basic common law damages rules will apply in common law based jurisdictions, which can seriously affect the value of such claims.

2.1.13 Political risk

In any cross-border financing, banks take a 'political' risk in the sense that a collapse of the existing political order in the borrower's country or the imposition of new taxes, exchange transfer restrictions, nationalisation or other laws may jeopardise the prospects of repayment and recovery.

In project financing, the political risks are more acute for many reasons, including:

■ the project itself may require governmental concessions, licences or permits to be in place and maintained, particularly where the project is for power generation, transport, infrastructure or the exploitation of the country's natural resources – oil, gas, minerals; and

■ the project may be crucial to the country's infrastructure or security and accordingly be more vulnerable to the threat of expropriation or requisition-power projects, airports, seaports, roads, railways, bridges and tunnels are obvious examples.

The term 'political risk' is widely used in relation to project finance. It can be defined to mean both the danger of political and financial instability within a given country and the danger that government action (or inaction) will have a negative impact on either the continued existence of the project or on the cash flow generating capacity of a project. Different projects and project structures will obviously encounter different types of political risk; however, examples of events that might be classified as political risks are set out below.

Types of political risks

■ expropriation or nationalisation of project assets (including the shares of a project company);

■ failure of a government department to grant a consent or permit necessary for commissioning, starting, completing and/or operating a project or any part of it;

■ imposition of increased taxes and tariffs in connection with the project, including products generated by the project or, perhaps the withdrawal of valuable tax holidays and/or concessions;

■ imposition of exchange controls, restricting the transfer of funds to outside the host country or the availability of foreign exchange;

■ changes in law having the effect of increasing the borrower's or any other relevant parties' obligations with respect to the project, for example the imposing of new safety, health or environment standards;

■ politically motivated strikes; and

■ terrorism.

There is no single way in which a lender can eliminate all project risks in connection with a particular project. One of the most effective ways of managing and reducing political risks, however, is to lend through, or in conjunction with, multilateral agencies such as the World Bank, the European Bank for Reconstruction and Development and other regional development banks such as the African Development Bank and the Asian Development Bank. There is a view that where one or more of these agencies is involved in a project, the risk of interference from the host government or its agencies is reduced since the host government is unlikely to want to offend any of these agencies for fear of cutting off a valuable source of credit in the future. This is a persuasive argument and certainly one that has some historical basis; for example, when countries such as Mexico and Brazil were defaulting on their external loans in the early 1980s, they went to some lengths to avoid defaulting on their multilateral debts, whether project related or not.

Other ways of mitigating against political risks include:

■ Private market insurance, although this can be expensive and subject to exclusions and the term that such insurance is available for will rarely be long enough.

- Insurance from national export credit agencies such as ECGD in the UK, COFAS in France, HERMES in Germany, etc. Export credit support comes in a variety of different forms and can include guarantees and/or direct loans and interest subsidies. However, these will only usually be given in connection with the export of goods and/or services by a supplier to the project and, as with lending in conjunction with multilateral agencies, co-financing involving national export credit agencies probably enjoys a similar 'protected' status.

- Obtaining assurances from the relevant government departments in the host country, especially as regards the availability of consents and permits.

- The Central Bank of the host government may be persuaded to guarantee the availability of hard currency for export in connection with the project.

- A final exercise, which should be undertaken in any event, is to carry out a thorough review of the legal and regulatory regime in the country where the project is to be located. This is so as to ensure that all laws and regulations are strictly complied with and all the correct procedures are followed, therefore reducing the scope for challenge at a future date.

In some countries, particularly developing countries, which are keen to attract foreign investment, host governments (or their agencies) may be prepared to provide firm assurances on some of the above matters to foreign investors and their lenders. Obviously such assurances are still subject to a performance risk on the part of the host government concerned. But at a minimum they can make it very difficult (as well as embarrassing) for a government to walk away from an assurance given earlier in connection with a specific project and on the basis of which foreign investors and banks have participated in a project.

2.1.14 Legal and structural risks

There may appear to be some overlap with both of these risks with some of the risks itemised above. By legal risk is meant the risk that the laws in the host jurisdiction (and any other relevant jurisdiction for that matter) will not be interpreted and applied in a way consistent with the legal advice obtained from lawyers in the relevant jurisdiction at the outset of the project. (Change of law has already been dealt with under political risks, above.)

Of particular concern will be the laws relating to security and, in particular, the security taken by project lenders over the assets of the project. Not all jurisdictions have available to them the concept of the 'floating charge' (or equivalent) nor the ability to appoint a receiver which is so convenient for project finance structures. In many jurisdictions, particularly in the lesser developed countries, many basic concepts of security are not well developed. Consequently, local legal opinions may only be of limited comfort and, in such cases, the lenders may have to discount the value of such security completely or in part.

Structural risk is the risk that all of the elements of a complex project structure do not fit together in the way envisaged or that the various legal advisers and other experts involved have not done their job properly. Complex projects can involve hundreds of interlocking documents running to many tens of thousands of pages and the possibility of errors and oversights cannot be completely ignored.

The availability of professional negligence insurance policies will obviously provide some comfort for lenders here, but even the largest firms of professional advisers are unlikely to have sufficient cover for the larger projects.

It might be thought, when reviewing the above list of risks involved in project financing, that it is a risky business. It is! However, the lenders (together with their advisers) in this particular market are experts at analysing and managing such risks and they earn a premium on their funds for lending in this market. The next section deals with one of the basic methods for lenders to reduce overall financial risk to themselves, that is, through the use of securities and guarantees.

2.2 INTRODUCTION TO SECURITIES AND GUARANTEES[2]

In a project financing, lenders require the sponsors or other creditworthy parties involved with the project to provide assurances, generally through contractual obligations, that:

■ the project will be completed, even if the costs exceed those originally projected (or, if the project is not completed, its debt will be repaid in full);

■ the project, when completed, will generate cash sufficient to meet all of its debt service obligations; and

■ if for any reason, including force majeure, the project's obligations are interrupted, suspended or terminated, the project will continue to service (and fully repay on schedule) its debt obligations.

There are several types of security arrangements, or combinations of them, which the lender may require for a specific project, depending on its nature and associated risks.

2.2.1 Security interest in project assets

It is common for banks to take security over the project assets if this is possible under the laws of the country where the assets are situated. In cases where this is inappropriate or impossible the lenders will have to rely on negative pledges – binding commitments on the part of the borrower not to create encumbrances over its assets in favour of any third party.

In some cases the bank can use the value of specific tangible assets, which can be separated from the project, to supplement its security. The value of such assets is evaluated on the basis of their open market price. Such tangible assets usually include:

■ tangible assets used in the facilities – equipment, machinery, plants and other physically movable assets;

■ land, buildings and other properties of the project company;

■ technology and process licences;

■ operating permits and licences;

■ rights under contractors' performance bonds or completion guarantees (see below);

■ goods produced by the project, sales and the project's bank accounts; and

■ other rights, eg energy or goods supply contracts, operating agreements, joint venture agreements, transportation contracts.

2 The source for the ideas on project securities and guarantees were borrowed from John Finnerty *Project Financing* (John Wiley, 1996) and Clifford Chance *Project Finance* (ISR, 1991, reprinted 1994).

2.2.2 Security arrangements covering completion

Such securities typically involve an obligation to bring the project to completion or else repay all project debt. The banks usually require that the sponsors or other creditworthy parties provide an unconditional undertaking to furnish any funds needed to complete the project in accordance with the design specifications and place it into service by a specified date.

On the other hand, the project sponsors have to secure the performance of contractors, sub-contractors and suppliers by requiring bonding from banks or surety companies. The bonds are usually unconditional on-demand payment obligations in favour of the project company in the form of a bond, guarantee or standby letter of credit. The most frequently used types of bonds include tender bonds – commitment to take on the contract; performance bonds – performance guarantee by the contractor; advance payment guarantees – a guarantee to refund an advance payment in the event of failure to perform; retention money guarantees – retention of money to cover rectification of defects; and maintenance bonds – to cover defects discovered after completion of construction.

2.2.3 Security arrangements covering debt service

After the project commences operation, contracts for the purchase and sale of the project's outputs normally constitute the principal security arrangements for the project debt. Lenders always require that these contractual obligations are in place, valid and binding (with the required governmental and regulatory approval) before any portion of their loans can be drawn down.

The banks normally need assurances that the debt can be fully serviced out of project revenues received from binding purchase and sales contracts. The main types of such contracts are: Take-if-Offered Contract, Take-or-Pay Contract, Supply-or-Pay Contract, Hell-or-High-Water Contract, Throughput Agreement, Cost-of-Service Contract and Tolling Agreement. For example, the contracts for power supply and purchase signed with RAO 'United Electricity System' of Russia represent a type of purchasing agreement which can be used as a security for covering debt service.

2.2.4 Supplemental credit support

The bank may want to have additional security arrangements in the event that purchase and sales contracts fail to provide enough cash to enable the project company to service its debt obligations. Examples of such agreements include: Financial Support Agreements (usually letter of credit); Cash Deficiency Agreements; Capital Subscription Agreements; Clawback Agreements (control over the project's dividends and/or tax benefits) and Escrow Fund Agreements (special deposit accounts). These agreements provide commitment from creditworthy party(ies) to supplement any cash deficiency in servicing the project's debt obligations.

2.2.5 Insurance

The bank will require an adequate insurance policy which provides that the project will be restored as a viable operating or commercial entity in the event of accident, force majeure or contractual failure.   In some cases the bank may require an insurance against business interruption.

2.2.6 Governmental support and guarantees

For projects critical to national security, infrastructure or where the project company is majority state owned, the bank will require governmental guarantee. The governmental guarantee may provide a supplemental credit support against the political risk, or the government may act as a principal borrower.

In many cases the lender will seek assurances from the national or local government that they will not take actions or impose policies that may adversely affect the project. Such policies include tariff setting, tax, duty and excise, etc. Depending on the project and the type of security required by the lender, the governmental support may be provided in the form of letter of support, support agreement or loan agreement. Such governmental commitments usually require some form of approval or ratification from the local or country parliament. For example, in the Russian Federation, loans with governmental guarantee on amounts above 100 million US dollars require ratification from the State Duma.

Checklist: Avoiding lender liability

Suggestions for reducing the risk of lender liability include:

- covenants in the documentation should be drafted carefully to ensure that the lender is not seen to be effectively exercising control;

- restrictions might be better expressed as events of default, rather than as directions to follow specific policies;

- lenders should be careful when proposing to take an equity interest in the borrower and/or to have a nominee director on their board;

- lenders should take care to minimise meetings with the project sponsors and borrower so as to reduce the risk of allegations of misrepresentation or failure to negotiate in good faith;

- offers of finance should be clearly stated to be subject to final documentation and to be indicative, rather than exhaustive, of the terms and conditions of the offer;

- events of default should be specific (it is perhaps dangerous to rely solely on the ground of 'material adverse change') and, where possible, subject to objective tests rather than simply being dependent on the discretion of the lender;

- financial covenants which could be regarded as imposing a 'business plan' on the borrower should be avoided; it might be preferable for the lender to ask the borrower to produce its own bankable proposal for approval and then to provide that failure to carry out that plan would be an event of default; and

- similarly, covenants prohibiting the borrower from removing existing management or board members might be better expressed in such a way that change of management constitutes an event of default.

2.3 CONCLUSION

One of the first tasks in setting up a project financing is to determine the types of risks and how they may be allocated amongst the participants. This is a complex problem which is solved through an interactive negotiated process amongst the participants.

3

Evaluating project economics

LEARNING OBJECTIVES

After reading this chapter you will be able to:

- *Analyse and calculate project related costs*
- *Understand how to determine capital costs and depreciation*
- *Determine operating costs, including any supply costs as well as fixed and variable costs*
- *Analyse project valuation using investment appraisal, cash flows, payback, discounted cash flow and internal rate of return methods*
- *Distinguish the criteria for making financing and investment decisions*

3.1   INTRODUCTION

Corporate and banking professionals use a variety of strategies to evaluate whether a project is financially viable. Each of these approaches has limitations, advantages and disadvantages. This chapter covers basic investment appraisal techniques used by project finance practitioners throughout the world, how these various methods are used and gives examples of how project costs and benefits are calculated and why. These are the fundamental building blocks of evaluating projects and provide a set of criteria for creating, analysing and improving the financial projections of bankable proposals.

In essence, each method of investment appraisal is about determining the costs and benefits of each project over time. While all major international financial institutions prefer to use a discounted cash flow model, it is unlikely that many companies follow this practice in their computations of project viability. They are likely to use simple payback methods to calculate the costs and benefits of small-sized projects with short-term completion horizons (within one to three years). This may be adequate for a thumbnail review of projects, but it is not sufficient nor does it lead to consistent answers for projects over different time horizons or for projects involving longer payback periods. It is crucially important therefore that the proposer understands how to do the discounted type of financial calculations since they are fundamental to the financial projections which are required under a bankable proposal. A good understanding of these various methods – how they work, their purpose, limitations and applications – will enable the proposer to set out financial projections and financial plans which meet the minimum professional standards required by most financial institutions.

We will first discuss project financial economics in terms of a simplified model on how to calculate costs. Many of the examples used in this chapter apply to energy efficiency schemes. Other types of project concepts could be substituted in place of energy efficiency to illustrate similar points. Energy efficiency examples are used here in order to show how a simple project concept can be developed and analysed using various types of models. We will then turn to the principles underlying financial assessment and investment appraisal. The key point is that the use of undiscounted methods for calculating the return on any type of investment may not be entirely appropriate and, therefore, discounted methods should be used wherever possible. Let us now turn to calculating project costs.

3.2 CALCULATING PROJECT RELATED COSTS[1]

The first step in assessing the financial viability of a project finance proposal is to determine all the obvious and hidden costs related to the project. For example, the various types of costs related to an energy efficiency project would include energy usage and the calculation of the economic value of energy savings such as:

■ **Capital costs of the project**   This is the initial investment in the project.

■ **Fuel costs**   This includes gas, oil and electricity.

■ **Operating costs**   Amongst the major items to consider are:
  – maintenance;
  – materials;
  – labour;
  – service utilities;
  – storage;
  – handling;
  – other items which are expended within one year.

For a listing of the types of transaction costs which a bank may require, see Section 6 of the Business Plan Form in Chapter 7. The costs of the project would include: land, buildings and facilities, equipment and machinery, installation, start-up expenses, training, professional fees, working capital, interest during construction and registering security and insurance policies. These costs should be split according to foreign currency, local currency and contributions in-kind. A detailed worksheet for these costs is found in Chapter 7. In this section we shall discuss the principles of capital costs.

---

1   The ideas in this chapter come from a number of sources. We have borrowed and adapted the major principles set out in chapter 2 of *The Economics of Energy-Saving Schemes* by Eastop and Croft (1990). Another excellent practical source which we have relied on is ETSU and Cheriton Technology Management Limited *Investment Appraisal for Industrial Energy Efficiency*, Guide 69 (1993) ETSU, Harwell, Oxfordshire OX11 ORA. For a most comprehensive guide on project finance analysis from a cash flow perspective, see Finnerty *Project Financing* (1996).

3.2.1   Capital costs and depreciation of the project

All projects normally require an initial investment for new equipment to achieve the project's financial goals. Capital costs can be viewed as the investment from which long-term benefits are expected. Capital costs would include land, buildings, facilities, equipment and machinery, which are bought and paid for in one year and reside in the business for subsequent years with the view that such items will make a contribution towards income for several years in the future.

The capital costs of the project will be accounted as an asset and depreciated over subsequent years. Depreciation can be defined as (a) the reduction in the book or market value of an asset (accounting depreciation), or (b) the portion of an investment that can be deducted from taxable income (taxable depreciation). Depreciation is a *non-cash expense* – it only reduces taxable income and provides an annual tax advantage (or tax shield) equal to the product of depreciation and the (marginal) tax rate.

The company may decide to sell the equipment or machinery after using it for a number of years: this amount is the investment's salvage value. The value of the equipment or machinery will be depreciated by a certain percentage per year until its ultimate salvage value is reached. The salvage value of the equipment is related to its initial capital cost. The most common method for depreciation is *straight-line depreciation*. Under this method, annual depreciation equals a constant proportion of the initial investment. Other methods of depreciation exist. For example, to benefit sooner from the tax advantages offered by depreciation, *accelerated depreciation* can be applied, an accelerated cost recovery system where the amount depreciated is larger in early years than the later years.

Example 3.1

Fan blades to a turbine at a power plant are in need of repairs or replacement. After four years of use, they show corrosion and with replacement with new blades a 7 to 10% increase in efficiency can be achieved. The initial cost of the installed blades is $500,000. Calculate the salvage value of the blades if:

1 the depreciation is set at $75,000 per year;
2 the depreciation is set at the rate of 20% reduction in value per year.

Solution

1 After four years, the total depreciation is:

4 years x US$75,000/year = US$300,000

The salvage value is given by:

initial value – depreciation

= US$500,000 – US$300,000
= US$200,000

In this case, if we assume that the corporate tax rate is 40%, the annual tax shield will amount to:

depreciation x tax rate

=   US$75,000 x 40%
=   US$30,000

2 In tabular form, the salvage value may be calculated as follows:

Table 3.1: Depreciation table (amounts in US dollars)			
Year	Value at start of year	20% depreciation	Residual value
1	500,000	100,000	400,000
2	400,000	80,000	320,000
3	320,000	64,000	256,000
4	256,000	51,200	204,800

In this particular example, the salvage value is therefore US$204,800. One should note that as depreciation is greater in the first years, the company will benefit from the tax shields sooner and these will be worth more (see 'Time value of money', p 40, below).

3.2.2 Operating costs

There are many other costs which are part of the operational costs of a project. Manufacturing costs include the direct costs of raw materials, labour and energy costs other than fuels and maintenance.

Indirect costs such as storage, rates and rent, insurance and handling also apply. There are further general overhead costs due to administration and distribution activities. These should be well detailed, since in many projects the estimation of costs devoted to support activities is too meagre to cover delays and unforeseen contingencies. Whatever the benign motivations may be for 'efficient costing', misestimations of indirect costs could lead to unnecessary costs (or losses) and ultimately to project failure. In practice, erring on the side of over-estimating costs and under-estimating benefits puts the proposer in the happy position of outperforming the expectations laid down in the project agreements.

Costs towards improving plant or facility efficiency

The main aim of the initial capital investment may be to reduce the material consumption of the company. Monetary savings can be achieved either by (a) installing new technology that reduces material consumption, and/or (b) raw material switching in order to benefit from another type of material that is cheaper. An example of a plant efficiency investment is a material switching investment that leads to a reduction in the company's raw materials bill without diminishing the company's overall use of raw materials.

The economic value of a raw materials savings project is related to how quickly the reduced raw material consumption (eg fuel costs savings) can cover the initial capital costs of the project. For example, fuel costs are crucial in the calculation of the running costs of projects and the determination of whether the proposed project is viable. The prices (tariffs) of electricity and fuels are important aspects of energy management. However, the specific value of the cost of a fuel is difficult to state with certainty for a number of reasons, some of the more common being:

- **Negotiability of price by large users** Large industrial users and power generators are heavy consumers of particular fuels and are able to negotiate prices for fuel which are considerably below that charged to the domestic consumer.

■ **Methods of extraction change fuel prices**   The method of extraction affects the prices of fuels and this is especially true for coal and gas. Open-cast coal, for example, generally costs less than deep-mined coal.

■ **Market demand alters fuel prices**   Market forces can play havoc on long-term forecasts— Witness the oil price shocks in the 1970s and then the considerable fall in fuel oil prices in the late 1980s and 1990s. There are also complex knock-on effects on the prices of natural gas and the viability of renewable energy projects.

The prices (tariffs) of fuels are a crucial aspect of energy management since they are the input factors which have the largest impact on the overall profitability of the operations. Fuel costs are a major factor in calculating the running costs of different kinds of schemes and in assessing the viability of proposed projects. To illustrate these concepts, consider the following example.

Example 3.2

The industrial company Rollon plc uses 10,000 MWh of electricity (5p per kWh) and 400,000 therms of gas (36p per therm) per year for its power and heating requirements. The company has traditionally purchased the electricity and used a gas-fired boiler to generate the heat. The management of Rollon is now considering whether to install a diesel engine to generate both the power and the heat. It is estimated that the diesel engine will consume 2 million litres of light fuel oil per year (11p per litre). Calculate the fuel costs of the two systems.

Solution

Present system: annual costs

Electricity cost

$$= \text{number of kWh} \times (\text{cost/kWh})$$
$$= (10,000 \times 1000) \times 0.05 = £0.5m$$

Gas cost

$$= \text{number of therms} \times (\text{cost/therm})$$
$$= 400,000 \times 0.36 = £0.144m$$

Therefore, the total fuel cost = £0.644m

Diesel engine scheme: annual cost

Fuel oil cost

$$= \text{number of litres} \times (\text{cost/litre})$$
$$= 2 \times 10^6 \times 0.11 = £0.22m$$

Therefore, the total savings in fuel cost—

$$= £(0.644 - 0.22)m$$
$$= £0.424m$$

Comment

The above figures indicate that the project would save a great deal of money on energy costs. However, many other costs, including the capital costs of the engine and operating costs, have not been included. The usefulness of this calculation is that it helps a company make a preliminary evaluation of new schemes and the savings in fuel costs will subsequently be compared to the initial investment required. A detailed analysis of what types of costs should be considered are found in Section 6 of the Business Plan Form in Chapter 7.

Relating costs to production: *fixed versus variable costs*[2]

The traditional method of classifying costs is to distinguish between *fixed* costs and *variable* costs. Fixed costs do not change with the output of the plant. These include:

- rent;

- rates;

- insurance;

- space heating and lighting;

- offices and administration;

- interest on capital invested such as interest charges on plant.

Variable costs are those which vary directly with the output of the plant. These include:

- raw materials;

- process energy;

- electricity and fuels;

- maintenance;

- packaging;

- labour costs.

The total cost of operating a project is the sum of the fixed and variable costs. The total costs can be worked out by first adding up the fixed cost items, which can be obtained from the financial records, and then adding the costs of variable items for any level of production:

$$\text{total costs} = \text{fixed costs} + \text{variable costs}$$

Individual cost items such as energy have both fixed and variable components. In many industrial processes, *energy is consumed even at zero output* through, for example, the standing losses of the furnace or boiler. The variable energy consumed for each additional unit of output must then be added to this baseline figure.

The relationship between energy and production is of utmost importance whenever energy saving measures are applied to an existing process. Energy saving measures seldom affect the fixed and variable energy costs equally. For example, insulation applied to a furnace affects the fixed consumption but not the variable consumption, and heat recovery affects the variable cost but not the fixed cost. It should be noted that when a measure does not affect the fixed and variable costs in equal proportions, it is not possible to express savings for any process in percentage terms, unless the production rate is also stated.

Since the total cost of operating an energy efficiency scheme will be the sum of fixed and variable costs, the total will vary with the output of the plant. It is possible in some cases,

2 The discussion on fixed versus variable costs stems from ETSU & Cheriton Technology *Investment Appraisal For Industrial Energy Efficiency* (ETSU, Harwell, 1993) pp 9–11.

therefore, to make a comparison of two energy supply schemes by calculating how the total costs vary with the level of supply.

Having examined the basic principles of how to calculate energy efficiency costs, it is important to note that the same principles would apply to projects involving refurbishments and re-equipment of plants where the goal is plant life extension. In such cases, the total costs compared to the total benefits should be gained from the extended life of the plant. This is also an important area in the project cycle of nuclear plants since, in many situations, the option of life extension may be economically the more feasible option to building new plants. For the improvement of major industrial processes, calculations of the efficiency gain of the plant would also begin by considering the above principles of costs. Having seen how costs are calculated, methods of calculating costs and benefits are considered using the principles of investment appraisal.

3.3   INTRODUCTION TO INVESTMENT APPRAISAL

Investment appraisal is the process whereby a range of projects is evaluated and ranked according to measures of financial return. These measures allow a company and its investors and lenders to use a common set of values to make financial comparisons between different projects. A company should first think about what projects to accept and then about how they should be financed. In general, we are faced with either corporate finance (which means financing a project of an existing company) or project finance (which means setting up a new company).

Some of the major objectives of investment appraisal are:

■   to determine which investments make the best use of the organisation's money;

■   to ensure optimum benefits from each of these investments;

■   to minimise risk to the enterprise; and

■   to provide a basis for the subsequent analysis of the performance of each investment.

The appraisal process produces measurements of the financial contribution each project is expected to make to the business, identifies the risks and uncertainties in each project and defines the expected costs and benefits. The decision-maker uses the results of the appraisal to select the 'best' project. Other strategic factors that need to be taken into account are:

■   quality of management;

■   cost structure of the business;

■   how the project relates to the core objectives of the business;

■   the relation of the project to the company's objectives in terms of capacity, quality, flexibility, product mix, logistics and so on.

It should be emphasised that investment appraisal does not determine whether or not a project should be approved. The main function of the appraisal process is that it allows for different people with different self-interests to agree on a ranking of a whole range of possible projects open to the company.

While there are many different possible ways to evaluate a project, the first focus will be on some basic concepts, gradually building up to a useful, if not sophisticated, model for assessment.

Our aim is to err on the side of usefulness rather than sophistication. The field of financial appraisal is underpinned by concepts in modern finance theory. However, in this discussion we will not review the history of modern corporate finance theory except on occasion where it is relevant.

3.3.1 Cash flows

The first step in any investment appraisal is to gather the appropriate information on project costs and benefits and calculate the cash flow. In simple terms, the cash flow is a statement of how much money will be spent or will be accumulated in each year of the project.

In basic terms, cash flow is the difference between money coming in and money going out of the investment project.

Cash flows are not to be confused with accounting profits and losses, which include some cash flows and exclude some others. As a consequence, some careful corrections will have to be made to transform the accounting earnings generated by the investment project (income statement) into the cash flows generated by the project. For example, depreciation charges have to be added as they do not correspond to a cash outflow at all, increases in account receivables and inventories which do not correspond to cash-inflows will have to be deducted and increases in account payables which do not correspond to cash outflows will have to be added.

It is important to note that cash flow statements can be derived from accounting figures, mainly the profit and loss (income) statement and balance sheet which contain all the necessary information. For details of how cash flow statements are constructed and are related to income statements and balance sheets, see the commentary to Section 11 of the Business Plan Form in Chapter 7.

Example 3.3

Suppose a project costs $100,000 and produces annual savings of $20,000 for six years. The cash flow is:

Table 3.2: Simplified cash flow	
Year	**Cash flow in US dollars**
0	(100,000)*
1	20,000
2	20,000
3	20,000
4	20,000
5	20,000
6	20,000
Total net cash flow	20,000**

*   Figures stated in parenthesis follow the standard accounting practice of being an outflow or a negative amount. The $100,000 is the capital cost.

**   Total cash flow is $20,000 per year x 6 years = $120,000. The capital cost was $100,000, therefore the total net cash flow is $120,000 − $100,000 = $20,000.

This is a very simplified example of cash flow. There is no reason to expect the savings to be the same in each year.

One of the principal points of the cash flow of a cost savings project is that the savings are achieved in a variety of ways, for example, by altering the way the product is made or by using resources, including all forms of input or operations, more efficiently.

Cash flows have to be evaluated on an incremental basis: the value of a project depends on all the additional cash flows that follow from project acceptance. In estimating the cash flows generated by a project, one should pay particular attention to the following points:

- **Marginal not average cash flows** Cash flow consequences of investment decisions should be rigorously assessed. Incremental Net Present Value (see below) in a loss-making division can be strongly positive and vice versa.

- **Forget sunk costs** These are costs which have been incurred and cannot be reversed. They are past and irreversible outflows. Because sunk costs are bygones, they cannot be affected by the decision to accept or reject a project and so they should be ignored.

- **Include opportunity costs** The cost of a resource may be relevant to the investment decision even when no cash changes hands. The proper comparison between investment projects is not 'before versus after' but rather 'with or without'.

3.3.2 Payback

The payback of a project is easy to calculate. It is defined as the length of time required for the running total of net savings before depreciation to equal the capital cost of the project or, even more simply, it is the capital cost divided by the average annual savings. The basic idea is that the shorter the payback time the more attractive the investment,

$$payback = capital\ cost/annual\ savings$$

The advantages of payback as a financial measure are:

- It is easy to calculate.

- It is interpreted in tangible terms, ie, years.

- It does not require any assumptions about the project in terms of timing, lifetime or interest rates.

- It favours projects with a short payback time, which reduces the uncertainty of calculating savings for periods a long time in the future. The effects of changing technology and fuel prices are reduced.

- It does take into account in a crude fashion the timing of the net savings.

The disadvantages to payback are:

- It takes no account of any cash flows after the payback period (cut-off date) and therefore does not assess the overall value of the project. If the company uses the same cut-off regardless of project life, it will tend to accept too many short-lived projects and too few long-lived ones.

- It does not indicate a rate of return on the money invested.

■   It takes no account of the residual value in the capital asset.

■   It takes no account of the time value of money.

To illustrate the above points, the following example sets out three different project opportunities.

Example 3.4

Calculate the payback times of each of the three projects given that the capital outlay (initial capital investment) is as described:

Table 3.3: Comparing schedule of costs of three projects

Capital costs ($)	Project 1		Project 2		Project 3	
	50,000		50,000		50,000	
Year	Net annual savings	Running total	Net annual savings	Running total	Net annual savings	Running total
0	(50,000)	(50,000)	(50,000)	(50,000)	(50,000)	(50,000)
1	10,000	(40,000)	12,000	(38,000)	8,000	(42,000)
2	10,000	(30,000)	9,000	(29,000)	9,000	(33,000)
3	10,000	(20,000)	11,000	(18,000)	10,000	(23,000)
4	10,000	(10,000)	10,000	(8,000)	9,000	(15,000)
5	10,000	0	10,000	2,000	9,000	(6,000)

Solution

The payback periods for each of the three projects are:

Project 1: exactly 5 years
Project 2: (by interpolation) 4.8 years
Project 3: (by interpolation) 5.6 years

The payback method takes into account the timing of the net savings but notice that interchanging years 2 and 4 for Project 2 makes no difference to the final outcome. It will be seen later that an explicit recognition of the timing must be taken into account. The above example, however, illustrates the basic virtues and disadvantages of the payback method. The table below summarises the advantages and disadvantages of the payback method.

Table 3.4: Payback Method – Summary of Advantages and Disadvantages	
Advantages	**Disadvantages**
• The method favours projects with short payback periods, thus reducing uncertainty associated with calculating savings over the long term in the future. • Favouring the shortened period means that effects such as changing technology and fuel prices are reduced. difference	• The payback method does not consider savings produced after the payback time and therefore fails to assess the overall value of the project. • The payback method does not indicate a rate of return on the money invested. • The payback method may give a misleading picture of the timing of net savings as in the above example under Project 2, as years with different payouts could be interchanged without any to the payback result.

As can be seen, payback is a 'quick and dirty' method which can give us some useful answers but it falls down when it is used for longer term projects where fluctuating prices and interest rates may need to be featured in the calculations. Later we shall see that the simple payback method is inversely related to the discounted rate of return. That is, the shorter the payback period, the higher the rate of return.

The fact that payback ignores the timing of net savings is a big flaw and, therefore, it is suggested that it should be used as only a rough indicator and preparatory to using a more detailed discounted technique of analysis.

The simplicity of payback makes it an easy device for describing investment projects, but it should by no means govern the investment decisions of the managers.

We turn now to discounted methods of appraisal and examine the principles underlying the method of discounted cash flow.

3.3.3   Discounted cash flow methods (DCF)

Time value of money: interest rate

In order to calculate the value of a project over a number of years, one needs to take into account the *time value of money*.

It is a basic principle of finance that money has time value. This means that a certain amount of money in hand today (that is, cash) is always worth more than an equivalent amount of money a year from now. The reason for charging interest on a loan is related to this concept of time value. In other words, the bank should be able to charge a market related price for the use of its money. The main charge for the use of the bank's money is called *interest*, which is stated as a percentage rate.

While the payback method of appraisal is easy to use, it fails to allow sufficiently for the timing of savings. A project which generates higher savings in the early years facilitates further investment in other schemes. DCF methods if properly applied add weight to the value of savings at certain times and, thus, *take into account the timing of investments.*

Basically, DCF methods are based on interest rates. For example, a deposit of $100 in a bank at 10 per cent will accrue $10 of interest in the first year and the account will be worth $110 at the end of year 1. A different way of looking at these figures is to say that an interest rate of 10 per cent, a figure of $110 in one year's time is worth $100 now – the $100 is its present value. We could also say that to get $110 in one year, we would have to deposit $100 in the bank today.

By repeating this process, if the $110 is left in the bank to accrue another year of 10 per cent interest, the account would be worth $121 at the end of year 2. Again, it could be said that at an interest rate of 10 per cent, an amount of $121 over a two year period has a present value of $100. The general formula for this concept is:

$$S = D \times (1 + i)^N$$

Where i = interest rate, in %

D = deposit

S = value of money saved.

The Present Value (PV) of an amount of money S saved in year N will be:

$$PV = S/(1 + i)^N.$$

Example 3.5

A project generates cash flows of $20,000 in years 2 and 4 of its operation. Calculate the present value of the savings for an interest rate of 12%.

Solution

Using the formula for Present Value:

$$PV = S/(1 + i)^N$$

We have for year 2:

$$PV = \$20,000/(1 + 0.12)^2$$
$$= \$15,943.88$$

For year 4:

$$= \$20,000/(1 + 0.12)^4$$
$$= \$12,710.36.$$

If we extend this concept to a complete project which generates savings over a sequence of years then for each year there will be a factor $1/(1 + \text{interest rate})^N$ which relates the savings at year N to a present value. This factor is called a *discount factor* (see Table below) and its effect is to reduce the value of savings achieved in the later years of project life. The Table gives discount factors for various interest rates (or discount rates) for a ten year range.

Table 3.5: Discount Factors

Year	Interest rates (or discount rates)							
	8%	10%	12%	14%	16%	18%	20%	24%
0	1.000	1.000	1.000	1.000	1.000	1.000	1.000	1.000
1	0.926	0.909	0.893	0.877	0.862	0.848	0.833	0.810
2	0.857	0.826	0.797	0.769	0.743	0.718	0.694	0.651
3	0.794	0.751	0.712	0.675	0.641	0.609	0.579	0.525
4	0.735	0.683	0.636	0.592	0.552	0.516	0.482	0.423
5	0.681	0.621	0.567	0.519	0.476	0.437	0.402	0.341
6	0.630	0.564	0.507	0.456	0.410	0.370	0.335	0.275
7	0.584	0.513	0.452	0.399	0.354	0.314	0.279	0.222
8	0.540	0.467	0.404	0.351	0.305	0.266	0.233	0.179
9	0.500	0.424	0.361	0.308	0.263	0.226	0.194	0.144
10	0.463	0.386	0.322	0.270	0.227	0.191	0.162	0.116

It is important to remember that year 0 is the current time and therefore will always have a discount factor of 1. The basic concept of 'discounting' cash flows of future years to a 'present value' is the basis for the project appraisal technique called 'Net Present Value' method. This method overcomes the disadvantages associated with the undiscounted and payback methods.

Net Present Value method (NPV)

NPV is a method for calculating the present value of all yearly capital costs and net savings throughout the life of a project. By summing all the present values (costs are represented as negative amounts and net savings as positive), a total will be obtained which is called the NPV of the project.

The basics of the NPV criteria are:

- forecasting all cash flows generated by the investment projects;

- discounting these cash flows with the appropriate opportunity cost of capital.

If the NPV is negative, it means that the present value of the net savings (cash inflows) generated by the project during its life-time are less than the initial capital costs (initial cash outflow). The project will then be rejected.

If the NPV is positive then it is not automatically accepted, but other factors are taken into account to assess the worthiness and value of the project. These other factors will be discussed later in the chapter.

To calculate the present value of an investment project, the expected future cash flows as discounted by the rate of return offered by comparable investment alternatives. This rate of return is often referred to as the *discount rate, hurdle rate* or *opportunity cost of capital* – it is the return forgone by investing in the project rather than investing in securities. If we invest in a riskless project, we will discount the forecasted cash flows with the risk-free rate of return (the interest rate offered by the bank on Treasury Bills, for example). But if we invest in a risky project, we will have to include a risk premium to the discount rate. This is so because the bigger the risk involved in a project, the bigger the return expected by the investor. The uncertainties in estimating the net savings of the project are offset by using a slightly pessimistic discount rate.

It is important to emphasise that each investment project should be evaluated at its own opportunity cost of capital. It would be clearly unreasonable to suggest that a company should demand the same rate of return from a very safe project as from a very risky one. This would lead the company to reject many good low-risk projects and accept many poor high-risk projects.

Treating inflation consistently

Discounting is designed to take account of the time value of money and thus is basically a forecast. The discount rate should not be confused with the general rate of inflation which is not selected but is given as a fact. This includes fuel prices, wages and maintenance, equipment and installation costs. In the UK the rate of inflation is formally associated with the Retail Price Index (RPI) which is published monthly by central government.

Inflation can be seen when the value of money decreases over time. For example, when prices of goods are rising by 10 per cent a year and the money rate of interest is 15 per cent then the real money rate of interest is 5 per cent – the difference between the money market rate (the nominal rate) and the inflation rate. In effect, the real rate of interest is the rate of interest that would be paid if prices were constant.

The object of expressing something in real terms is to adjust for the effect of rising prices throughout an economic system. To differentiate between actual money and money with constant purchasing power, economists refer to the latter as money in real terms. When the annual rate of inflation is 10 per cent the real purchasing power of $110 received in one year's time is $100. This is equivalent to another form of discounting which must be clearly differentiated from the effect of time value of money. In other words, the inflation rate can influence our decision on what type of discount rates are appropriate.

There is no absolutely objective method for taking account of the effects of inflation when discounting the money value of net savings. In general, many financial practitioners use the RPI as the discount factor for inflation and forecast that this inflation rate will prevail during the life-time of the project.

It is important to remember to apply a consistent treatment of inflation in your calculations.

If the discount rate is stated in nominal terms then consistency requires that forecasted cash flows be estimated in nominal terms, taking account of trends in selling price, labour, material costs, etc. Of course, there is nothing wrong with discounting real cash flows at a real discount rate.

Discount rate	Cash flows	
	Nominal	*Real*
Nominal	Yes	No
Real	No	Yes

Discounting nominal cash flows (taking into account the effect of inflation and price variation) with a nominal discount rate will always yield the same results as discounting real cash flows with a real discount rate. The following example shows how this is true.

Example 3.6

A company plans to invest $50,000 in an energy efficiency project with a life-time of four years. It is estimated that the savings and costs of the project will be as follows:

> Energy savings = $50,000 in the first year escalating by 5% per year
> Labour costs = $20,000 in the first year escalating by 8% per year
> Material and other costs = $10,000 in the first year escalating by 10% per year

Assume the inflation rate (Retail Price Index) is currently 7% and the nominal rate of interest is 15%. Calculate the present value of the project in nominal and real terms.

Solution

You will first need to evaluate the net savings of the project by subtracting the costs from the energy savings, allowing for the escalation in value of savings and costs.

Table 3.6: Net savings (energy savings – costs)

Year	Capital costs ($) (A)	Energy savings (5%/yr) ($) (B)	Labour costs (8%/yr)($) (C)	Material and other costs (10%/yr) ($) (D)	Actual money value of savings ($) (E)
0	– 50,000	None	None	None	– 50,000
1	none	50,000	– 20,000	– 10,000	20,000
2	none	52,500	– 21,600	– 11,000	19,900
3	none	55,125	– 23,328	– 12,100	19,697
4	none	57,881.25	– 25,194.24	– 13,310	19,377.01

Columns A–E represent the following:

A $ – 50,000: this is the initial capital investment of the project.
B Energy savings: with escalation factor of 1.05.
C Labour costs: the escalation factor is 1.08.
D Material and other costs: escalation factor is 1.10.
E Actual money and value of savings = net savings = (A + B + C + D).

This example shows clearly that the value used as the inflation rate is an average value and that energy, labour and other costs can escalate at a rate different than inflation.

Method 1: NPV analysis in nominal (money) terms

This method works by discounting the actual values of the net savings with a discount factor which is based on an interest rate which includes an allowance for inflation. In this case the discount rate R is the combined effect of the real rate of interest I_R and the overall inflation rate (Retail Price Index). The Bank tends to favour calculations in nominal terms.

The discount rate R is the combined effect of the real rate of interest I_R and the overall rate of inflation as measured by the inflation rate.[3] In this case, we have agreed that the discount rate is 15 per cent.

The NPV is calculated as follows:

Table 3.7: Calculating Nominal Net Present Value

Year	Capital ($) (A)	Net savings (money terms) ($) (B)	Discount factor (15%) (C)	Present value (money terms) ($) (D)
0	– 50,000	none	1.000	– 50,000
1	none	20,000	0.869	17,391.30
2	none	19,900	0.756	15,047.26
3	none	19,697	0.657	12,951.10
4	none	19,377.01	0.571	11,078.87
				Total: 56,468.53
				NPV = 6,468.53

Columns A–D represent the following:

A $ – 50,000 is the initial capital investment.
B   Column B is from Column B of the previous table.
C   Discount factor.
D   D = C x A; or D = C x B.

Method 2: NPV analysis in real terms

It is also possible to calculate the real values of the net savings using a discount factor which is based on the real rate of interest.

Table 3.8: NPV Analysis in real terms

Year	Capital ($) (A)	Net savings (money) (B)	Inflation deflator ($) (C)	Net savings (real terms) ($) (D) = B x C	Discount factor (real terms, 7.4766%) (E)	Present value (real terms) (F) = D x E
0	– 50,000	None	1.000	– 50,000	1.000	– 50,000
1	none	20,000	0.935	18,700	0.930435	17,399.14
2	none	19,900	0.873	17,372.70	0.865709	15,039.71
3	none	19,697	0.816	16,072.75	0.805486	12,946.38
4		19,377.01	0.763	14,784.66	0.749453	11,080.41
						56,465.64
						NPV =
						6,465.64

3   To calculate the inflation rate, use the following relationship:
$$(1 + R) = (1 + I_R)(1 + RPI)$$
$$= (1 + 0.08)(1 + 0.07) = 1.1556$$
ie R   = 0.1556 or (15.56%).
For purposes of simplification, we will round the value of R to 15%.

Columns A–F represent:

A $ – 50,000 equals the initial capital investment.
B This is the same as column E from Table 4.6.
C The factor = $1/(1 + \text{inflation rate})^N$, where the inflation rate = 0.07.
D This is an application of the equation for computing the real value of a sum of money:
real value = $S/(1 + RPI)^N$.
In this case, D = C x A or D = C x B.
E The factor = $1/(1 + \text{real interest rate})^N$, where the real interest rate = 0.08.
The real interest rate is calculated according to the following formula:
(1 + nominal interest rate) = (1 + real interest rate) x (1 + inflation rate)
(1 + 15%) = (1 + 7.4766%) x (1 + 7%).
F This is the present value in real terms. Notice that the net present value in real terms
is 6,465.64, which is substantially the same as the one calculated above in nominal
terms – 6,468.53. In theory, they should be precisely the same – their small difference
is due to rounding off estimations in the calculations.

Even if the results under the two methods are the same, it is preferable always to use nominal
cash flows and nominal discount rate.

The following example sets out the capital costs and net savings of three projects. For a nominal
discount rate of 14 per cent, calculate the NPV of each project.

Example 3.7

Consider three projects with initial capital costs of $120,000, $120,000 and $160,000
respectively. The net annual savings are stated in the Table below. Given a discount rate of
14 per cent, calculate the NPVs for each of the projects.

Table 3.9: Comparison of net annual savings of three projects

	Project 1	Project 2	Project 3
Capital cost ($)	120,000	120,000	160,000
Year	Net annual savings	Net annual savings	Net annual savings
1	30,000	36,000	35,000
2	30,000	34,000	37,000
3	30,000	32,000	40,000
4	30,000	30,000	42,000
5	30,000	28,000	45,000
6	30,000	26,000	47,000

Solution

The discount factors for a rate of 14 per cent are taken from Table 3.5 above. The columns
of present values in the Table below are obtained by multiplying the net saving by the
appropriate discount factor. The NPV is obtained by subtracting the capital cost from the
sum of the discounted net savings.

Year	Discount factor for 14%	Project 1		Project 2		Project 3	
		Net savings ($)	PV ($)	Net savings ($)	PV ($)	Net savings ($)	PV ($)
	(A)	(B)	(A x B)	(C)	(A x C)	(D)	(A x D)
0	1.000	-120,000	-120,000	-120,000	-120,000	-160,000	-160,000
1	0.877	32,000	28,064	36,000	31,572	35,000	30,695
2	0.769	32,000	24,608	34,000	26,146	37,000	28,453
3	0.675	32,000	21,600	32,000	21,600	40,000	27,000
4	0.592	32,000	18,944	30,000	17,760	45,000	26,640
5	0.519	32,000	16,608	28,000	14,532	48,000	24,912
6	0.456	32,000	14,592	26,000	11,856	50,000	22,800
		Gross PV = 124,416		Gross PV = 123,466		Gross PV = 160,500	
		NPV = +4,416		NPV = +3,466		NPV = +500	

Table 3.10: Comparison of NPVs of three projects at 14% discount rate

The projects can be ranked in the following order:

Project 1: NPV = +4,416

Project 2: NPV = +3,466

Project 3: NPV = +500.

Project 1 has the highest NPV and would therefore be the one selected amongst the three proposed schemes.

The NPV of a project should be positive for the project to be accepted. The magnitude of the NPV represents the extra money made available by the project. For example, with project 2, the NPV of $3,466 could be regarded as money which is available now if the $3,466 is borrowed against the project surplus. In this sense the NPV is immediately available.

In the above example, projects 1 and 2 have the same initial capital investment and the NPV affords a direct comparison between these two projects.

Internal rate of return (IRR) method

The Internal Rate of Return (IRR) is defined as the discount rate which will make the NPV of a project equal to zero. It is a handy measure and widely used in finance.

This represents the rate of interest that money would have to earn outside or elsewhere in the organisation to be a better investment. The higher the IRR on a project, the better the project.

47

The IRR rule states that companies should accept any investment offering an IRR in excess of the opportunity cost of capital. This technique is based on discounted cash flows and will give a correct answer if properly used.

There is no easy and direct way of calculating IRR (except by successive approximations or by using a computer programmed to do these approximations on an automatic basis). We shall show how to derive the IRR using a graphical means.

The calculation method is identical to that of the NPV method described by systematically repeating the calculation with different discount rates until the NPV is zero. The graphical method requires less calculation and is illustrated by the example below.

Example 3.8

Using the cash flow data of project 2 in Example 3.7, calculate the NPV for discount rates of 10%, 14% and 16%. Draw the graph of the NPV against discount rate and approximate the IRR of the project.

Solution

The discount factors for 10%, 14% and 16% are taken from Table 3.5. The present values in the Table are obtained by multiplying the net savings (cash flow) by the appropriate discount factor. The NPV is obtained by subtracting the capital cost from the sum of the discounted net savings.

Table 3.11: NPVs of project using different discount rates

Year	Cash flow (A)	10% Discount rate		14% Discount rate		16% Discount rate	
		Discount factor (B)	Present value ($) = (A) x (B)	Discount factor (C)	Present value ($) = (A) x (C)	Discount factor (D)	Present value ($) = (A) x (D)
0	-120,000	1.000	-120,000	1.000	-120,000	1.000	-120,000
1	36,000	0.909	32,724	0.877	31,572	0.862	31,032
2	34,000	0.826	28,084	0.769	26,146	0.743	25,262
3	32,000	0.751	24,032	0.675	21,600	0.641	20,512
4	30,000	0.683	20,490	0.592	17,760	0.552	16,560
5	28,000	0.621	17,388	0.519	14,532	0.476	13,328
6	26,000	0.564	14,664	0.456	11,856	0.410	10,660
		Gross PV = 137,382 NPV = 17,382		Gross PV = 123,466 NPV = 3,466		Gross PV = 117,354 NPV = -2,646	

The NPVs for the three different discount rates can be plotted on a graph of NPV (y-axis) versus discount rate (x-axis). The IRR for project 2 of example 3.7 above is approximately 15.1 per cent.

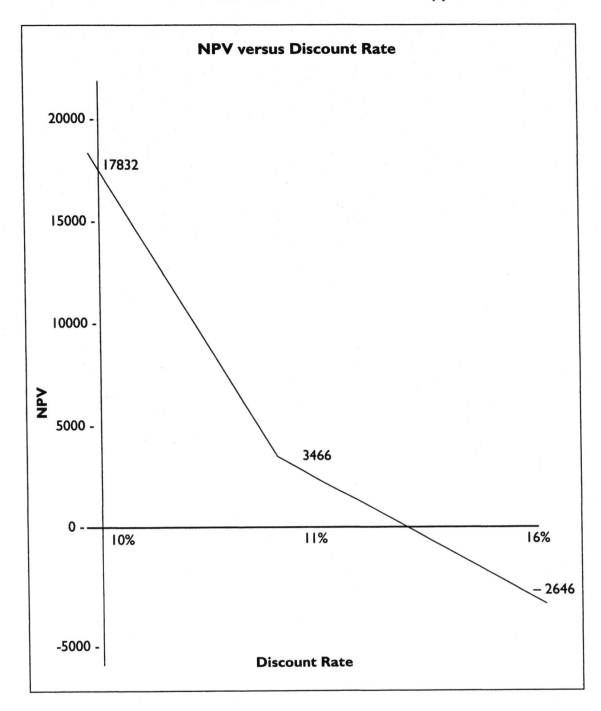

If this calculation is repeated for projects 1 and 3 in Example 4.7, then the following values are obtained for the IRR:

Project 1 = 15.34%

Project 3 = 13.91%

This is the same ranking order as the above NPV calculations. Although it is not necessarily always the case, in general the NPV and IRR methods lead to the same acceptance or rejection decision.

It should be noted that they are some pitfalls in applying the IRR rule.

Lending or borrowing?

Consider the following projects A and B:

Cash flows ($)				
Project	C0	C1	IRR per cent	NPV at 10 per cent
A (Lending)	-1,000	+1,500	+50	+364
B (Borrowing)	+1,000	-1,500	+50	-364

In the case of project A, we are lending money at 50 per cent. In the case of B, we are borrowing money at 50 per cent. When one lends money, one wants a high rate of return. For Project B, NPV increases as the discount rate increases. Obviously, the IRR rule will not work in this case: we have to look for an IRR less than the opportunity cost of capital.

■ **Multiple rates of return** This case might occur when there is more than one change in the sign (ie inflow or outflow) of the cash flows. There can be as many IRRs for a project as there are changes in the sign of the cash flows. There are also cases in which no IRR exists.

■ **Mutually exclusive projects** Firms often have to choose from among several alternative ways of doing the same job or using the same facility. In other words, they have to choose from among mutually exclusive projects. Here too the IRR rule can be misleading.

Consider projects A and B:

Cash flows ($)				
Project	C0	C1	IRR per cent	NPV at 10 per cent
A	-10,000	+20,000	+100	+8,182
B	-20,000	-35,000	+75	+11,818

The IRR rule seems to indicate that if there is a choice, project A is preferable since it has the higher IRR. Following the NPV rule, the choice will be project B and an additional $11,818. The solution to this is to look at the IRR in relation to the *incremental flows*: consider the smaller project first. If its IRR is higher than the opportunity cost of capital, then it is acceptable. Then, question if it is worth making the additional investment in Project B. If the IRR on the incremental investment is in excess of the opportunity cost of capital, project B is preferable. If the IRR on the incremental investment is in excess of the opportunity cost of capital, project A is preferable to project B. Unless the incremental expenditure is considered, IRR is unreliable in ranking projects of different scale. Note that the IRR rule is also unreliable in ranking projects which offer different patterns of cash flows over time.

As a conclusion, it can be seen that IRR is a less easy rule to use than NPV but, used properly, it gives the same answer. Once you know the pitfalls, you should be able to use the IRR rule properly.

The four-step procedure to value a capital investment

> 1 Forecast the project's incremental (after-tax) cash flows.
>
> 2 Assess the project's risk.
>
> 3 Estimate the opportunity cost of capital, that is, the expected rate of return offered to investors by the equivalent-risk investments traded in the capital markets.
>
> 4 Calculate NPV using the discounted cash flow formula.

In fact, each project needs to be considered as a mini-company and the question asked: how much would that mini-company be worth if it were spun off as a separate, all equity-financed company? How much would investors be willing to pay for shares in the project?

It is important to emphasise that in order to convince an investor that an investment project is a good project, a *sensitivity analysis* should be conducted to identify the principal threats to the project's success. Each of the determinants of the project's success should be considered in turn and estimates made of how far the present value of the project would be altered by taking a very optimistic view or a very pessimistic view of that variable. The net present value of the investment project should be estimated under different scenarios and this estimate compared with the base case.

Factors affecting investment appraisal: a detailed example

In discussing investment appraisal, it is important to realise that there are a number of factors which bear on the final outcome. There are practical considerations which must be taken into account. Other costs or contributions such as tax or grants can have a considerable impact on the feasibility of the project. The major factors impacting investment appraisal on an energy efficiency project are:

■ government grants;

■ tax;

■ variability of supply material and commodity prices.

Government grant schemes from a national government or from, say, the European Commission are considered capital contributions. While they may not be given at the beginning of the project, they may be used in its later years. Obviously, in either case, NPVs will be improved by diminishing the initial capital costs of the project.

Tax is a two-edged sword. On the one hand, the additional cost of tax on net savings will decrease the attractiveness of a project, on the other hand, tax incentives (eg tax allowances) will enhance attractiveness. Cash flows will always have to be forecast on an after-tax basis. A delay in tax payment will of course increase the NPV of the project.

Supply material and commodity prices are very volatile and may be difficult to predict over the life-time of a project. For example, after the oil price shocks of the 1970s, there was a surge in oil price. In the late 1980s and 1990s, the price of fuel oils dropped and oil prices have remained relatively low. The low prices caused many companies to simply switch fuels rather than invest in new measures for existing equipment. While preparing cash flows forecasts, assume the expected variation in commodity prices during the expected life-time of the project: it is best to use statistical methods to determine a benchmark or index of future prices.

Example 3.9

Energy Works plc is planning to invest in a number of energy savings measures. The initial investment is estimated at $100,000. Additional investment if the scheme proves a success is planned for year 2. The additional investment amounts to $50,000 which will come from a regional development grant.

According to a technical study, the running costs of the current compared to the improved heat recovery system generate the savings over the course of five years.

Year	Savings
1	30,000
2	35,000
3	28,000
4	25,000
5	23,000

According to the tax regulations, the proposed project would have the following tax liability:

1 Corporation tax = 40% of net savings. This means that the tax will be paid by the company at the end of each year of operation.

2 Tax allowance of 50% for first year. This tax allowance means that 50% of the tax on the capital investment can be offset against tax paid on the project.

For example, the calculation of tax is:

$$0.40 \times \$30,000 = \$12,000$$

The tax allowance is:

$$50\% \times \$12,000 = \$6,000$$

The $6,000 is directly related to the capital investment in the energy efficiency project but its application against any tax which the company may incur.

Other data to Example:

Depreciation is over the five-year life of the project at $18,000 per year and the salvage value will therefore be $10,000. The salvage value is considered as a savings in year 5. A discount rate of 12% is assumed based on current interest rates and no inflation.

Year	Capital investment ($) (A)	Net savings ($) (B)	Depreciation ($) (C)	Tax incentive ($) (D)	Tax at 40% ($) (E)	Additional grant ($) (F)	Net after tax ($) (G)	Discount factor (12%) (H)	Present value ($) (I)
0	-100,000	none	none	none	none	none	-100,000	1.000	-100,000
1	none	30,000	18,000	6,000	-2,400	none	27,600	0.893	24,646.80
2	none	35,000	18,000	none	-6,800	50,000	28,200	0.797	72,475.40
3	none	28,000	18,000	none	-4,000	none	22,200	0.712	14,119.20
4	none	25,000	18,000	none	-2,800	none	13,800	0.636	7,824.60
5	10,000	23,000	none	none	-9,200	none	13,800	0.567	7,824.60
									136,154
								NPV =	36,154

Table 3.12: Effect of tax and grant on NPV

Columns A–H represent:

A $ – 100,000 is the initial capital investment and $ 2,500 is the salvage value.

B   Net savings on the new scheme compared to the existing scheme.

C   Depreciation.

D   Tax allowance for year 1 only.

E   Tax for year 1 onwards = – (B – C + D) x .40.

F   Additional tax-free grant of $50,000 for year 2 only.

G   Net after tax = B + E.

H   Discount factors for 12%.

I   Present value = (G x H).

3.4   FINANCIAL APPRAISAL

Financing is principally a marketing problem. The company tries to split the cash flows generated by its assets into different streams that will appeal to investors with different tastes, wealth and tax rates.

It is very difficult to find financing schemes with NPVs significantly different from zero. This is because of the nature of competition in the financial markets. Still, remember that a good financing decision will generate a positive NPV. It will be one where the amount of cash raised exceeds the value of the liability created. However, if selling a security generates a positive NPV for you, it must generate a negative NPV for the buyer. For example, getting a subsidised loan from the government is a good deal for your firm, but a negative NPV investment from the government's point of view (see below).

The different sources of finance are the following:

- The simplest and most important source of finance is *shareholders' equity*, raised either by stock issues or retained earnings.

- The next most important source of finance is *debt*. Debtholders are entitled a fixed regular payment of interest and the final repayment of the principal. But the company's liability is not unlimited. If it cannot pay its debts, it can file for bankruptcy.

It is important to note that tax authorities treat interest payments as a cost. This means *the company can deduct interest when calculating its taxable income*. Interest is paid from pre-tax income. Dividends and retained earnings come from after-tax income.

A look at the ways in which companies raise and spend money reveals in general:

- internally generated cash is the principal source of funds;

- internally generated cash does not provide all the money companies need and, as a consequence, companies come to the capital markets for more money; and

- there are cycles in company financing – sometimes companies prefer to issue debt, sometimes equity. In part, this reflects their attempt to maintain a targeted debt-equity ratio.

Modigliani and Miller have stated that *the value of a company* (the value of all its assets) *is independent of its capital structure*.[4] They agree that borrowing increases the expected rate of return on shareholders' investment but also increases the risk of the company's shares. The risk increase exactly offsets the increase in expected return, leaving the investors no better or worse off. Modigliani's and Miller's proposition depends on a very strong assumption – the existence of perfect capital markets. We will see below that once distorting facts such as taxes are introduced, their proposition no longer holds true. Yet, it remains a powerful proposition which is useful in calculating Net Present Value of investment projects.

3.4.1 Choosing the company's debt–equity ratio

When taxes are taken into account, the value (V) of the investment project increases creating the following relationship:

V = Value if all-equity financed + PV of tax shield[5] – PV of costs of financial distress

---

4 See F Modigliani and M H Miller 'The Cost of Capital, Corporation Finance and the Theory of Investment' in *The American Economic Review*, XLVII (3), 261–297.

5 In simple terms the tax shield reduces the company's tax obligations. It is defined as the impact on a company's income tax obligations from a change in a tax-deductible expense, such as depreciation or interest and, specifically, it is the amount of change multiplied by the applicable tax rate. The tax shield assumes the company has sufficient taxable income to offset the change in the expense. See E A Helfert, *Techniques of Financial Analysis* (8th edn, 1994), Irwin: Burr Ridge, Illinois) p 498.

The tax shield is due to the fact that interest payments are considered in many jurisdictions as tax deductible expenses. As a consequence, tax shields can be valuable assets as they decrease the tax bill of the company. Usually, tax shields depend only on the marginal corporate tax rate and on the ability of the company to earn enough to cover interest payments. Tax shields, therefore, are usually discounted at a relatively low discount rate, the most common assumption being that the risk of the tax shields is the same as that of the interest payments generating them.

Debt may be better than equity in some cases, worse in others. Investments should be financed with debt up to the point where the present value of financial distress is equal to the present value of the tax shield. When financial distress becomes all too significant, it will offset the advantages of the tax shield and decrease the value of the company. Despite this, keep the following four points in mind when considering the capital structure of a company:

- **Taxes** If a company is in a taxpaying position, an increase in leverage reduces the income tax paid by the company. There is a tax advantage to borrowing for companies that are able (or reasonably certain of being able) to use the interest tax shields.[6]

- **Risk** With or without bankruptcy, financial distress is costly. Other things being equal, financial distress is more likely for firms with high business risk than with low business risk. For this reason high business risk companies generally issue less debt than companies with low business risk.[7]

- **Asset type** The costs of distress are likely to be greater for firms whose value depends on growth opportunities or intangible assets as they are more likely to forego profitable investment opportunities and, if default occurs, their assets may erode rapidly. Hence, firms whose assets are weighted toward intangible assets will be able to borrow significantly less, on average, than firms holding assets you can kick!

- **Financial slack** In the long run, a company's value rests more on its capital investment and operating decisions than on financing. Therefore, make sure your firm has sufficient financial slack, so that financing is quickly accessible when good investment opportunities arise. Financial slack is most valuable to firms that have ample positive NPV growth opportunities. This is another reason why growth companies usually aspire to conservative capital structure.

3.4.2 Anticipating the banker's advice

When companies issue debt, they have to persuade lenders that they will be able to repay their loan. Therefore, companies seeking debt financing usually draw up a set of pro forma income statement and balance sheets. When completing these statements, you are simply making your best forecasts of the firm's profit, assets and liabilities. These forecasts are regarded with the utmost importance by bankers and are key to a successful business plan.

These forecasts may reveal that the firm is unlikely to generate sufficient cash internally to repay the loan. That is not in itself a cause for alarm. But such a result should prompt two questions:

---

6 Note that borrowing is not the only way to shield income. For example, accelerated write-offs of plant and equipment can be used to reduce corporate taxes.

7 The risk of a common stock reflects the business risk of the real assets held by a firm, but shareholders also bear financial risk to the extent that the firm issues debt to finance its real investments. The more a firm relies on debt financing, the riskier is its common stock.

■   Can the maturity of the proposed loan be extended so that the firm can repay the loan out of income?

■   Is the firm likely to be able to raise the additional debt or equity that it will need to repay the proposed loan?

The financial manager should conduct a sensitivity analysis to see how far the profits could decline without imperilling the company's ability to service the loan.

3.5   INTERACTION OF INVESTMENT AND FINANCING DECISIONS

In an ideal world with no taxes, transaction costs, or other market imperfections, only investment decisions would affect the value of a company. In such a world, companies could analyse all investment opportunities as if they were equity financed. They could decide which assets to buy and then worry about getting the money to pay for them. No one would worry about where the money would come from because debt policy, dividend policy and all other financing choices would have no impact on the stockholder's wealth.

However, the side effects of financing cannot be ignored in practice. A simple technique takes them into account:

Step 1:   start by estimating the project's base-case value as an all equity-financed mini-firm;

Step 2:   then adjust this project's base-case NPV to account for the project's impact on the firm's capital structure.

Adjusted NPV or APV = Base-case NPV + NPV of financing decisions caused by project acceptance.

Once the side effects of financing a project are identified and valued, calculating its APV is no more than addition or subtraction. The rule is then to *accept projects if APV is positive.*

Here are some examples of side-effects:

■   **Issue costs**   If accepting the project forces the firm to issue securities, then the present value of issue costs should be subtracted from the base-case NPV.

■   **Interest tax shields**   Debt interest is a tax-deductible expense. Most people believe that interest tax shields contribute to a firm's value, thus a project that prompts the firm to borrow more generates additional value. The project's APV is increased by the present value of interest tax shields on debt the project supports.

■   **Special financing**   (interest rate subvention, subsidies)   Sometimes special financing opportunities are tied to project acceptance. For example, the government might offer subsidised financing for socially desirable projects. Simply compute the present value of the financing opportunity and add it to the base-case NPV.

Calculating APV, therefore, may require several steps: one for the base-case NPV and one for each financing side effect.

3.6 CONCLUSION

In order to determine the overall financial viability of a project, it is best to start with an estimation of total costs. After determining the costs, it then becomes a matter of estimating the total benefits over the life-time of the project. The decision of whether to invest in any particular project means assessing various alternatives under the same method. In this chapter, we reviewed cash flow methods that allow for a consistency in approach. While payback and internal rate of return methods are generally favoured by companies for their convenience, there are severe limitations and disadvantages in their use. Therefore, for the purposes of obtaining finance from financial institutions, proposers are most likely to be asked to use the discounted cash flow method to conduct their investment appraisal. It is this method which underlies the pro-forma cash flow analysis of the Business Plan Form in Chapter 7.

4

Understanding lender procedures

LEARNING OBJECTIVES

After reading this chapter you will be able to understand the basic procedural steps lenders take in order to approve a loan. These steps include:

- *The initial proposal*
- *Concept clearance*
- *Initial review*
- *Final review*
- *Board review*
- *Signing*

4.1   INTRODUCTION TO THE APPROVAL PROCESS

Each lender has its own procedures for appraising the financial, economic, technical and environmental feasibility of projects proposed for financing. Proposers should be aware of the basic process before constructing a proposal and this chapter contains an outline of the major steps that would be taken by a multi-lateral bank such as the European Bank for Reconstruction and Development (EBRD) in assessing financial feasibility. The lender's formal project approval process consists of concept clearance, initial review, final review and review by the Board of Directors. The main elements of each of these steps is set out with particular emphasis on the areas in which environmental due diligence is incorporated in each of the project development stages. As a first step, the sponsor may approach the lender with an initial proposal.

4.2   PROJECT SIZE

Normally, a lender does not finance projects where its involvement (limited to 35 per cent of long-term capital) is smaller than US$5 million. Proposals for smaller projects amalgamated into a larger structure would, however, be welcomed in order to build up a pipeline of projects and justify the development of a dedicated instrument.

4.3 INITIAL PROPOSAL

In the initial proposal to the lender, the sponsor should have sufficient information to satisfy the requirements of the lender. The sponsor has two choices: either to prepare a synopsis of the business or the bankable proposal itself. If the sponsor prepares a synopsis of the business, then it must also prepare a cover letter with a synopsis of the bankable proposal which includes the following information:

■ Information on the sponsors who may be a public company or joint venture or government entity and whether the enterprise is registered as a local or foreign organisation.

■ Business and project rationale:

  – a clear explanation of the investment proposal;

  – whether it is a public service such as schools and hospitals;

  – technical aspects;

  – economic and commercial aspects;

■ Initial proposal as to the type and amount of lender involvement the client requires:

  – as an equity partner;

  – as a source of credit (debt financing); or

  – as a combination of both.

However, the sponsor may wish to send a complete bankable proposal to the lender since the lender will in any case request a complete bankable proposal if the concept is of any interest.

4.4 CONCEPT CLEARANCE

The information provided in the initial proposal should be sufficient to enable the lender to determine whether the project fits within its guidelines and strategies and deserves further involvement and work on the part of the lender. This will lead to the first step in the lender's approval process, the concept clearance. Concept clearance is an internal procedure which all projects must pass before detailed work can commence.

The concept of the project is presented to the relevant Banking Vice President and/or Deputy Vice President for approval to begin work on it. The project sponsors should supply details of the proposed project to the lender. These details include a description of the property (size and location of each site), a description of major processes, raw materials and wastestreams, the historical and current environmental status of the property, available environmental reports and a description of the proposed modernisation (if any) and the associated environmental impacts. The information should highlight any potential environmental concerns associated with the property. A copy of a corporate environmental policy can also be helpful.

If the project concept is accepted, a mandate letter will be required from the sponsor which forms the basis of a working agreement with the lender. It needs to be signed by both parties and sets out the basic working practices of the lender and the requirements for entering into a working relationship, including allocation of expenses and procedures in the event that the sponsor or the lender subsequently decides to withdraw from the project.

4.5 INITIAL REVIEW

The next stage is the initial review which involves the Operations Committee of the lender's senior management. At this level, much more detailed information is required as the lender will make its assessment of the project by analysing the bankable proposal and financial projections and assessing the ability of the project sponsors to implement them. The initial review normally occurs one to two months after concept clearance. The initial review will usually incorporate the following points:

- **A detailed description of the client enterprise** This should include:
    - its history;
    - a description of production activities;
    - the names and biographies of principal managers;
    - lender references;
    - other relevant information.

- **Financial statements audited to international standards**
    - it is in the client's own long-term interests to seek guidance from reputable accounting firms;
    - the lender will ask for full disclosure and will respect confidentiality.

- **Financial projections**
    - the purpose of these projections is to inform the lender of the ultimate financial viability of the project;
    - these include realistic assumptions about costs, prices, etc.

- **Relevant laws** Information on the relevant laws and export/import duties applicable to the project.

- **Environmental information** The environmental specialist in the Lender's Environmental Appraisal Unit (EAU) will review the preliminary information and the description of the project, identify the environmental concerns and opportunities typically associated with such projects and define the investigations that will be required. The EAU prepares an Environmental Screening Memorandum (ESM) for the project team, which is incorporated in the documentation presented to the lender's senior management at the time that they undertake the initial review of the project. An overview of the investigations and information frequently required is found in the section on 'Environmental due diligence', below.

- **Project preparation** The investigations are always the responsibility of the project sponsor, but the lender can assist, where necessary, in the preparation of consultancy Terms of

Reference for environmental studies and in the identification of environmental consultants. If properly integrated in the overall due diligence process, environmental investigations should not delay project processing.

■ **Letter of information** The lender will provide a format for the disclosure of this information. This letter will detail the legal basis of the company. It will also provide information on contracts relevant to the future of the company. The letter should be completed by the company's lawyers and accountants. It should be started as soon as possible after the signing of the mandate letter.

4.6 FINAL REVIEW

A final review by the lender's Operations Committee on the basis of a negotiated Term Sheet for private sector projects is carried out before going to the lender's Board of Directors for its approval. This evaluation process covers financial, legal, economic, technical and environmental issues.

The final review normally occurs two to six months after the initial review.

It is important to note that the final review follows a very detailed preparation of all aspects of the proposed loan, including indicative terms, although these will not be formally agreed until after the final review and just prior to Board approval.

4.7 BOARD REVIEW

The project documentation is presented to the Board of Directors for their consideration. This documentation includes a section on the project's environmental implications and summarises the work that was done on the project.

4.8 SIGNING

Following Board approval, loan documentation can be signed and the loan may be disbursed.

4.9 CONCLUSION

The proposer of a bankable proposal needs to understand the procedures of the target funder. This chapter reviewed one example of the procedures found in an international lending institution, the EBRD. The proposer should check to see what types of advisory services the target bank offers, the types of operational procedures and normal deadlines, timetables and schedules. The bank may also have its own established guidelines for proposals and criteria for acceptance. Armed with this information, the proposer may plan an approach which is tailored to the financial institution's requirements, thereby enhancing the chances for success.

5

Constructing bankable proposals: feasibility studies

LEARNING OBJECTIVES

After reading this chapter you will be able to identify major factors affecting the feasibility of projects including:

- *Reserves*
- *Throughputs*
- *Access*
- *Permits*
- *Value adding potential*
- *Insurance*
- *Foreign exchange*

5.1   INTRODUCTION

In constructing a bankable proposal, it is necessary to gather the relevant information in a documented form which provides strong technical and economic justification for the project. It is not possible in the space allowed to list every type of technical or economic factor that would need to be identified, assessed and resolved in a satisfactory way in a project financing. This chapter indicates some of the major types of issues that need to be resolved prior to completing a bankable proposal.

These issues should be addressed as a minimum in the form of feasibility studies that are conducted by relevant experts who are able to express an opinion in a documented report. The feasibility studies are usually referred to within the body of the business plan and attached to it in the form of appendices. Needless to say, technical and economic feasibility studies form the basis for critical assumptions in the business model of the project and will be closely assessed by the bankers. The bankers may also request further information about these technical and economic studies or conduct their own in order to confirm or deny the findings of the original studies.

This section lists some of the major areas for feasibility studies with a brief commentary on each.

5.2   MAJOR ISSUES ADDRESSED IN FEASIBILITY STUDIES

The feasibility study should address:

- the extent and certainty of the reserves in extraction projects;

- the likely throughput in pipeline or tolling (processing) projects;

- the likely passenger or traffic flows in transport projects;

- the cost of acquiring the project site, construction and development;

- the availability and cost of services to the project site: energy, water, transportation and communications;

- access to supplies of raw materials, from either domestic or foreign sources;

- whether there are tariff or foreign exchange barriers to imports;

- the existence of accessible markets – domestic and/or foreign – for the product or service and the demand within those markets;

- the availability and transferability of operating licences and other official permits;

- projection of costs and returns, based on assumptions as to interest rates, exchange rates, inflation, taxes, delays and other contingencies;

- the existence of any potential for added value, eg property development or by-product sales;

- the environmental impact of the project and the need to comply with environmental protection legislation;

- the availability and convertibility of currencies and the effect of foreign exchange controls; and

- the availability of insurance against project and country risks.

5.2.1   Extent and certainty of the reserves

The reserves to any extraction scheme are critical to the projected life of the project. The specialist engineering or geological team will provide an opinion as to the quantity of the reserves which will form the basis for the calculation of the total potential output of the extraction project. This estimation may form the basis for the calculation of the total value of the project. However, estimates will usually be couched in terms of likelihood or probability. The feasibility study will also usually disclaim any precision as to the actual amount that could be found. For large extraction projects, it is not unusual to have at least three feasibility studies conducted by various experts before the bank is ready to grant any credits.

5.2.2   Likely throughput

In pipeline or tolling (processing) projects, the critical element is the actual throughput since the project economics will usually be dependent on the charge per quantity passing through the completed project, whether a pipeline or tolling bridge, road or tunnel. The throughput will be based on models of the general region and factors determining the frequency of use, such as population, local businesses, border restrictions, demographics, tourism, climatic conditions, competition, economic growth and politics. The price of the per unit throughput will also have a dynamic impact on the throughput since pipeline and tolling projects are price sensitive unless the projects hold monopolistic positions.

5.2.3   Likely passenger or traffic flows

Projections in passenger and traffic flows are the basic assumptions to any highway, railway or airport construction project. Similar to throughput projections, the factors that may be considered important include, amongst others the population characteristics, proximity to alternative means of transport and growth of the local economy. Estimations of passenger or traffic flows will be based on historical measures and are known to be notoriously difficult to predict, especially for new projects.

5.2.4   Cost of the project site, construction and development

The cost of acquisition of the site together with construction and development costs are normally agreed to and set out in the form of written contracts. Preliminary or draft construction and development agreements including architectural drawings would also need to be available at the time of submission of the business plan. Except for build-operate-transfer contracts where the total construction and maintenance of the facility is completely transferred to one contractor, total costs are often made subject to certain events occurring in the course of the completion of construction, or the passage of time. It is important that these events be foreseeable and controllable within reasonable objective standards, otherwise the description of the costs would be said to be too indefinite or uncertain to be enforceable.

5.2.5   Services to the project site

The typical types of services necessary for project development include energy, water, transportation and communications systems. A critical assessment needs to be made about their availability for the project. If for any reason a key resource is in jeopardy of becoming defunct or severely curtailed, then there may be additional costs for monitoring and actively managing this exposure. A statement concerning the availability and cost of services made in a feasibility study will be used as an assumption in the business model for the project. At the initial stage the basis for this statement is likely to involve 'letters of intent' to participate in the project signed by the utilities, public authorities or private bodies in charge of particular services. At a later date these intentions will need to be crystallised into agreements which will be made part of the bankable proposal.

5.2.6   Access to supplies of raw materials

Access to supplies of raw materials can be divided into domestic or foreign sources. Sometimes governments granting a concession for a specific development, say, the development of a mine, will also control access to domestic supplies for other strategic raw materials, such as oil or gas. In these cases, the government may agree to make the raw materials available to the project at a certain price. Obviously, where access to critical raw materials is threatened or cut off, there is no possibility for the project to continue. Guarantees or insurance should be included wherever possible with penalties for failure to comply with agreements to access. In cases where access is not controlled by the government, such as in foreign sources of raw materials, there may be a means of making such materials more accessible to the project by the government reducing the tariffs for such items or linking their import price to the price paid to the government for the concession. Here the risk of lack of access is transformed into a market risk. In any case, the feasibility study will need to address how raw materials may be accessed and at what price.

5.2.7   Tariff or foreign exchange barriers to imports

Where high tariffs or foreign exchange barriers to imports exist, the economic viability of the project is decreased. While tariffs and foreign exchange barriers might be altered swiftly by a change in law, the residual underlying risk remains, that is, political risk. In this case, the feasibility study should address the likelihood of changes of attitude by the government and the factors that are likely to cause such changes to occur. The profitability and therefore the project's acceptability from a financial standpoint may depend on whether such barriers be overcome or reduced.

5.2.8   Existence of accessible markets

The major, perhaps, primary concern of the project managers is whether there is an accessible market – domestic and/or foreign – for the product or service and the demand within those markets. This information should be included in a market analysis or market feasibility study. This will usually require a survey of the relevant major buyers of the project's production, with estimations and details of their requirements over a period of years. Letters of intent or signed offtake agreements would be relevant to proving market demand.

5.2.9   Operating licences and other official permits

The operating licences and other official permits constitute perhaps the most valuable property of the project in the initial stage. Their availability is evidenced by documents of transfer signed by the highest level official in the government who have the authority to grant such licences and permits. These should be made part of the bankable proposal. The issue of their transferability is important in determining the on-sale value of the project. If the licences and permits are not transferable, then the owners of the project have in effect no market value for their assets, except perhaps for the salvage value of the equipment and raw materials. One way to handle the transferability issue is to offer a first right of refusal at a certain price to the original owner of the asset (in most cases, the local government) and if the original owner does not accept then the project owner can sell his equity to others. In any case, the availability and transferability issues will need to be specifically addressed in the bankable proposal and backed up by transfer of ownership documentation signed by the original owner.

5.2.10   Projection of costs and returns

The projection of costs and returns is part of the business plan for the project. It is based on a number of factors including assumptions as to interest rates, exchange rates, inflation, taxes, delays and other contingencies. For a full description of the pro forma financial projections required for a project, see Chapter 7.

5.2.11   Added value potential

It is currently in vogue amongst some corporate financiers to consider the 'real option value' of assets. Basically, any asset can be considered in terms of an option pricing model. This concept may be especially helpful in thinking through the potential added value of projects which consequentially flow from the main project. For example, the original facility may involve future property development or by-product sales which will provide additional positive net cash flow streams. It is important that the feasibility study distinguish between the primary business (or primary cash flow streams) and the secondary business, which may or may not be implemented, but which exists by virtue of the completion of the main project.

5.2.12   Compliance with environmental protection legislation

In most jurisdictions, governments have laws and regulations that require environmental compliance. This may be in the form of obtaining permits, conducting environmental impact assessments or participating in a monitoring and control scheme for pollution. Whatever the requirements, the project owner needs to assure the bank that all such requirements will be fulfilled. The bank may condition its approval of the loan application on successful completion of all the necessary environmental requirements. Details of the types of environmental information required can be found in Chapter 7.

5.2.13   Currencies and foreign exchange controls

In many countries there still exist laws and regulations that limit the exchange of funds into foreign currencies. Obviously, without an explicit lifting of this type of foreign exchange control, it will not be possible for foreign owners of the project to receive a return on their equity and lenders of foreign currency to be paid back in their own currency. There are many ways to overcome this obstacle. The most direct route is for the government to lift foreign exchange controls. For large projects, this may be necessary in order for the project to have any chance of success. However, for smaller projects this might not be a politically viable solution. In such cases, alternative mechanisms may be necessary in order to ensure smooth foreign exchange transactions. For example, counter-trade of goods that have genuine market value or where other valuable commodities exist (such as oil or minerals) may be exchanged through a third party broker. Foreign exchange risk is not to be taken lightly since, as we have seen in the Asian crisis during 1997 and the Russian crisis in 1998, large sections of the economy can come to a near halt, driving up interest rates and making dollar-denominated projects prohibitively expensive.

5.2.14   Project and country risks insurance

Whether insurance is available for the project to completion is critical for giving confidence to bankers that there are sufficient layers of capital to bring the project to operational status. Obviously, if the project cannot meet completion, there will be no funds to pay back the loan and the loan might then have to be written off as a dead loss.   Therefore, insurance against project risks is critically important for the initiation of the project and insurance policies should be made part of the bankable proposal.

To mitigate the impact of foreign exchange turmoil, such as that generated by a series of crises during the 1990s, it appears that insurance against country risks would be a necessary requirement before lenders will consider entering into major project financings. In the same vein, it is possible to structure deals where country risks are transformed into the credit risk of the counterparties concerned through use of credit derivatives. It is becoming more fashionable for such instruments to be used by banks at the time of financings to manage their own exposures to country risks. There is no reason why such financial products might not be structured for the project owners allowing them to pass some of the benefits of their risk management programme to their bankers and insurers.

5.3   CONCLUSION

This brief chapter has highlighted some of the major issues that need to be addressed in project feasibility studies. Not all these issues need to be addressed in every project and there are many other issues that will need to be addressed that have not been discussed. The main point is that feasibility studies should provide sufficient credible evidence for assumptions that are used in the business model of the bankable proposal. Armed with these studies, the proposer will have a better chance of convincing the banker of the economic viability of the project.

6

Legal considerations to project finance

LEARNING OBJECTIVES

After reading this chapter you will be able to:

- *Identify major risk allocation issues in a project finance transaction amongst the major participants*
- *Assess the major project risk issues in terms of their legal implications*
- *Determine in a comprehensive way how risks might be allocated using legal means of risk transfer*

6.1   STRUCTURING THE PROJECT SPONSOR

There are a number of different structures available to sponsors in deciding how to finance a particular project. The most commonly utilised are:

■   joint venture;

■   partnership;

■   limited partnership;

■   limited company.

A joint venture set-up would normally be used in cases where the sponsors wish to hold the project assets directly. Where the assets are to be held indirectly, a project company – a special purpose vehicle (SPV) – would be established. The sponsor's right to the assets would exist in the form of a shareholding in the project company.

The choice of structure will depend upon a number of commercial, legal, taxation and financial issues including, for example:

■   the sponsors' desire to isolate the project, ie utilise the concept of no recourse;

- the need to consolidate the project assets on the sponsors' balance sheets can be avoided through the use of an SPV, the benefit being the impact of cross-default clauses within loan documentation, be it in respect of the project or of additional financing;

- the granting of government concessions may require the structure to be in a particular form, usually an SPV.

The art of project finance is to analyse and evaluate correctly the risks associated with a particular project. The science is to create a pattern of agreements among all the potential players that puts sufficient controls on the risks so that a passive investor or lender will provide funds and can expect to receive a reasonable market return.

In analysing each project, the starting-point is the financial projections for the project showing profit and loss, cash flow and pro forma balance sheets. Each project must have the ability to generate sufficient cash flow to retire the debt incurred for the project plus a sufficient cushion so that reasonable variations in the projections do not result in financial disaster. The financial projections will be used to determine how much debt can be incurred, the amount of the equity investment needed and the expected return on equity.

Reliability of the projections is crucial and must be examined in the light of assumed project costs, the project capacity and completion date, operating costs, revenues (including market demand and price for the product) and costs of raw materials. Beyond these basic risk factors, country risk, currency exchange risk and currency valuation risks may also need to be taken into account. The projections are then analysed in terms of these risk factors and various scenarios are explored showing the consequences of the occurrence of certain risks. To the extent that the risks can be shifted away from the project, the projections are that much more reliable for the financing. For example, will the contractor cover additional costs or delays due to strikes? What if the delay is due to shipping interruptions? Can the project perform satisfactorily if total costs are 20 per cent higher than expected? What if customers take 120 days to pay instead of the projected 60 days? Typical risks and the parties to whom some or all of the risk is allocated are shown below.

Risk	Candidates
Project cost	Contractor; Project owner; Project sponsor guarantees
Timely completion	Contractor; Project owner; Project sponsor guarantees
Project output below design	Contractor; Project owner; Project sponsor guarantees
Cost of raw material	Suppliers; Project sponsor guarantees
Market demand or price of	Project owner; Customer contracts; Project sponsor product guarantees
Operating costs	Project owner; Customer contract; Management or technical services agreement

Risk	Candidates
Currency exchange	Project owner; Customer contract; Project sponsor guarantees
Currency valuation	Project owner; Customer contract; Project sponsor guarantees
Regulatory changes	Project owner; Insurance
Damage to project	Project owner; Insurance
Force majeure	Project owner; Insurance

In all the above risk areas, lenders may assume some part of the risk and the allocation of risk among the parties for any one risk is subject to extensive negotiation. Project sponsor guarantees may take different forms depending on the risk covered. For example, the guarantee relating to cost overruns or delays may be a limited obligation to invest more equity or make subordinated loans to the project owner. Another example is the guarantee relating to currency exchange or product sales which may be to purchase certain volumes of product with payment in an off-shore escrow used to repay debt.

Once the risks directly related to the reliability of the financial projections are allocated satisfactorily, an analysis of the parties' abilities to fulfil their commitments is almost complete. Since the project owner has no source of revenue except the project, his obligation can be backed only by mortgaging the project, pledging its revenues and equipment and assigning various key contracts such as long-term customer and/or supply contracts. The value of the mortgage rights depends heavily on the enforceability of the mortgage under local law and the resale potential if the project fails. In many developing countries, mortgages and similar property rights are new and untested. Likewise, in many projects, the ability to resell a project to cover its outstanding debt is highly questionable. The package of security or collateral the lenders will require for a particular project is then developed based on the creditworthiness of the various parties, their contractual obligations, the location and nature of the project and the expected sources of its revenues.

6.2   BUILD-OPERATE-TRANSFER (BOT)

The basis for all BOT model projects is likely to be the granting of a concession or licence for a period of years involving the transfer and retransfer of all or some of the project's assets. The key features are:

■   the grant of a concession;

■   the assumption of responsibility by the promoter;

- the construction, operation and financing of the project; and

- the retransfer of the project at the end of the concession period to the grantor.

A common variant of the BOT model is the BOO (build-own-operate) project structured on similar lines to the BOT but without the obligation of transferring the project at the end of the concessions.

The advantages of a BOT project to the concession grantor, are:

- it offers a form of off-balance sheet financing as the borrowing will be undertaken by the project company;

- because the concession guarantor will not borrow there will be a favourable impact on public sector borrowing rate;

- it enables the concession grantor to transfer construction risks; and

- it is a method of attracting foreign investment.

6.3 FINANCIAL STRUCTURING

6.3.1 Bond financing

The main attraction to bond financing is the long-term nature of fixed rate funding which is generally cheaper than bank borrowing but also offers possibilities of lengthening repayment profiles so as to considerably improve project economics. There are conversely a number of disadvantages to bond financing including:

- Consents and waivers from lenders are sought in project financings and it is considerably more difficult to obtain these from bondholders. Bond trustees have a certain amount of discretionary authority but this may not be wide enough to cover material changes to loan terms, etc.

- Bonds tend to be structures where the payment by the bondholders is in one large sum at closing. Project financings generally require periodic drawdowns. The solution in this case is *to deposit* the proceeds of the bond offering with a bond security trustee and allow withdrawals as and when required. The problem here revolves around what happens when a default occurs prior to drawdown. To whom do the funds belong – the bondholders, the lenders or the project company? Second, in respect to interest payments, the bond interest will surely be more than that obtained from placing the proceeds of the bond offering on deposit.

- Bonds have less onerous warranties, covenants and events of default compared with, for example, syndicated loans. Typically, owing to the fact that there are a number of bondholders, the structure of the documentation is such that insignificant events do not amount to an event of default. This is in direct conflict with the concept of a project financing in that any misperformance or non-performance under a loan agreement would be considered a technical breach of strict warranties and covenants and trigger default clauses in order to catch all.

Similarly, bond investors' appetite, for risk is much lower and they are not attracted per se to pure project risk. Bond market investors typically invest in sound companies with strong balance sheets rather than relatively speculative investments.

A major development over the past few years has been the liberalisation of the US securities market by the introduction of Rule 144a of the Securities Act 1933. The rule allows non-US issuers to issue securities in the US to 'Qualified Institutional Buyers' without registration of securities under the 1933 Act. An example of a major Rule 144a project is the US$1 billion Petroziata issue in Venezuela where sponsors did not even seek political risk cover.

Project bonds represent a great opportunity for investment bankers, however, for lawyers the situation is quite the opposite. It was mentioned above that going to a bond market will produce longer term funding. Caution must be taken when considering a bond offering in that even before the deal is done it may be sunk. Confidentiality clauses, for example, in fuel supply agreements may mean that breaches of such clauses may occur when coming to list the offering on the relevant stock exchange. The scenario of the Salt End power deal is a recent example of how a deal can fail. BP, the lessor of the site, pulled the plug on Entergy's planned bond issue, refusing to allow the terms of their agreement to be disclosed. Not only would it not be possible to list the bonds in London but it would not be possible to satisfy US market disclosure requirements nor obtain a rating for your bonds, for anyone in Entergy's shoes. It is imperative therefore that all project agreements conform consistently in all their provisions.

6.3.2 Leveraged leasing

A typical leveraged lease involves six groups of parties:

- the owner or equity participants
- the owner trustee,
- the lenders or loan participants,
- the secured or indenture trustee;
- the manufacturer or supplier; and
- the lessee.

There may also be a guarantor of the lessee or an owner participant undertakings or another credit enhancement party for the lessee, such as a letter of credit issuer, a sublessee, or a purchaser of products of the leased asset.

For example, an investor seeking to acquire capital equipment costing $20 million might invest $5 million of his own money and borrow the rest on a non-recourse basis from one or more lenders. The parties agree that repayment can be made exclusively from the rentals produced by the equipment lease and, upon the lessee's default, from the proceeds of sale. Although the owner invests as little as 20 per cent of the cost the income tax benefits, from investment tax credit (if still available) and depreciation deductions, are calculated on 100 per cent of the cost, assuming that the lease is a true lease and not a conditional or instalment sale agreement. In addition, even if the owner is not personally liable to repay the debt, in most cases the owner is entitled to deduct the full amount of the interest component. For tax purposes, therefore, the owner has made his $5 million do the work of $20 million.

Owner participants are usually one or more commercial banks, bank affiliates, leasing companies or finance companies that desire to acquire title to capital equipment or real property, to obtain the tax benefits of ownership and ultimately to realise an additional return from the disposition of the leased asset. For reasons discussed below, the owner participants often do not take legal title to the property directly but instead appoint a trustee, generally a commercial bank (the owner trustee), to hold legal title for their benefit. The owner participants contribute to the trust the amount of their investment, generally at least 20 per cent (but occasionally as high as 50 per cent) of the acquisition cost, which may include such expenses as legal costs for themselves and the lenders, appraisal expenses and any commissions payable to a third party for arranging the project.

Concurrently with receipt of the owner participant's investments, the owner trustee borrows the balance of the purchase price by issuing its promissory notes, loan certificates or bonds to the third group of parties, the lenders, usually in a private placement. Normally an exemption from registration is available under the Securities Act 1933 – public debt placement is extremely expensive and generally avoided except in very large projects.

The debt incurred by the owner trustee is without recourse to the institution acting as owner trustee or to the general assets of the owner participants; the purchasers of the debt instruments agree to look exclusively to the rentals under the lease for repayment and, upon default, to their security interest or mortgage in the leased property and to any credit enhancements offered by the lessee.

Because an assignment of the lease and a security interest or mortgage in the property is invariably created for the benefit of the lenders to secure repayment of the borrowings, the lenders generally appoint a second trustee, called a secured or indenture trustee, to act for them in holding the security interests. Use of such a trustee has at least two advantages. First, all rent is usually paid to the indenture trustee, who is then responsible for dividing it among the various lenders and owner participants – this is a task lenders are usually loath to do. Second, the notes or bonds are more readily transferable if the secured party or mortgagee on the various documents and filings or recordings need not change as a result of such a transfer.

The owner trustee, immediately upon receipt of the investments from the owner participants and borrowings from the lenders:

■ purchases the property from the manufacturer or supplier pursuant to an underlying construction or purchase agreement, the rights under which are assigned by the lessee to the owner trustee, or purchases from the lessee if the lessee initially took title from the manufacturer or supplier;

■ pays the expenses being financed in the project; and

■ leases the property to the lessee.

The term of the lease is usually identical to the amortisation period of the debt, with monthly, quarterly or semi-annual lease payments due on, or occasionally on the day immediately preceding, each day on which a payment of interest, principal, or both is due on the debt. Occasionally the lease term survives the final debt maturity date by a year or two in order to produce additional cash flow for the benefit of the owner participants.

Since the lenders do not enjoy recourse to the general assets of the owner participants, it is evident that the financial merits of the project rest entirely upon the value of the leased property and the creditworthiness of either the lessee or a seventh party to the project that acts as a credit enhancer. Credit enhancement falls into several categories.

Most often a full guaranty by a parent or affiliate of the lessee is used. Variations on a guaranty that are often seen include comfort letters, keep-well agreements and limited guaranties. These documents normally are in the same form as would be used in any other kind of financing.

A second source of guarantees or guaranteed cash flow is an unrelated private business enterprise, such as either a major customer of the lessee who is willing to support the lessee's obligations because it is a substantial principal consumer of the products to be manufactured or transported by the leased equipment, or the manufacturer of the leased asset who is willing to support the lessee's credit if the lessee acquires the asset from that manufacturer. In lieu of reliance on a guarantee, the manufacturer might act as the lessee of the asset with an identical (or very different) sublease to its customer, which is the real user of the asset. In such cases the equity and debt investors need look only to the manufacturer's credit and may not even deal with the user.

Two other ways in which a lessee can enhance its credit are by, first, supplying a letter of credit from a friendly commercial bank and, second, by arranging either for subleases of part or all of the leased asset or for someone to agree to purchase the products of the leased asset and then to have the subleases or purchase contracts assigned to the owner trustee as collateral for the lessee's lease obligations.

Occasionally, to save some expenses and reduce the cast of characters, the separate functions of the owner trustee and the indenture trustee have been combined in a single institution which, pursuant to a trust agreement with the owner participants as settlers, agrees to hold legal title to the equipment and to receive the rentals and other payments under the lease for the benefit, first, of the lenders and, second, of the owner participants. Because of the obvious conflict of interest thereby created, as well as the mechanical problems arising from having the debtor and secured party be the same entity, this device is rarely used.

There are several variations on the standard leveraged lease structure described above. In railroad equipment financing, it is still traditional to use a conditional sale agreement to evidence the obligations to the lenders. The owner trustee initially enters into a conditional sale agreement directly with the supplier, under which the owner trustee makes an initial payment equal to the aggregate investments made by the owner participants and agrees to pay the balance, plus interest, in instalments over a period of years, each instalment being payable concurrently with each rental payment under the proposed lease.

The supplier, on the delivery date, assigns its rights to receive future payments to the lenders (or a bank acting as their agent) in exchange for a full payment by the lenders of the remaining amounts to which the supplier is entitled. The supplier is thus taken out of the project immediately and the lender steps into its shoes. The lenders become entitled to receive further instalments of the conditional sale indebtedness in repayment of their loans-the payments are supported by the lessee's obligations under a lease of the equipment simultaneously entered into between the owner trustee and the railroad. The conditional sale agreement specifically provides that the indebtedness is payable exclusively out of payments under the lease and the other assets of the owner trust estate.

A variation on the foregoing arises when Japanese leasing companies provide the debt financing for a leveraged lease. As such companies are not permitted by Japanese law to make loans, the manufacturer or supplier sells the asset to the lenders, which then resell the asset to the owner trustee, with the purchase price payable in instalments and secured by a purchase money lien. The initial down payment is provided by the equity investment. The owner trustee then leases the asset to the lessee.

Another structure quite often seen is the so-called wrap lease. Here an entity (usually a lease broker) arranges a leveraged lease with itself as the lessor/borrower. Afterwards this entity sells the asset to an equity investor or an owner trust which immediately leases back the asset to the seller (now a lessee/sublessor). All these steps are subject to the existing sublease to the user and the debt documents with the lender, the debt remaining an obligation of the sublessor. The equity investor pays for the asset by making a down payment (frequently equal to the original equity investment made by the sublessor) and issuing a note to the sublessor for the balance. The rent due on the head lease is frequently equal to the debt service on this note so that no real money changes hands for part or all of the term of the head lease. The term of the head lease often exceeds the term of the user lease, thereby giving the sublessor an opportunity to realise profit after the end of the user lease by remarketing the residual. This structure has been used most often for tax shelters offered to the public and hence will probably not be seen much in the future. Institutional equity investors tend to avoid wrap leases because of the heightened tax risks.

6.3.3 Structured finance

Structured finance could encompass any of the following:

- limited recourse or project financing;
- buyer credit export financing;
- tax driven financing;
- multi-sourced financing;
- defeasance;
- asset securitisation;
- cross-border lease;
- acquisition finance;
- ESOPS (Employee Share Option Plan);
- derivative enhanced or equity linked financing.

6.4 SECURITY FOR PROJECTS

6.4.1 Approach of lenders

Security plays an important role in project financing and problems encountered in perfecting security can often necessitate changes in how a project is to be structured. As in most project financings, the lenders will have no recourse to assets of the project company other than the project assets and will look primarily to the cash flow generated by the project to repay loans to the project company. It is therefore crucial in project financing for lenders to ensure that valid and effective security interests are taken over all the project assets. If problems do arise with the project and the lenders are forced to pursue their security interests then, in the absence of any shareholder guarantees or other tangible support, the enforcing of their security over the project assets will be the only opportunity for the lenders to recover their loans.

If the project company is a special purpose vehicle, it is likely that the lenders will have taken security over all its property and assets and will have control of those assets to the exclusion of other creditors. In this case they may be able to petition to wind up the project company and prove as a creditor in the winding-up. However, if there are no assets outside the project, then this is not likely to prove a fruitful course of action for the lenders. Because the value of the project assets is primarily determined by their cash-generating power and because the project lenders are only likely to seek to wind up the project company if something has gone wrong with the project, a winding-up is unlikely to recover the full amount of any loan to the project company, particularly if the project is incomplete – a half-built power station, for example, will produce a negative cash flow.

Where the project company is not a special purchase vehicle and has other assets apart from the project assets, then it is likely that those assets will have been ring-fenced so that the lenders' actions will be limited strictly to enforcing their security against the project assets alone. Normally this is achieved by providing in the loan documentation that the lenders are prevented from petitioning to wind up the project company or taking other similar action which would allow them to threaten the continued existence of the project company or to pursue the other assets of the project company. This principle of ring-fencing individual projects is of fundamental importance to sponsors and project companies. Indeed, it is also important for a sponsor's lenders which may be concerned to ensure that projects they have financed are not allowed to stand as collateral for, or be threatened by, other lenders to the project company. This is one of the main reasons why special purpose vehicles are used for project financing – the more so given that in most jurisdictions a shareholder will not be responsible for the debts of its subsidiaries (although in certain jurisdictions there are limited circumstances in which it is possible to pierce the corporate veil of limited liability and this will be something that sponsors will need to investigate in each jurisdiction in which they participate in projects).

6.4.2   Reasons for taking security

In most cases where lenders take security over assets they have financed (for example, ships and aircraft), the prime motivation for taking such security will be aggressive, that is, to ensure that the lenders are able to sell the asset in question on any enforcement of their security. In most jurisdictions movable assets such as ships and aircrafts will not pose insurmountable problems for the lenders (although in some jurisdictions this can be an expensive and time-consuming exercise). Likewise, with most real property there will usually be a buyer, at a price, depending on the state of the local property market and the type of property in question. However, selling a half-built tunnel or power station is likely to prove considerably more difficult, if not impossible – there is unlikely to be a long queue of interested buyers and the position may be made even more difficult for the lenders in those countries where the consent of government agencies or public sector bodies is required. It may well be the case that the only buyer is the host (or local) government and then at a fire-sale price! The predicament of the lenders can be further exacerbated in those jurisdictions where sale is not a remedy directly available to the lenders and can only be undertaken through cumbersome, time-consuming and expensive judicial proceedings.

With most projects, however, the ability to sell the project assets will not be the prime motivation for taking security in the first place. Instead, lenders will have two aims through the taking of security. First, they will see a comprehensive security package as a defensive mechanism designed both to prevent other (possibly unsecured) creditors taking security over the assets which they have financed and to prevent other creditors trying to attach those assets or take other enforcement action in respect of them. The reasoning is that if the lenders cannot sell the project assets and repay themselves out of the proceeds, then they certainly do not want any other creditors interfering with those assets in any way. This is a fine principle insofar as it goes, but often it is not watertight. For example, the mere existence of the lender's security over the project assets would not ordinarily prevent another creditor of the project company, for example, petitioning to wind up the project company for non-payment of a debt or non-performance of an obligation. Ordinarily, the project lenders will attempt to structure matters such that there are no significant creditors apart from within the project itself.

One way in which lenders will seek to achieve this is by limiting the activities of the project company to the project in question. This is one of the reasons why special purpose vehicles are so popular in the financing of projects. However, it is likely to prove impossible to eliminate all third party creditors and, therefore, there will always be a risk that third party creditors will threaten a project, for instance by obtaining a charging order against a vital project asset so as to enforce a judgment debt owed by the project company. If there are one or two particularly large creditors, it may be possible to bring them within the security package in some way, but this is likely to be more difficult, if not impossible, with smaller trade creditors. In practice this is a risk that most lenders will accept and in the worst case they may simply face the prospect of paying off a difficult creditor.

The existence of other security interests over the same assets can also be an important issue, especially in those jurisdictions where effective subordination of security interests is either not recognised or not effective. Whether or not other creditors can take a competing (or subordinate) security interest in the same project assets will, of course, depend on the security laws in the jurisdiction relevant to the particular security (usually the jurisdiction where the asset is located). The position is likely to be more precarious in those jurisdictions which do not have a central public registration system for the registering of security.

The other prime motivation for taking security over project assets is a desire on the part of the lenders to be able to control the destiny of the project should things start to go wrong. The lenders will hope that through their security interests they will be able to wrest control from the project company and themselves determine how the project should proceed. They then have the option to complete the project (if necessary) and operate it in order to generate the cash flows needed to repay themselves. However, the ability of the lenders to be able to achieve this aim will depend to a large extent on the jurisdiction in which the principal project assets are located.

In those jurisdictions which allow secured lenders to appoint a receiver to step in and effectively run a company's business as part of an enforcement of security, the lenders should be able to achieve their objectives. This is likely to be possible to a greater or lesser extent in most common law-based jurisdictions where secured lenders are given the right, either through the security document itself or under the general law, to appoint a receiver or receiver and manager over the assets over which they have security. However, where the relevant local law does not recognise the concept of receivers or other creditors' representatives taking control of the project assets then the aims of the lenders are likely to be frustrated. For example, this is likely to be the case in many civil law jurisdictions and in the US, where possessory management of a company through a receiver cannot displace the powers of the directors of the company. In these circumstances, the lenders only likely protection is through the local courts or judicially appointed officials, unless they have the opportunity to obtain an equivalent degree of control by taking security over the shares in the project company. This would (in theory) enable the lenders to exercise rights of shareholders in the event of default and take over management of the project company assuming that the applicable law of the jurisdiction concerned confers a right of possession rather than judicial sale. The lenders will, however, need to be aware that, by assuming control through the project company's equity, in certain jurisdictions they risk taking on liabilities of the project company (eg in the UK by becoming shadow directors of the project company).

6.4.3 Universal security interests

It will be readily apparent from the above that jurisdictions in which universal security over all of a company's property and assets (whether through a floating charge or a similar instrument) is coupled with the ability to be able to appoint receivers to take control of the project assets are a significant advantage for lenders involved in the financing of projects. However, for the most part, these advantages are enjoyed mainly in the common law-based jurisdictions. Where lenders are financing projects in other jurisdictions they will frequently find they have to accept a less complete security package, which in some cases will fall well short of giving either effective control over the project assets or acting as an effective defence against other creditors.

In some jurisdictions, it may be possible for the lenders to achieve some of these advantages through a pledge of the shares of the project company or other security devices, but the position will seldom be as effective or secure as a right to appoint a receiver.

English security law allows the taking of universal security, is extremely flexible and is generally thought to favour lenders. Some of the more important features of English security law from the point of view of a lender are:

- it allows enforcement to be effected without involving the courts and sale is not the only enforcement remedy since a secured lender can also operate an asset (either by taking possession of the asset himself or by appointing a receiver);

- certain types of security (fixed security) will rank ahead of preferential creditors;

- it allows security to be taken over virtually all types of assets, including security over assets which do not yet exist; this ability to take security over future assets can be of fundamental importance in the context of a project financing, especially those projects where future receivables form an important part of the project security;

- it allows security to be taken by means of a floating charge over all of a company's assets; thus, it is necessary to create different types of security interests over different categories of assets – for the most part English law will not concern itself with the form of a security interest and will be more concerned with the scope and issues of priorities;

- security can be taken over virtually all classes of asset without taking possession of that asset (in other words, English law recognises non-possessory security interests);

- it allows security to be taken over all of a company's property, assets and business, through the use of the floating charge, without the need separately to identify and list all such property and assets;

- there is a central registration system for most categories of security interests which enables creditors and prospective lenders to check what security a company has already created in favour of other creditors;

- it does not for the most part impose liabilities on the lenders as mere holders of the security (unless, for example, they have become shadow directors of the project company);

- only minimal fees and duties are payable on the creation of security and only the normal transfer taxes (for example, stamp duty) are payable on its enforcement; and

- the trust concept allows interests in security to be transferred relatively simply (and, in a secured syndicated loan, the security is usually vested in the agent as agent and trustee).

For a discussion regarding the scope of security interests taken in a project financing, please refer to Chapter 8.

6.4.4   Security trusts

It is now common in large-scale project financing to see arrangements where the security is held by, and project revenues paid to accounts in the name of, a security trustee. Security trusts represent a convenient way of taking and holding security in those jurisdictions where the concept of a trust is recognised. Two particular advantages of security trusts are, first, that they facilitate the trading of loans by the lenders without any danger of releasing security and, second, they remove the insolvency risk of an agent or other third party holding the security. In those jurisdictions where trusts are not recognised, it may still be possible for one of the banks to act as security agent on behalf of the other lenders, although the insolvency of the security agent becomes a risk for the lenders. Failing this, it will be necessary for all the individual lenders to be a party to each of the security documents, which is both cumbersome and inflexible, especially as this would inhibit the trading of debt by the lenders.

6.4.5　Formalities

Whatever security is taken, it will need to satisfy the security formalities in the relevant jurisdiction. Because the laws of England and other common law jurisdictions are generally more amenable to the granting and taking of security (allowing, amongst other things and to varying degrees, the granting of a universal security, the granting of security over future assets and the appointment of a receiver over international project contracts, insurance, offtake contracts and possibly the construction contract) and over the bank accounts, security will typically be governed by English or New York law. However, security over the assets situated in the project company's jurisdiction, and often any concession agreement or licence, will generally be governed by local law. The relevant jurisdiction may require registrations, filings, translations, notarisations, the payment of stamp duties and other formalities, depending upon the jurisdiction in question. Local law considerations will have to be investigated by the lender's lawyers at the outset so as to ensure that the security package finally agreed upon is both properly constituted (not least that the project company has the power to grant the security being taken) and perfected in accordance with local laws. Such formalities may be relevant both at the time the security is taken and also at the time of enforcement. Failure to comply with these formalities will, in many jurisdictions, result in the security being unenforceable.

6.4.6　Problem areas

In many jurisdictions around the world lenders will encounter difficulties in structuring an effective overall security package for a project financing. These difficulties are usually as a result of the local security laws that either do not recognise the type of security that the lenders are trying to create or, where a particular type of security is possible, local procedural rules frustrate or obstruct the perfection or enforcement of such security. Some of the problem areas are:

- certain jurisdictions impose a total block on creditors enforcing their security during bankruptcy proceedings (eg UK administration procedure, US Chapter 11 procedure);

- certain jurisdictions do not recognise the concept of trusts with the result that security trusts are unlikely to work (many civil law jurisdictions);

- certain jurisdictions do not recognise security contract assignments (many civil law jurisdictions);

- certain jurisdictions require that any sale of security assets must take place through a judicial auction procedure;

- certain jurisdictions are problematical for certain types of loans, eg revolving loans or foreign currency loans; and

- certain jurisdictions give preference to certain categories of creditors (most common law jurisdictions).

Faced with such difficulties the lenders will either have to accept a tainted security package or seek comfort from third parties (usually the sponsors).

6.4.7 Checklist

Checklist: Taking security

The lenders' lawyers should establish:

- which assets the borrower owns and which it merely has a right to use (eg under a licence);
- whether security can be created over user rights as well as ownership rights;
- over what project assets a fixed security can be created;
- whether floating charges are possible;
- whether security can be created over assets not in existence at the time of creation of the charge;
- whether security over movable assets can be created without physical transfer of those assets to the mortgagee or pledgee;
- what degree of control the chargee must exercise over the assets to constitute a fixed, as opposed to floating, charge;
- whether there are restrictions on foreigners taking security, especially overland;
- what creditors will, by law, be preferred over a secured creditor;
- whether third parties (including joint ventures under terms of pre-emption or similar rights in underlying documents) or a liquidator can interfere with the grant of security or with its enforcement;
- whether, on a default, the lenders will be able to appoint a receiver over the assets;
- whether the banks will be responsible for the receiver's actions or whether the receiver can be appointed as agent for the borrower;
- whether, on enforcement, the lenders will be able to control the sale of the assets or there must be a court sale or public auction;
- whether the ability to enforce security over claims against third parties (eg debts, receivables, shares, bonds, notes) depends on obtaining the third party's consent or, at least, ensuring that it is aware of the security;
- what formalities need to be complied with to perfect security-notarisations, registrations, filings and stamp duties; and
- whether the security can be held by an agent or trustee for a group of creditors whose members might change from time to time (eg through transfer of their participation in the facility to another bank).

6.5 INSURANCE ISSUES

6.5.1 Role of project insurance

Insurance is a very important aspect of most projects and certainly one that will concern the project sponsors and the lenders equally. Lenders will view the insurance as an integral and key element of their overall security package for a project. Should a major casualty or disaster occur with respect to all or a material part of the project, then the lenders may be left with little else to proceed against. It is, therefore, perhaps surprising that in many project financings the subject of insurance is deferred until the last minute and then not always given the attention it warrants.

6.5.2 Who insures?

One of the first issues to resolve is which party will be responsible for arranging and maintaining the insurance for the project during its various stages. The responsibility for this will vary from project to project. For example, in a construction-related project, the principal insurance cover during the construction period will often be arranged by the contractor through a Contractor's All Risks (CAR) Policy, with the responsibility for maintaining insurances during the operating period then moving to the project company or perhaps the operator of the facility. Some sponsors prefer to leave insurance arrangements to individual project companies to arrange on a project-by-project basis, others prefer to centralise all insurance arrangements. The latter is so particularly with some of the larger international contractors who do this to ensure that they get the finest rates for their cover and also provide themselves with the means of effectively managing their risks more thoroughly and efficiently.

6.5.3 Scope of cover

Cover will vary between the construction and operating phases of a project. Details of typical insurance cover applicable to each of these phases is set out below:

■ Construction phase:

  – physical damage to project facilities during the course of construction;

  – physical damage to other assets such as offices, vehicles etc;

  – transit insurance, eg parts in transit;

  – employers, workmen's compensation and third party liability insurance;

  – environmental liability insurance; and

  – delay in start-up insurance against increased costs resulting from delay caused by an insured loss.

■ Operating phase:

  – insurance against physical damage to project facilities;

  – insurance against physical damage to other assets such as plant, equipment or motor vehicles;

  – transit insurance covering the periods until point of sale;

  – employers' and workmen's compensation and third party liability insurance;

  – environmental liability insurance; and

  – business interruption or loss of profits insurance.

6.5.4 Additional insurance issues

Additional insurance may, depending on the precise nature of the project, be required. For example, in projects connected with the development of oil, insurance against the cost of controlling a blow-out might be required.

6.5.5 Problem areas

It is almost certainly impossible to list all the potential problems that could arise with the insurance aspects of a project, but some of the principal concerns from a lender's perspective would be:

■ The policy may be cancelled, either in accordance with its terms by agreement between the insured and the insurers, or by the brokers for non-payment of premiums.

■ The policy may expire and not be renewed.

■ The policy may be changed so as adversely to affect the cover provided – for example, the scope of the policy may be narrowed, policy limits may be reduced or deductibles may be increased (deductibles are, of course, a form of self-insurance).

■ The loss may be caused by a peril which was not insured, and so (for example) a policy which covers political risks such as war, revolution and insurrection should be checked further to ensure that it also covers politically motivated violent acts such as terrorism or sabotage.

■ The policy may be avoided by the insurers on grounds of misrepresentation or non-disclosure. Insurers, in deciding whether to accept the risk, rely on the information presented to them by the insured or their representatives and lawyers acting for the insurers may well elect one of these grounds so that the claim need not be paid because a contract of insurance is a contract said to be *uberrimae fidae* (of the utmost good faith) and so can be disclaimed for seemingly minor non-disclosure or misrepresentation. Understandably, this type of clausing has been strongly resisted by the banking community, which could be faced with the principal cover falling away on the basis of a non-disclosure or misrepresentation of which they were completely ignorant. In the past, many insurers were prepared to waive these clauses following pressure from the banking community, but recently the position of the insurance industry has hardened. Faced with this, one source of reassurance to the lenders in these circumstances is to follow the co-insured route (see below). Another is to take out additional cover to protect the lenders against invalidity of a policy on grounds of non-disclosure or misrepresentation (so-called non-variation cover). Such policies are a relatively new entrant to the insurance world but should not necessarily be viewed as the complete solution. In the first place, the cover is expensive (70 per cent to 15 per cent of the sum insured) and, more importantly, insurers will only pay out in circumstances where the only reason why the insurers have not paid out on the main policy is as a result of a non-disclosure by the project company or other insured party. In other words they are not a general cure for all defences that an insurer may have and if an insurer is otherwise entitled not to pay or only to part pay, the non-vitiation insurance will not protect the lenders.

■ The policy may be avoided by the insurers on the grounds of breach of warranty by the insured.

■ The insured may not make any (or any timely) claim for indemnity under the policy.

■ The insurers may be insolvent and unable to pay a claim.

■ The claim may be paid by the insurers to the brokers but somehow lost in the broker's insolvency.

■ The broker may assert a lien (ie a special proprietary claim) against any unpaid premiums which are due from the insured.

■ A claim may be paid to the insured by the brokers but somehow lost in the borrower's insolvency.

The occurrence of any or a combination of these events could result in the insurance moneys not being received by the lenders, as expected, with the result that the lenders could find themselves unsecured for all or part of the project loan.

6.5.6   Reinsurance

It is often the case that all or a significant part of an insurance policy is reinsured with other insurers. Usually this is simply because the principal insurer does not have the capacity to absorb the full risk insured against. It is also the case that some jurisdictions have a legal requirement that all or a part of the insurance is arranged through domestic insurers. With larger projects this will frequently pose a problem for local insurers who will not be able to underwrite the full amount required. Also, lenders may have a concern with all the insurance being placed locally as this exposes them potentially to additional risks that the payment of insurance claims may be blocked or otherwise interfered with (ie a form of political risk).

Reinsurance with offshore insurers is therefore frequently called for by both lenders and local insurers. However, there is a serious security issue for lenders to consider with reinsurance. The issue concerns the possible insolvency of the principal insurer. Since the contract of reinsurance will have been taken out by the principal insurer with the reinsurance company, should the principal insurer become insolvent all proceeds payable under a reinsurance contract will be paid to the estate of the principal insurer and distributed to its creditors according to the normal bankruptcy laws in its jurisdiction of incorporation. In other words, neither the project company nor the lenders are likely to have any priority interest in these insurance moneys since they form part of the insurer's bankruptcy estate.

There are two possible ways of dealing with this issue:

- ■ The most satisfactory route is to require the principal insurer to execute an assignment of the reinsurance proceeds in favour of the project company thereby removing the reinsurance proceeds from the principal insurer's bankruptcy estate. Notice of assignment would be served on the reinsurer in the normal way and the reinsurance proceeds would be paid direct to the project company (or, more likely, the security trustee). Although this is the best protection for the project company and the lenders it is relatively rare that an insurance company can be persuaded to create a security assignment in these terms.

- ■ The alternative, less satisfactory, approach is to arrange for the reinsurance contract to have endorsed on it a 'cut-through' undertaking. The effect of this undertaking is that the reinsurer would be irrevocably directed by the principal insurer to pay the proceeds of all claims direct to the project company (or, more probably, the security trustee) thereby by-passing (or cutting through) the principal insurer. The problem with this approach, however, is that it is doubtful that such an undertaking would be enforceable against a liquidator of the principal insurer as it does not amount to a security interest but simply an unsecured payment direction.

6.6   CONCLUSION

This chapter has reviewed how project risks might be legally assessed, transferred or mitigated mainly from the perspective and for the benefit of the lender. As in previous chapters, it has been emphasised how understanding the lender's perspective and concerns enables the proposer to write a proposal which may be found acceptable to the lender. Having cut a path through a complex forest of financial and legal issues, a clearing is near where the foundations for a project financing can be laid. In the next chapter, a Business Plan Form is presented which can be used to help construct bankable proposals.

7

Bankable Proposal Form

IMPORTANT NOTE

Please note that the various Sections and paragraphs of the Bankable Proposal Form are just guidelines and, depending on the particular circumstances of your project, it may not be possible to fill in the whole form. Therefore, we recommend you complete those parts of the form which you feel will help others understand the merits of your project. A commentary explaining each section of the form follows on p 120.

Commentary to the Bankable Proposal Form

The purpose of the commentary is to explain each of the sections and paragraphs of the Bankable Proposal Form. The commentary offers guidance on how and why each component of the form should be completed. However, should you have any doubts about whether any section or paragraph is relevant, you should ask yourself whether the information sought is necessary for the bank to understand the merits of your proposal. If not, then do not complete it. This rule also applies whenever you feel that you may be repeating yourself or making your proposal unnecessarily complex. Every effort has been made to make the Bankable Proposal Form simple and straightforward in order to encourage you to do the same.

SECTION 1   PROJECT SUMMARY

Sponsor

1.1   Legal name of sponsor (main contact person for proposal)

1.2   Contact person and location of sponsor

Contact person:		
Address:		
Country:	Region:	Town:
Tel:	Fax:	Email (if any):

1.3   Legal status of sponsor (mark appropriate box)

[ ] Public company	[ ] To be privatised
[ ] Private company	[ ] Other (specify)

The sponsors

1.4   Describe the main parties to the transaction

1.4.1   Personal details, background and experience of main parties and top management to the transaction

(Use additional sheets if necessary)

Name:		
Address:		
Telephone (home):	Telephone (work):	Fax:
Business experience, qualifications and training:		

1.4.2 Financial data

1.4.2.1 Past track record

1.4.2 Future projections

Project partners

1.5 Identity and location of partners

(Attach separate page if necessary)

Name:	
Address:	
Tel:	Fax:
Name:	
Address:	
Tel:	Fax:
Name:	
Address:	
Tel:	Fax:
Name:	
Address:	
Tel:	Fax:

1.5.1 Proposed financial contributions and exposures of partners

Name of partner	Financial contribution ($)	Exposure to financial risk (recourse or non-recourse)

1.5.2 Rationale for the involvement of other partners, if any

1.6 Sector (please tick relevant box(es) and specify)

[ ] Building   Specify:..

[ ] Industry   Specify:..

[ ] Transport Specify:..

[ ] Services   Specify:..

[ ] Others   Specify:..

1.7 Brief project description

1.8   Objectives

1.8.1   What are the objectives of the business itself?

1.8.1.1   Short-term (from today until end of first year)
1.8.1.2   Medium (from end of first year to end of fifth year)
1.8.1.3   How are these objectives going to be achieved?

1.8.2   What are the long-term objectives of the business (if any)?

1.8.2.1   From the end of fifth year
1.8.2.2   How are these objectives to be achieved?

1.9 Type and amount of finance required

Type of finance requested (tick appropriate box): [ ] Debt [ ] Equity	Total project cost (ECU):	
	Amount of finance requested (ECU):	
	Amount requested as percentage of total project cost	%

Other sources of finance (as percentage of total project cost)

Sponsor's own resources	%
Local commercial bank	%
Grants	%
Other international financial institutions	%

Total 100%

1.10 Summary Cash Flow Analysis

Year	0	1	2	3	4	5	6	7	8	9	10
1 Capital investment											
2 Revenue											
3 Efficiency savings											
4 Other benefits											
5 Operation & maintenance costs											
6 Other costs											
7 Depreciation of installed equipment											
8 Pre-tax profit (2+3+4) −(5+6)											
9 Tax											
10 Profit after tax											
11 Net cash flow											

SECTION 2   INTRODUCTION TO THE BUSINESS

Company history, activities and prospects

(Attach separate page if necessary)

Briefly discuss the nature, strengths, risks, current situation and future plans of the business:

1.1   **Nature of business**

1.2   **Strengths of business**

1.3   **Risks**

1.4 Current situation

1.5 Future plans

SECTION 3 NATURE OF THE PROPOSED PROJECT

1 Scope of the project

2 Arrangements for implementation

3 Asset collateral

(Attach separate sheets if necessary)

3.1 Plants, machinery, lands, buildings, other	Location	Age

SECTION 4   BENEFITS TO HOST GOVERNMENT AND LOCAL ECONOMY

Describe the benefits to the local economy expected from the project, covering the specific impact on:

1   Job creation

2   Export promotion

3 Import substitution

4   Technology transfer

5   Management development

6   Productivity improvements

7   Energy and environmental improvements, if any

SECTION 5 PROJECT COSTS AND TIMETABLE

This section sets out in detail the total costs of the project and its justification.

1   Project costs

(Use additional sheets, if necessary)

Item	Local currency	% of Total cost
a.		
b.		
c.		
d.		
e.		
f.		
g.		
h.		
i.		

2.1   Cost estimates

2.2   Technology and equipment

Name and short technical description of proposed technology and equipment	Estimated value	Condition (new, good, fair, poor)	Age (in years)
a.			
b.			
c.			
d.			
e.			
f.			
g.			
h.			
i.			
j.			

3   Timetable of implementation and disbursements
(Estimated cash flow out. This should be provided in detail.)

Expected of value purchase or cost incurred (month/year)	Short technical description of item to be purchased or cost to be incurred	Estimated amount

4   Description of agencies in charge of implementing major components of project and rationale for their selection

(For projects involving government concessions)

Component of project	Name of agency in charge of implementation	Reasons for selecting agency and track record

5   Nature of the contracts with agencies in charge of implementation of project

(For projects involving government concessions)

Major terms and conditions of the contracts:

6   Cost contingencies

6.1   Built-in contingency costs to the project?

6.2   Justifications for these contingency costs?

6.3   If there are provisions for cost overruns, what are the reasons for assuming that such overrun smay occur?

6.4   How has the company ensured that there is sufficient back-up funding in the event of cost overruns?

7   Procurement issues

7.1   What are the proposed means for purchasing goods, services and equipment with the proposed lender's funds?

SECTION 6   PRODUCTS, SERVICES AND MARKET

1 Description of products or services to be supplied by the business
(Attach separate sheet if necessary)

Name of product or service	Brief technical description of product or service	Contribution to total turnover (%)
A		
B		
C		
D		

TOTAL 100%

2 Pricing and costs (breakdown of the cost of materials)

Product or service	Variable costs of product or service	Selling price of product*
A		
B		
C		
D		

* Note: these are assumptions.

2.1 Sources of cost estimates

Product	Source of information for cost estimates of materials to product
A	
B	
C	
D	

2.2 Explanation of price estimates

a. Cost-plus price

b. Competitor prices

c. Market price

d. Other

The nature of the market for the enterprise's products or services

3 Market description, location and size

3.1 Description of the market the business is in

3.2 Geographical area of the company's market

3.3 Size of the company's market ($ per year)

3.4 Description of the market environment

4 Type of customers

4.1 Characteristics of customers of business

5　Competitor analysis

Name of competitor	Name of competitor's product or service	market share (%)
A		
B		
C		
D		
E		
F		
G		
H		

6.1   What is special about your own product or service? (What is its unique selling point, if any?)

6.2   Advantages of your product or service over the competition

7   Factors affecting the growth of demand

7.1   Description of factors affecting growth of demand

7.2   Is the company's market growing, stable or in decline?

7.3   Financial position of buyers

SECTION 7   ROLE OF THE LENDER

Concise description of the proposed role of the Lender*

* The lender may play any one or more of the following roles in the transaction:

■   principal lender;

■   syndicater of loans to other lenders;

■   guarantor;

■   underwriter;

■   equity investor; and

■   financial and investment advisor.

SECTION 8   FINANCING PLAN

Details on the structure of the financing, including:

I Current and required sources of finance

Financing Source	Amount in local currency (if relevant)	Amount in $	Total in $	% of total project costs
Sponsor's own resources				
Supplier				
Local loans				
Foreign loans				
Foreign equity				
Others:				
Total current sources (A)				
Total project costs (B)				100%
Total financing required (B – A)				

2 Type of financing required

Type of financing required	Amount (local currency)	Amount ($)
Debt		
Equity		
Other		
TOTAL		

3 Security, if any, that sponsor will put up for the project

	Description of item(s)	Estimated value (local currency)	Estimated value ($)
a.			
b.			
c.			
d.			
e.			
f.			
g.			
h.			
i.			
j.			
k.			

SECTION 9 CASH FLOW PROJECTIONS AND FINANCIAL VIABILITY

Provide annual estimates for each of the items listed below over the life of the project finance

(Use additional sheets, if necessary)

1 Operating profit

Year	0	1	2	3	4	5	6	7	8	9	10
1.1 Total turnover											
1.2 Turnover on investments											
1.3 Raw material											
1.4 Other direct operating costs											
1.5 Gross profit											
1.6 Indirect costs											
1.6.1 Sales and marketing											
1.6.2 Utilities and maintenance											
1.6.3 Overheads											
1.6.4 Other											
1.6.5 Total Operating Expenses (excluding depreciation)											
1.7 Operating profit (excluding depreciation)											

2 Working capital

2.1 Decrease (increase) in stock											
2.2 Decrease (increase) in debtors											
2.3 Increase (decrease) in creditors											

3 Taxation

	Year	0	1	2	3	4	5	6	7	8	9	10
3.1 Taxes paid												

4 Servicing of Finance

4.1 Free cash flow (pre-finance)											
4.2 Interest paid											
4.3 Lender fees paid											
4.4 Net cash flow before financing											

5 Financing

5.1 Issue of ordinary share capital											
5.2 Others long-term loan payment											
5.3 Lender long-term repayment											
5.4 Long-term loan requirement											
5.5 Short-term loan											
5.6 Net cash flow from financing											

6 Ratios

8.1 Gross profit margin											
8.2 Net profit margin											
8.3 Return on equity											
8.4 Current ratio											
8.5 Acid test (quick ratio)											
8.6 Cash flow to debt service ratio											

SECTION 10 APPENDIX: PROFORMA FINANCIAL STATEMENTS

The proforma financial statements consist of:

- Income statement (profit and loss account);
- Balance sheet;
- Cash flow;
- Financial ratios.

Sample of these forms are found below.

Forecasted income statement including bank loan (in thousand US$)

	Historical				Forecasted						
1 Turnover on fuel, operation and maintenance											
2 Turnover on investments											
3 Total turnover											
4 Raw material											
5 Other direct operating costs											
6 Gross profit											
7 Indirect costs											
8 Sales & marketing											
9 Utilities & maintenance											
10 Overheads											
11 Other											
12 Total operating expenses (excl. depreciation)											
13 Operating profit (excl. depreciation)											
14 Depreciation											

		Historical				Forecasted		
15	Operating profit							
16	Interest expense							
17	Bank fees							
18	**Net profit before tax**							
19	Taxation							
20	Net profit after tax							

Forecasted balance sheet including bank loan (in thousand US$)

	Historical				Forecasted				
ASSETS									
1 Tangible assets									
2 Accumulated depreciation									
3 **Net book value**									
4 Stocks									
5 Debtors									
6 Cash									
7 Current assets									
8 **Total assets**									
LIABILITIES									
9 Called-up share capital									
10 Profit and loss account									
11 Shareholders' equity									

	Historical			Forecasted					
12	**Long-term debt**								
13	Trade creditors								
14	Short-term debt								
15	Current liabilities								
16	Total liabilities								

Forecasted cash flow including bank loan (in thousand US$)

	Historical					Forecasted					
1	Operating profits										
2	Add back depreciation										
3	Decrease (increase) in stock										
4	Decrease (increase) in debtors										
5	Increase (decrease) in creditors										
6	**OPERATING CASH FLOW**										
7	Taxation paid										
8	Capital expenditures										
9	FREE CASH FLOW										
10	Servicing of finance										
11	Interest paid										
12	Bank fees paid										
13	Dividends paid										
14	NET CASH FLOW BEFORE FINANCING										

Historical | Forecaste

15	Financing									
16	Issue of ordinary share capital									
17	Others long-term loan payment									
18	Bank long-term repayment									
19	Long-term loan requirement									
20	Short-term loan									
21	**NET CASH FLOW FROM FINANCING**									

Financial ratios

1	Gross profit margin									
2	Net profit margin									
3	Return on equity									
4	Current ratio									
5	Acid test (quick ratio)									
6	Cash flow to debt service ratio									

Commentary to bankable proposal form

SECTION I

Sponsor

1.1 Legal name of sponsor

This is the full legal name of the entity which is applying for finance from the bank.

1.2 Contact person and location of sponsor

The contact person is the person who understands the contents of the Bankable Proposal and who has authority to act on behalf of the sponsor to explain the Bankable Proposal to the bank. The location of the sponsor is usually the official headquarters of the sponsor. The contact person should be reachable at or through the sponsor's address, telephone and fax. The email code, if available, enhances communication.

1.3 Legal status of sponsor

Insert here the official name of the enterprise which is included in the business licence, entrepreneur's certificate, or company record or, if it has not yet been recorded, in the Syndicate Agreement, Articles of Association, or Memorandum of Foundation. If the company is in the process of being registered, these documents should be provided together with the receipt of the Court of Registration of the submission of these documents.

The various types of legal status include:

■ Sole trader: This is a business owned by a single person such as an individual entrepreneur or a industrial entrepreneur, salesman.

■ Partnership: This is a business owned by multiple persons. This may have many different forms, such as unlimited partnership, business associations or limited partnership.

■ Limited liability company.

■ Joint stock company.

■ State-owned enterprise or institution, local government's institution.

■ Co-operative.

If the sponsor's legal status is complex (for example, a joint venture with public and private elements) then this should be explained fully on a separate sheet and attached as an Appendix to the Bankable Proposal Form. The sponsor should also consider setting out the current and future ownership of the business.

The Sponsors

1.4   Describe the main parties to the transaction

1.4.1   Personal details, background and experience of main parties and top management to the transaction

This section should be written with the purpose of convincing the bank that the management to the project can be trusted to complete the job.   What kind of technical credibility does the management have? Have they completed other similar projects?

How does their background enable them to accomplish the objectives of the project?

1.4.2   Financial data

This gives the bank a view on the financial strength of the sponsor. More financial information will be included in Sections 9 and 10 of the Bankable Proposal Form.

There are many complexities to financial risk but the question here is whether the partner will be personally liable for payment on default. If the partner is personally liable then the bank has full recourse against the partner and therefore the bank has greater comfort. Technically, recourse means that, in case of default on the loan, the lender has the right to sue an endorser or guarantor for payment. Non-recourse means that the lender has no right to sue for any of the underlying assets beyond that which was pledged by the defaulting party.

1.4.2.1   Past track record

The past track record of the sponsor would include any relevant business experience and, especially, any businesses which the sponsor has successfully brought to market or sold. The track record evidences the sponsor's business acumen, judgment and expertise.

1.4.2.2   Future projections

These are highlights of the sponsor's own future business potential. Are the sponsor's prospects in the future stable, in a growth phase or declining. The bank will make its own assessment of the creditworthiness of the individuals, but this is a summary indication of the sponsor's future financial capability. The expected future projections of the sponsor's own business potential should match the expected growth of the project.

Project partners

1.5   Identity and location of partners

These are the names, addresses, telephone and fax numbers of consultants, suppliers, local banks and others who have contracts with the sponsor and who may share in the financial benefit of the project.

1.5.1   Proposed financial contributions and exposures of partners

Each partner's contribution shows a measured vote of confidence for the project and shows that the partner is willing to stake funds which are at risk. The funds which are lent to the project may be in the form of recourse or non-recourse. This means that if the funds are not repaid, then either the project company itself and no others are liable for repayment of the financial obligation (non-recourse), or, others besides the project company are liable for repayment (recourse).

1.5.2 Rationale for the involvement of other partners, if any

There are many different rationales for a local enterprise to involve other partners. For example, the local enterprise may need a foreign partner in order to meet certain contractual requirements for hard currency. Or, the enterprise may be relatively unknown and thus, in order to bolster its credibility, it may enter a joint venture with a well-known international company. Another rationale may be that the company wishes to enhance its political security by teaming up with politically powerful entities.

1.6 Sector

This is the economic sector in which the project can most appropriately be categorised. To 'specify' means to describe in some detail the type of project within the economic sector. For example, if the project is new space heating for municipal buildings, then you should tick (mark with an 'X' [ ] Building and specify with 'new space heating for municipal buildings').

One of the reasons for this section is to help the bank determine what type of technical expertise is required to evaluate the Bankable Proposal. Obviously, a proposal for retrofit of a nuclear power station will require different expertise from a project that aims to enhance the efficiency of rail transport.

1.7 Brief project description

This description should avoid technical details! The first sentence should state in lay language the purpose of the project and the remainder should focus on the financial and environmental benefits of the project to the sponsor, the local community, the nation and the bank. You should be able to say all this in less than 100 words.

You will discuss details of the project in Sections 3, 5, 6 and 7 of the Bankable Proposal Form. It is very likely that after you finish writing these sections you will have a clearer view of the project than when you first began. It is therefore recommended that initially you merely note a few salient points in the 'brief project description' until you have finished writing the rest of the proposal and then return to this section to fill in the details.

1.8 Objectives

These objectives may include business, economic, social and environmental goals. It would be helpful to the bank if these objectives were stated in specific enough language so that they can be ascertained, measured, monitored and controlled.

1.8.1 What are the objectives of the business itself?

1.8.1.1 Short-term (from the start of the project until the end of the first year)

This might include the hiring of personnel, completion of design, preliminary testing, set up of offices and other types of preparatory work for the initiation of the project. This would also include the beginning phase of the construction of the project.

1.8.1.2 Medium term (from end of first year to end of fifth year)

Here, the construction phase of the project is likely to occur as well as final testing of the facility for completion and the beginning of positive net cash flows from production sales.

1.8.1.3 How are these objectives going to be achieved?

A brief description of how the plans will be achieved and who will be responsible would need to be considered.

1.8.2 What are the long-term objectives of the business (if any)?

1.8.2.1 *(From the end of the fifth year)*

The main concern of the banker is when he will receive return from the project. If there is a possibility of a pay-down of the principal, then this should be stated. Also, the year in which break-even will occur should also be indicated.

1.8.2.2 *How are these objectives to be achieved?*

Achieving the long-term objectives may require a strong sense of how the project will be returned to the concession grantor, or when it might be sold to a wider group of equity holders. A favourite expression amongst bankers is the favourable time for 'exit', or the time when the equity holders are most likely to realise profits. The managers involved are likely to need further financial advice at those times and, therefore, the main consideration here is what type of managerial role the equity holders are likely to have in place. This should be a planned transition to managers who would be capable of handling buy-outs, mergers, acquisitions and further expansion.

1.9 Type and amount of finance required

Type of finance requested

You will normally select either debt or equity.

The basic distinction between debt and equity is that debt requires the borrower to repay the amount of the loan (principal balance) plus interest over a certain period of time while in an equity deal the sponsor has no obligation to pay back the loan or any interest. In the equity deal, the sponsor pays only dividends and the investor hopes that the sponsor will be successful in the enterprise and the market will recognise this success by bidding up the value of the shares. To cover the bank's equity exposure there will normally be shareholder agreements which place certain conditions on the way the sponsor runs the business, but the bank in turn gets to own a part of the business.

Total project cost

Details of how you determine this figure are found in Section 6 on 'Transaction costs'.

Amount of finance requested

This is the amount which the sponsor seeks from the bank and is a portion of total project costs. Since banks may set upper and lower limits on the amount of money they can loan to clients, the sponsor should check with his banks about what these limits are. The sponsor should be very careful to state an amount of finance requested which is within the bank's limits.

Other sources of finance

- Sponsor's own resources Since banks are generally risk averse, they like to see sponsors risk their own money or capital. The more money or capital the sponsor puts into the project, the greater comfort for the bank. (See Chapter 3, Section 3, for discussion on project risks.)

- Local commercial bank Multi-national banks and international development banks may have established credit lines with local banks and the local bank therefore may have a strong interest in lending for certain types of projects, such as small and medium enterprise development.

■ **Grants** Outright grants (with no requirement for repayment) increase the net cash flow of the project and thus lower the risk of the project and enhance its attractiveness to the potential lender. For example, grants for technology development may be available through programmes of the European Commission.

■ **Other international financial institutions** In a similar vein, other financial institutions may offer loans or preferential finance for projects involving infrastructure development, energy efficiency, renewables and ecologically sound developments.

1.10   Summary cash flow analysis

The figures in this form should be consistent with the figures provided under Section 10 – Cash flow projections of the Bankable Proposal Form. A brief explanation of the terms used in the summary cash flow analysis are:

■ **Capital investment**   The total cost of the installed equipment (excluding Value Added Taxes).

■ **Revenue**   This is any incremental change in revenue due to the project.

■ **Efficiency savings**   The quantity of commodities, goods or services saved through efficiency multiplied by the expected prevailing energy prices including taxes.

■ **Other benefits**   The additional benefits to energy savings generated by the investment, if any. These benefits should be explained in more detail in Section 10 of the Bankable Proposal Form or on separate sheets attached as an appendix to the Form.

■ **Operation and maintenance costs**   The net additional costs or the net cost reductions to operate and maintain the newly installed equipment.

■ **Other costs**   Miscellaneous costs incurred to run the project, if any. These should be explained in detail in section 10 of the Bankable Proposal Form or on separate sheets attached as an appendix to the Form. It is important to note that none of these costs are distinct from and not duplicated in the costs of the installed equipment stated above as capital investment.

■ **Depreciation of the installed equipment**   Not a cash cost but a non-cash expense that reduces taxable income.

■ **Tax: corporate tax rate**   The impact of tax is twofold. On the one hand, if the investment is successful and the company has a net profit, the company's taxes will increase. On the other hand, where the project has involved capital expenditure, the company may be able to claim capital allowances from the government which will help reduce the tax burden. To calculate the tax cash flows accurately, you will need to forecast the profits from the investment. In any case, once the incremental cash flow has been forecast, then the payment of taxes should be automatically included in your cash flow forecasts.

SECTION 2

Company history, activities and prospects

1.1 Nature of business

What is the core business activity that the sponsor is engaged in? For example, it may be the supply of electricity or it may be cement manufacturing. The business is defined by the products it makes and sells for its customers and clients. In market economies, businesses exist on the strength of market demand. Ultimately, market demand defines the genuine nature of the business.

There are a number of areas to draw from when making a statement which defines the nature of the business. You may wish to consider the answers to the following questions to make a brief statement about the nature of your business, its strengths, risks, current and future plans:

- **What do you intend to sell?**
  - Products
  - Services

- **What is your position in the market?**
  - Will it be based on high quality and high price? or
  - High volume and low price?

- **Who will be your customers?**
  - Individual members of public: what are their social class,
  - geographical area and particular interests?
  - Manufacturing: what is the size, area and nature?

- **How will you find new customers?**
  - Passers-by who walk into business location?
  - Press advertisements?
  - Direct mail?
  - Referrals?
  - Salesmen?

- **How will you increase the sales from your existing customers?**
  - Market survey and analysis

- **How will you obtain products?**
  - Manufacture from raw materials
  - Assemble from intermediaries
  - Purchase from manufacturers

- **Who will provide your company's services to customers?**
  - Just yourself
  - Yourself and partners or fellow directors
  - Employees
  - Sub-contractors or franchisees

- **How will you sell?**
  - Direct to the public
  - Direct to manufacturers
  - Through large chain stores

- Through individual shops

- By mail order

- Through a distributor

■ How will you support your sales?

- What delivery will you provide?

- In what geographical area?

- What is the after-sales service?

- What are the trade terms? For example, what is the financial assistance for leasing or loans?

1.2 Strengths of business

The strengths of the business can be divided into internal strengths or capabilities of personnel and plant and external opportunities in the marketplace. Amongst the major questions you should consider are:

■ Are your personnel and senior management equipped with proper technical, marketing, selling and negotiating skills?

■ Does the business have a unique selling point? In other words, does your company offer a special benefit in its products or services, which are not offered by competitors?

■ Does your company have strong customer loyalty?

■ Does your company enjoy a special licence or subsidy from the government?

■ Is your business in close proximity to the markets?

1.3 Risks

The risks are both internal and external—that is, factors which the management can control and factors which are beyond the control of management. Efforts by management should focus on controllable and critical risks. The critical risks to the business are those events, activities or persons without which the business is not likely to survive. For example, if the power generator enjoys a monopoly in the market then the major risk to the business is political and perhaps regulatory.

1.4 Current situation

The current situation is a description of recent events in light of current cash flows. Is the company improving or is it facing difficulties? Does it have good prospects in the near term or no new prospects?

1.5 Future plans

The future plans should describe ways in which the sponsor may use the strengths of the business or decrease the business risks.

SECTION 3

1 Scope of the project

This describes the breadth of the project in terms of time, space and number of personnel directly and indirectly involved.

2 Arrangements for implementation

This is a summary of the planning and contractual arrangements necessary for the completion of the project. For large infrastructure projects, tendering for contracts will ensure that fair and competitive prices are obtained. The bank will be looking to protect its investment capital from any possible conflict of interest or fraud. Details of any off-take agreements (contracts that begin with the approval of finance) should be noted.

3 Asset collateral

Locations and age of owned or rented fixed capital assets including:

- plants;
- warehouses;
- offices;
- other;

These properties may be used as collateral for financing the loan amount for the project.

SECTION 4

Introduction

In this Section, it is important to have an imagination. You will need to think of how the project will benefit the local and national economy and environment as well as your own commercial prospects. The greater the number and depth of the benefits, the more likely that the project will have both short and long-term local support and thus an increased likelihood of success.

Commentary on Form

1 Job creation

How many and what types of jobs will be created directly and indirectly by the project?

2 Export promotion

Will the project result in an increase in exports or support exports and therefore result in net gains to the local community and nation?

3 Import substitution

Will the project provide for the substitution of current imports with goods or services produced locally?

4   Technology transfer

Will the project involve the transfer of technology to and from the local community?

5   Management development

Will the project involve the enhancement of skills, knowledge and competence of the workforce?

6   Productivity improvements

Will the project result in enhanced performance and increased productivity of plant and workers?

7   Energy savings and environmental improvements, if any

The types of benefits that come from energy efficiency are many and varied. It is important to recognise those which can be directly quantified in money terms, such as savings in raw materials, fuel savings, reduced labour, etc. and those which may be only indirectly quantifiable, including improved product quality or marketability, and which might produce a benefit in terms of increased sales. There may also be other benefits, which are not quantifiable at all in money terms, but may have a bearing on the project. These include aspects such as improved working conditions and environmental benefits.

The benefits likely to arise from energy and environmental investments may include:

■   lower energy consumption;

■   lower fuel costs;

■   lower water costs;

■   lower labour requirements;

■   reduced overtime;

■   reduced maintenance;

■   fewer rejects;

■   reduced product finishing;

■   improved throughput rate;

■   savings in floor space;

■   improved scheduling;

■   improved quality;

■   improved product specification;

■   improved product range;

■   reduced greenhouse emissions;

■   reduced harmful emissions;

■   improved health and safety;

■   reduced environmental fees;

■   provide qualitative better services.

These are some of the considerations that may be taken into account in describing the benefits of the project.

SECTION 5

1 Project costs

In this Section, you will provide an estimate of the costs of all raw materials, technology, equipment, assets, goods and fees that will be necessary in order to implement and complete the project—basically, all contract costs and operating costs. This should be a fairly detailed breakdown of costs and the major items should be listed first, with smaller or minor costs listed last.

The types of typical costs incurred are outlined in the table below which can be used as a worksheet to estimate project costs. This worksheet is merely indicative and you should take care to make your own list as complete and comprehensive as possible.

Transaction costs worksheet			
Items	Value in local currency	Value in $	Contributions in-kind in $
Land			
Building and facilities			
Equipment & machinery (includes customs duty & fitting costs)			
Transport of equipment or goods, insurance and handling			
Installation			
Start-up expenses			
Training			
Professional fees			
Working capital			
Costs of registering security			
Cost of insurance policies			
Rental right			
Refurbishment			
Design and consultation			
Others:			
TOTAL			

* Contributions in-kind refer to elements within the project that do not need to be purchased but represent contributions (usually in exchange for equity) such as land, buildings, equipment, know-how, licences. This type of contribution often occurs in joint-venture projects.

Background information

All banks require an accurate breakdown of the project costs and the use of funds, especially the use of the lender's funds. This information should be available early in the project preparation.

Typically, the allocation of costs should be amongst land, building, facilities, equipment and machinery, installation, start-up expenses, training, professional fees, working capital, registering security, cost of insurance policies and others. These costs should be split according to local currency, foreign currency ($) and contributions in-kind ($).

It is important to take into account *all costs* related to the project and the key is to identify incremental costs—those costs which are directly related to the proposed project. Some of the areas which may be of direct relevance to project efficiency projects include:

■ **Raw materials** The raw materials are inputs to the production process. The sponsor needs to show that the assumptions made relating to the quantities and pricing of the raw materials is conservative and that even on this basis the proposed debt can be paid off with a significant margin of comfort. Where there are large raw material contracts, the lender may wish to take security over any of the supply contracts and this factor should be kept in mind when the contracts are being negotiated.

In considering the costs of the raw materials, it is important to note whether the supply of the raw materials is guaranteed in terms of price and quantity. For example, in municipal waste to energy projects, a critical factor to success is the price and volume guarantee on the waste given by the municipal authority to the operator. The operator needs a certain amount of raw material input in order to produce sufficient cash flow. Or, it may be the case that the operator does not need a guaranteed source of raw materials because there is a variety of sources for the raw materials and therefore service can depend on the market price.

The question of raw materials relates to the issue of mitigating or avoiding supplier risk, that is, failure of the supplier to supply the raw materials to the operator. Another consideration you may need to keep in mind is how the raw materials (their use, conversion, waste and disposal) relate to the physical environment, which may need to be reported.

■ **Incremental costs to the production process, premises or personnel** Normally, fixed overheads are not included in the costs of the project. However, if the project requires additional production processes, premises or personnel, then these should be included as incremental costs.

■ **Waste disposal costs and pollution cleanup** If the project reduces fuel consumption per unit of production, it may spur the increase of production of goods and polluting by-products. By increasing production, there may be costs associated with the greater amount of waste disposal and pollution clean-up.

■ **Energy consumption** It is important to note that energy efficient technology may pay for itself in terms of energy savings. An awareness of the fuel and electricity usage and the expected cost savings are important factors for the overall efficiency of the plant. For example, new energy efficient technology or equipment may lead to a reduction in operating costs, including less maintenance and repair, or it may result in helping to increase the flexibility of the production process, thus reducing overall production costs. Energy efficiency also reflects on the quality of management—pro-active modern management techniques will strive continuously to improve the efficiency of equipment, machinery and plant. Whilst it may be difficult to quantify, you need to be aware how much time it will take to train staff to act in a different way and to consider whether the morale of the workforce improves or deteriorates in response to the technology.

It is important to note that cost-reduction investment decisions are often a matter of deciding amongst different courses of action. If the costs are the same but the potential benefits are different, it would be easy. But more normally you have to decide amongst two or more investments with differing costs and life expectancies—for example, different types of boilers with different kinds of fuel efficiencies—so your method of investment appraisal must be able to compare these investments across similar time-frames.

While in many instances the cost of technology and equipment required for the efficiency savings may be incurred immediately at the start of the project, the resulting efficiency savings will be spread out over a period of time. More details of how to account for the timing of the cash flows will be found in Section 10, Cash Flow Projections and financial viability. Any technical assessments or engineering reports regarding the amount of energy savings should be included as an Appendix to the Bankable Proposal Form.

2.1   Cost estimates

The bank will require the 'basis' of the cost estimate, which means that the bank will require justifications for the figures stated in the cost estimate. How have the costs been estimated? In order to meet this requirement, the client might consider his answers to the questions in the table below.

Basis for the cost estimate

- Have they come from supplier costs?
- Have they come from engineering quotes?
- Have they been featured quotes?
- Have they come from some other means?
- Who gave you the information on costs? (Name(s) of person(s) and their qualifications)
    - Did the estimate come from someone within the company?
    - Did the estimate come from an independent contractor?
- How reliable are these cost estimates?
    - Would they be useful as firm market price quotations?
    - Would they be used as the basis for further negotiations with large buyers?
- How accurate are the cost estimates? (within 1 to 2%/3 to 5%/5 to 10%/10 to 20%/ only half accurate)

Evaluating costs: levels of estimate[1]

Financial appraisal is usually introduced when the project costs are only estimated. Depending on how far the project has progressed, the estimate will have different measures of accuracy. We might distinguish amongst five levels of estimate:

■ **Order of magnitude**   This is a very crude estimate derived by an inspired guess. The inspiration often comes from a similar project which someone else has undertaken and which has known costs, perhaps published.

■ **Study estimate**   This will approximately quantify the costs of the major components, perhaps by telephone calls to possible suppliers, 'rule of thumb' calculations and using blanket figures for installation and civil engineering works.

■ **Authorisation estimate**   At this stage most of the items of cost are known to a sufficient level of accuracy for the project to be submitted for approval by the financial management. The technical feasibility of the project will have been established, the components identified and costed and the scale of assembly and installation work established.

■ **Definitive estimate**   All outgoings on the project and the timing of those costs will have been established to an extent that the progress of the project could be measured from the costs incurred at any time. The price at which suppliers will deliver components or carry out work will have been agreed and any major designs or other alterations since the preliminary estimate will have been incorporated. The only margins allowed are those for cost that cannot be established until an appropriate point in the physical installation of the project is reached.

■ **Detailed estimate**   This sets an exact amount for the authorisation of payment of invoices on the project. It is in most cases the final cost. So far as possible, all the causes of cost outside those defined in the estimate have been reduced to zero.

2.2   Technology and equipment

This is a description of the technology and equipment and their sources and dependability (ie condition and age). If the technology is old and in poor condition, then it is unlikely to have very much value. New technology and equipment in new or good condition is likely to carry the best value. Obviously, out-of-date technology may need more frequent repairs and carry an increased risk of breakdown which leads to plant ineffectiveness and inefficiency. The bank will look to the company to decrease this risk of old and undependable technology and equipment.

Note: assistance to be provided by the technology supplier

The technology supplier may provide advice and training on how to operate and maintain the equipment and machinery. The terms of the training as part of the technology transfer should be examined closely since the value of the asset will be detrimentally affected if this training is inadequate or sub-standard. What specific assistance will the technology supplier provide?

---

1 See ETSU and Cheriton Technology Management Limited *Investment Appraisal for Industrial Energy Efficiency* ((1993) Energy Efficiency Enquiries Bureau, ETSU, Harwell, Oxfordshire OX11 ORA, Tel: +44 1235 436747, Fax: +44 1235 432923).

How long will this training be provided? How will your company measure the adequacy and competency of the training assistance?

3 Timetable of implementation and disbursements

The timetable for implementation and disbursements describes in chronological order the major payments that must be made in order to complete the project. These payments should correspond to specific phases in the project. The major disbursements are payments to specific entities, mainly contractors, sub-contractors and suppliers. While these disbursements may be made in local currency, you are asked to specify the amount in $.

The timing issue of when costs will be incurred may be critical to the financial viability of the project. In brief, the company should be looking to maximise its resources and the longer these outflows can be delayed the less costly they are in present value terms. The timing of the costs thus will have an impact on the valuation of total project. What is important here is that the timing of the costs (cash outflows) will need to be co-ordinated with the cash inflows.

In this paragraph, you will need to identify each of the major items to be purchased with a 'short technical description'. For example, 'automatic control systems' or 'flue gas analysers' would be sufficient if it is clear that these are major items to be purchased. Technical descriptions of the items to be purchased should be included in a Technical Purchase Appendix.

4 Description of agencies in charge of implementing major components of project and rationale for their selection

The bank will rely on the sponsor to implement the project directly, or to appoint contractors to implement it in a timely manner and in a cost-effective way. In order for the bank to assess the risks connected with the implementation of the project, you will be required to provide a description of the arrangements for implementation which includes the major components of the project, the names of the agency in charge of each component and the reasons for selecting the particular agency and its relevant track record. The major components of the project include amongst other things the sourcing of raw materials, construction of buildings and plant, delivery of fuel stock, marketing and after-sales support. In general, a major component can be thought of as any process which adds value to the product and which is within the control of the company and represents a major cost in the project.

The reasons for selecting any particular agency should include business confidence and trust in the agency's performance. Perhaps the agency has done business before with the company. In any case, the track record of the agency is important because it qualifies the agency in terms of its experience in work of a similar kind. Dates and types of contracts in which the agency was previously engaged would be relevant.

5 Nature of the contracts with agencies in charge of implementation of project

In this paragraph, you are asked to summarise some of the major features (terms and conditions) of the contracts with the agencies in charge of implementation. Some of the major points, which you should cover include:

■ What are the terms and conditions of the completion covenants? Are there any penalties for late completion or bonuses for early completion?

■ What are the terms of the progress payment schedules? These payments should be conditioned upon the completion of specific tasks or events. What are those specific events?

- Performance bonds associated with implementation What types of performance bonds are required for implementation?

- Is the agreement with implementing agency a turnkey contract? In other words, is the agency in charge of constructing and implementing the whole business process?

- Other types of special or unusual conditions These can be any kind of events which are critical to the performance of the contract.

6 Cost contingencies

In recognition that there may be events outside the control of the company, contingency costs are usually built into the project costs in order to help ensure that project funding will be available in case these events occur. From the perspective of the lender, the bank would like to know what types of risks are foreseen by the applicant for funds and what contingencies are included.

6.1 Built-in contingency costs to the project?

This is a listing of the contingency costs, their amount and the conditions under which they take effect.

6.2 Justifications for these contingency costs?

There may, for example, be cost contingencies built into equipment purchases and working capital. These assumptions should be explained.

6.3 If there are provisions for cost overruns, what are the reasons for assuming that such overruns may occur?

While provisions for cost overruns are normal in project finance, it is important that this risk is covered to ensure the successful completion of the project.

6.4 How has the company ensured that there is sufficient back-up funding in the event of cost overruns?

It is usually the case that the sponsor will need to have extra facilities that will sufficiently cover any extra costs.

7 Procurement issues

The bank requires transparency and arm's length procurement when approving the funding of a project so the sponsor is asked to address this area carefully. At an early stage, the bank will identify procurement issues and, in particular, the bank will:

- determine whether public sector or private sector procurement rules are applicable;

- indicate uses of proceeds and likely procurement procedure;

- highlight exceptions to open tendering if it is a public sector operation;

- ascertain whether or not there is a likelihood of advance procurement action or contracting (ie before operation approval);

- ascertain the need for special implementation and contracting risks and arrangements;

- determine whether the sponsor is likely to be a supplier or contractor;

- ascertain if used equipment is to be procured.

According to the bank's internal rules for procurement, public sector operations are operations:

- to or for the benefit of a government or an entity or undertaking that is controlled or majority financed by the public sector of the country of operation, or the procurement procedures of which are subject to regulation or control by a government or public agency, other than such entities or undertakings that, in the bank's judgment, are operating autonomously in a competitive market environment and are subject to bankruptcy or insolvency law; or

- guaranteed by the state or a public agency or instrumentality of the country of operations.

Operations that do not fall within the definition of 'public sector operations' or 'concessions' (as granted by the bank) are deemed by the bank to be 'private' for procurement purposes.

7.1 What are the proposed means for purchasing goods, services and equipment with the proposed lender's funds?

Whenever possible the preferred method is by tender. That is, at least three contractors should bid for the work and the procedure should allow for the best price and quality as possible. However, exceptions to this general rule should also be explained.

SECTION 6

1 Description of products or services to be supplied by the business

You may provide the names of each of your products or services, a brief technical description and the proportion each will contribute to the total turnover. The total percentage contribution of all the products and services should add up to 100 per cent and these figures should correspond to information you will supply on the profit and loss statement in the Appendix Proforma Financial Statements to the Bankable Proposal Form. If your company is selling more than four products or services then use separate sheets to provide the relevant information.

2 Pricing and costs (breakdown of the cost of materials)

For each product or service, you may wish to provide the variable costs associated with the product or service.

2.1 Sources of cost estimates

In nearly all cases, the source of cost estimates will be the costs the company actually pays. Therefore, if you yourself do not pay for the costs, then how are the costs estimated?

2.2 Explanation of price estimates

You may also wish to provide information on how you arrived at the sales forecast estimates. For example, perhaps you have conducted a market survey? If so, then a summary of this report should be included here and the market survey report should be attached as an Appendix to the Bankable Proposal form. Whatever information you supply, this will provide the bank with a basis to check the actual costs.

While there are many different ways to make price estimates, there are three good ways you may use:

- Cost-plus price What does it cost you to produce or provide?

- Competitor's price What do your competitors charge?

- Market price What the market will bear?

The nature of the market for the enterprise's products or services

The purpose of this section is to describe the market of the company, its general characteristics, customers, competitors and factors affecting the growth of the market and the position of the company within the market.

3   Market description, location and size

3.1   Description of the market that the business is in

A company is usually described in terms of the industrial or commercial sector in which the company is engaged accompanied by a brief description of whom the company sells to. For example, the company may be a electric power company that sells electricity to a region or the company may be a copper smelter that sells copper goods to a wide variety of appliance manufacturers. For this paragraph, it is sufficient to describe what the company sells and to whom.

The survival and existence of a business in a market economy is wholly dependent on market demand. That is, in simple terms, the company survives because it satisfies the needs of customers. Thus, a deeper description of your business market entails a description of your customers' needs. These should be detailed in the paragraphs below.

3.2   Geographical area of the company's market

The geographical area of the market can potentially be the population of the whole world. But this is not what is meant here. The geographical area should be limited to the area where you think your primary customers reside. Where do you see most of your income coming from? Where do your customers typically reside?

3.3   Size of the company's market ($ per year)

The question here is 'how big is your market?' This means not just your company's sales but the size of the total market in which you compete in. You should calculate how many units can be sold to potential customers per year and multiply this by the price per unit. This will be a gross figure. If you have various estimates of the size of the total market, you may mark these in terms of a range from pessimistic to optimistic.

3.4   Description of the market environment

Some of the questions to consider are:

- Is the market price sensitive?

- Is it very competitive or not competitive?

- Is it a mature market with established market leaders or a relatively new market with no clear market leaders?

4 Type of customers

4.1 Characteristics of customers of the business

This is fundamental information which your company must clarify and re-clarify if it is to survive and thrive. You should provide a customer profile. Who are your customers? Describe your customers as specifically as you can. This should include the names, type or profile. If, for example, the company plans to supply electricity to a region then it is sufficient to describe the major users of electricity in the region, eg residences, major industries, etc. In order to determine the characteristics of your customers, you may need to gather the following information:

- List of the geographical areas in which you plan to trade.

- List of the characteristics of people most likely to buy your goods.

- List characteristics and requirements of intermediaries you hope to do business with.

- Indicate the particular type of intermediaries who favour your products or services.

- List the characteristics of the organisations you want to do business with:

  - within these organisations, identify the types of people (by position or job title) you will have to convince of the value of your product/service in order to gain sales.

5 Competitor analysis

In this section, you are asked to identify your main competitors in terms of product or service and their respective market shares.

6.1 What is special about your own product or service? (What is its unique selling point, if any?)

Since the survival of a company in a market economy depends on market demand, it follows that the particular niche or special requirements which the company fulfils for the customers is its most important characteristic. Its so-called 'unique selling point' gives the company's products and services a unique psychological label within the minds of customers and enables them to identify the products and services to some particular need which the customers need fulfilled. Without this unique selling point, why should the customer buy your product or service over your competitors?

For example, a district heating company may have to compete against established domestic oil and gas companies for individual boilers. The district heating company may wish to emphasise not only its relatively low cost to the customers but the fact that it offers a less damaging alternative to the environment.

6.2 Advantages of your product or service over the competition

This is similar to the issue of the 'unique selling point' except that here the focus is on the particular advantage which your product or service has over competing products and services. For example, in one case, your advantage may be in price. But in other instances, your advantage may be in terms of quality, delivery, after-sales service, finance and so on. It is important to remember that a price advantage can be quickly eroded and therefore may not be an advantage for very long. It is therefore recommended that the company look to have a comparative advantage based on other factors which is really part of the definition of the product and integral to the definition of the customers' needs.

You may wish to refer to the 'Benefits' stated in Section 4 of the Bankable Proposal Form. For example, products produced from energy efficiency projects have an enhanced environmental quality and are therefore more likely to appeal to environmentally aware customers.

7   Factors affecting the growth of demand

7.1   Description of factors affecting growth of demand

What are the factors affecting the growth of demand for your company's products and services? There are two types of factors: general market factors and specific market factors. General market factors are those over which the company has no control and include interest rates, whether the product is a necessary (such as food) or a luxury, business and consumer confidence and the inflation or deflation rate. Specific market factors are those which the company can control or strongly influence. For example, there is the image of the company and the product via advertising. The limitation on the growth of demand is likely to be related to communications or the lack thereof to the appropriate target audience. In this paragraph, it is important to show both general market factors and specific factors which limit the growth of demand.

7.2   Is the company's market growing, stable or in decline?

This information will give the lender an idea of the market risk of the company. That is, if the company is in a growing area then it is likely to have more opportunities for growth in profits. On the other hand, if the market is declining then the company may be on a slippery slope and may be in danger of closing after a few years. A stable market implies that there may be intense competition amongst competitors and little opportunity for growth except at the expense of competitors losing market share.

7.3   Financial position of buyers

The stronger and more secure the financial position of the buyers of the company's products, the better it is for the company. The company, in other words, will carry less of a risk of buyers' default and a greater likelihood of continuing business if the buyers are financially strong and financially stable. The major questions to consider include:

■   What is the financial position of the buyers of the company's products and services?

■   Are the buyers financially strong or weak?

■   Do they command any credit from the business?

SECTION 7

Concise description of the proposed role of the lender

In this section, you will describe the role, which you wish the bank to play in this transaction. The major types of roles which the bank can play are set out below and are not mutually exclusive. In other words, the bank can play more than one role in the same project:

■   **Lender**   The Bank loans money to the borrower at a fixed or variable rate of interest for a fixed period of years.

- **Syndicator of loans to other lenders** This is where the bank repackages the loan and acts to spread the risk of the project across a number of lenders.

- **Guarantor** The Bank guarantees a certain portion of the project funds. This enables other banks and investors to participate in the funding of the project. Guarantees are an effective mechanism to induce other commercial banks to participate in the project funding.

- **Underwriter** This is where the bank acts to indemnify parties for the loss incurred by non-performance of the project. In effect, the Bank acts as a type of insurer.

- **Equity investor** In this case, the bank invests risk capital for which the company has no obligation of repayment in terms of principal and interest, but it may have certain contractual obligations to pay dividends.

- **Financial and investment adviser** The bank plays a role of advising the client on what types of financing and investment options are open and may be appropriate for the proposed project.

SECTION 8

Introduction

The financing plan sets out how the transaction costs identified in Section 5 will be met. Normally, the bank will be only one of several sources of financing. In fact, the bank will require the sponsor both to invest in the equity of the project and to identify other potential sources of financing. In the case where the project involves the expansion of an existing facility, the bank may be prepared to finance the project itself provided the bank's exposure in the company remains within 20 to 40 per cent of the long-term capitalisation of the company.

Why does the bank require other investors to co-finance the project?

- Risk sharing The bank has an interest to reduce its risks and at the same time to see that entities with direct experirience of the busniess are willing to risk their money in suppport of the project as a worthwhile venture. .

- Additionality The bank seeks to encourage other financing entities by having them participate in projects either through loans or through equity.

If the sponsor is experiencing difficulty in attracting other financing, especially debt, it is advisable to contact the bank at an early stage. The bank may be able to offer assistance in attracting other lending institutions once the financing structure has been agreed.

Commentary on Form

1 Current and required sources of finance

The purpose of this paragraph is to present the current and required sources of finance. The total financing required is simply the total current sources (A) less the total project costs (B).

The column entitled 'Financing source' includes major types of finance. They are as follows:

- **Sponsor's own resources**   The bank will require cash of at least 20 per cent of the project costs. The bank is looking to see its own risk minimised and may look to the sponsor for further cash injections. The valuation of the in-kind contributions should be the actual current market value (re-sale value) and not historical costs.

- **Supplier**   The supplier may extend credit for the purchase of necessary materials.

- **Local loans**   For example, these loans may come from local banks or consumer credit institutions.

- **Foreign loans**   These generally include loans from international financial institutions such as the World Bank, the EBRD and international commercial banks.

- **Foreign equity**   Cash from other investors.

- **Others**   These may be grants, cash contributions or new financial instruments which are combination of debt and equity, such as convertible bonds.

The layout of the financing plan should be described as in the table below:

Financing plan of infrastructure project

Financing plan (ECU million)				
Financing source	Local	Foreign	Total	% of total
Debt				
a.				
b.				
c.				
Equity				
a.				
b.				
c.				
Total project financing				

The object of the above table is to identify the major financial contributors to the project and its purpose is to help the bank assess the quality and adequacy of the financing.

2   Type of financing required

The sponsor should discuss the possibilities with the bank directly. Note that the total of the type of financing required stated in this paragraph should match the total financing required stated under paragraph 1.

3 Security, if any, that sponsor will put up for the project

As we have stated earlier, there is rarely a 'pure' project financing deal which looks only at the cash flow of the project for repayment of the loan. Therefore, any properties that may be used as security for the loan amount would be stated here.

SECTION 9

Introduction

This Section focuses on the cash flow projections of the project. We will describe cash flow projections and explain how cash flow is related to the financial viability of the project.

In this Section, the proposer's principal aim is to describe the financial viability of the project. This section assumes that the proposer is thoroughly acquainted with the principles stated in Chapter 3 on the financial economics of energy efficiency and has a grasp of how to carry out net present value (NPV) calculations. Here the emphasis is on the concept of cash flow, how it is determined and why it is important.

As a preliminary consideration, it is important to note that the project to be implemented by the proposer will be either (a) a stand-alone project, or (b) a corporate finance project. A stand-alone project will require the creation of a special purpose company. In this situation, the bank will analyse the cash flows of the proposed new company which does not yet exist. In the corporate finance situation, the bank will analyse the financial statements of the existing company with and without the cash flows brought about by the project.

In either case the bank's major concern is that the cash flow from the project be amply sufficient to cover the total debt service (all payments of interest and balance of the loan). The strength of the cash flow indicates the financial viability of the project.

Investment in the capital project may have company-wide cash flow implications. There is the danger that those involved in forecasting cash flows may not realise how the project affects other parts of the business. The proposer should therefore carefully consider whether there are any additional cash flows associated with the investment decision. For example, the decision to invest in refurbishment or energy efficiency equipment may influence the quantity and quality of the product, potentially increasing sales and working capital requirements.

Definition of operating cash flow[1]

Cash flow generated by an investment project is the difference between the money coming in and going out of the project. Cash flow should not be confused with accounting profits which include some cash flow items and exclude some others and are reduced by depreciation which is not cash flow at all. The cash flow indicates whether the investment is worthwhile. The timing of payments is very important to the value of the project. Net cash flows are a measure of the cash that comes into the investment and the cash that goes out. Depreciation is ignored because the capital outlay is already accounted for in the first year(s) of the investment project. Interest charges are ignored because they are taken into account by the discount rate that is used to discount the cash flows.

---

1 The following discussion on cash flow techniques borrows the line of argument from K Moran *Investment Appraisal for Non-Financial Managers* (Pitman Publishing, London 1995).

There are two other major reasons why cash flow from an investment does not equal accounting profit. First, the tax is usually payable in arrears but is deducted from the profit in the year that they are incurred. Second, the income statement does not take into account working capital outlay.

The differences between cash flows and accounting profit are set out below:

Cash flows versus accounting profit

	Cash flows	Accounting profit
Revenues	When cash comes in	When sale occurs
Operating expenses	When cash goes out	When expenses occurs
Depreciation	Not included	Included in Income statement added back for tax accounts
Capital allowances	Tax shield included as cash inflow	Included in tax accounts
Taxes	When tax is paid (one year time lag)	Recognized when tax incurred

There are two main ways to derive cash flows for investment appraisals:

■ from the raw data; and

■ from pro forma financial statements such as the income statement and the balance sheet.

Deriving cash flows from raw data

The ideal situation would be for you to analyse cash flows without looking at the income statement figures and to examine the cash flows from the actual operations of the firm.

As you consider your sales forecasts and operating cost forecasts, you may keep in mind to:

■ Include a cash outflow when it is likely to leave the business, not when it will be shown as an expense.

■ Include a cash inflow from sales when your customers will *actually pay*, not when the accountants will recognise the sale.

■ Include incremental tax, which has occurred due to the incremental cash flow from the investment. It is important to remember not to include a cash outflow for tax in the year in which the tax expense occurred but rather forecast the tax outflow for the following year when those taxes will actually be paid.

Deriving cash flows from projected financial statements

While deriving cash flow from raw data is ideal, it is likely that the data will come to you in the form of an Income Statement and Balance Sheet provided by the company accountant. You can derive a cash flow statement from accounting data by taking into account the following points.

Working capital

By focusing on cash you should automatically include *working capital expenses*. Working capital is the capital needed by any new project, for example, to pay for inventories or to allow for customers paying on credit, indeed all the expenses required by the investment before cash is received from the customers. The longer the production cycle and the longer your customers will take to pay, the greater your working capital requirements are likely to be.

Working capital requirements can be *derived from the balance sheet*. The total investment for capital projects can be considerably more than the fixed asset outlay. Normally, a capital project gives rise to increased stocks and debts to support the increase in sales. The increase in working capital (ie stocks plus debtors less creditors) brought about by the capital project forms part of the investment outlay, but it is a common error in appraisal to neglect this often crucial component. If the project takes a number of years to reach its full capacity, it is likely that there will be additional working capital requirements in the early years, especially for new products where the seller may have to tempt purchasers by offering more than usually generous credit terms. It is likely that as the investment increases its sales through its lifetime, there will be additional expenditure on working capital each year. The reason for this is that the ratio between accounts receivable and accounts payable will remain fairly constant. (If you do not have this information broken down into these components, a reasonable proxy from working capital is current assets minus current liabilities.)

The investment decision implies that the firm ties up fixed and working capital for the life of the project. At the end of the project, whatever is realised is returned to the firm. For fixed assets, this will be scrap or residual value which is usually considerably less than the original cost, except in the case of land and some premises. For working capital, the whole figure—less the value of damaged stock and bad debts – is treated as a cash inflow in the final year.

The introduction of new equipment or technology may reduce stock requirements. Here the stock reduction is a positive cash flow in the start year; but you should only include an equivalent negative outflow at the end of the project if it is assumed that the firm will revert to the previous stock levels. A more realistic assumption may be to assume that any replacement would at least maintain existing stock levels, in which case no cash flow for stock in the final year is necessary.

Interest: not included in cash flow

Capital projects financed by borrowing require a series of cash outflows in the form of interest payments. Interest payments, however, *should not be included* because they relate to the *financing* rather than the *investment* decision. Were interest payments to be deducted from the cash flows, it would amount to double counting since the discounting process already considers the cost of capital in the form of the discount rate. To include interest charges as a cash outflow would seriously understate the true NPV.

Only fixed overheads included in cash flow

Only *additional* fixed overheads incurred as a result of the capital project should be included in the analysis. In the short-term, there will often be sufficient factory space to house new equipment without incurring additional overheads, but ultimately some additional fixed costs (for rent, heating and lighting, etc) will be incurred. Most factories operate an accounting system whereby all costs, including fixed overheads, are charged on some agreed basis to cost centres. Investment in a new process or machine frequently attracts a share of these overheads. While this may be appropriate for accounting purposes, only *incremental* fixed overheads incurred by the decision should be included in the project analysis.

Taxation

Taxation for most organisations is a cash flow. It includes any cash benefits from tax relief on the initial capital expenditure and tax payable on additional cash flows. Attention should be given to estimating the timing of the tax cash flows. Generally, tax is assumed to be paid one year following the cash flow upon which it is based, while the tax benefit on capital expenditure occurs one year after the year-end following the end of the accounting period.

Impact of tax

Tax has two main implications for investment appraisals. On the one hand, if the investment is successful and has a net profit, company taxes will increase. On the other hand, if the investment has involved capital expenditure, the company may be able to claim capital allowances from the government and this will help to reduce its tax burden.

Taxable profit

In order to calculate the tax, you will need to forecast the profit of the investment. How accurate this estimate needs to be will depend on how large the investment is, and how far the investment proposal has progressed through the review and approval process. Once the incremental cash flow has been forecast, the payment of taxes should automatically be included in the cash flow forecasts.

Timing of tax cash flows

In some countries, the actual payment of corporation taxes, payable on the profits of one year, does not normally occur until the following year. For example, if it is currently due six months after the end of the financial year then the company only pays tax one year after the tax expense was incurred.

Example 7.1
Deriving cash flow from financial statements

The following simple example shows how data from the balance sheet and the income statement can be used to derive cash flow.

Cash flow from the forecasted income and the balance sheet (in $)

Year	0	1	2	3	
From the balance sheet:					
Investments	(120,000)				
Stocks	0	80,000	100,000	110,000	
Debtors	0	40,000	48,000	46,000	
Creditors	0	60,000	72,000	84,000	
From the income statement:					
Revenues	0	400,000	480,000	560,000	
Operating profit	0	60,000	96,000	120,000	
Depreciation (straight line)	0	(40,000)	(40,000)	(40,000)	
Interest charges	0	(10,000)	(8,000)	(3,000)	
Tax payable at 33%		(3,300)	(15,840)	(24,420)	
Net profit	0	6,700	32,160	49,580	
Dividends	0	0	(2,000)	(3,000)	
Retained profit		6,700	36,860	83,440	
Add back:					
Depreciation, interestcharges & dividends	0	50,000	50,000	49,000	
Delayed tax charge*	0	3,300	12,540	9,840	(24,420)
Add investment	(120,000)	0	0	0	0
Add changes in working capital**	(120,000)	(60,000)	(16,000)	(6,000)	82,000
Cash flows		(6,700)	46,540	52,840	57,580

*   This shows the difference between tax payable in one year and when the tax is actually paid in the next year. So in Year 2 tax is paid on Year 1 profits ($3,300) and not on Year 2 profits ($) and the difference is added back ($15,840 minus $3,300 is $12,540).
** Add in the initial working capital expenses in Year 1 (stocks plus debtors minus creditors), and then any changes in working capital. Add back the working capital outlay for the investment to Year 3's cash flow, as those funds are released at the end of the investment.

Other considerations in cash flow analysis

Forget 'sunk costs'

This is money that has already been spent and should have no bearing on whether, if further money was invested, it would gain a good return for shareholders. For example, if you are considering whether to build a block of energy efficient apartment blocks on land that you already own, you do not need to include the cost of the original land purchase as part of the investment cost, as that is a sunk cost.

All incidental costs and benefits should be included

An example of incidental cost that is often overlooked is the management time involved in the investment project that leads to a temporary decline in sales elsewhere in the business. That cost (lost sales) should be included as an incidental cost.

Opportunity cash flows

Capital projects often give rise to opportunity cash flows. For example, a company owns land which is not being used for any commercial purpose and intends to build a wind farm on it offering an NPV of $100,000. If the market value of the land is $120,000, this new use imposes an opportunity cost—the cost of denying its sale by building the wind farm. This opportunity cash flow is a fundamental component to the investment decision and should be deducted from the $100,000. The wind farm option is not wealth-creating—other alternatives should be explored, including that of selling the land.

We frequently see opportunity cash flows in *replacement decisions*. For example, a water treatment facility at a power plant can be replaced by an improved model costing $5 million, which generates cash savings of $1 million per year for five years when it will have a $500,000 scrap value. The equipment manufacturers are prepared to give an allowance on the existing machine of $1.5 million. The net initial cash outlay is therefore $3.5 million. However, by taking this course of action, the company prevents the existing machine from continuing its intended life when in three years' time it would yield a $300,000 scrap value. The scrap value denied three years from now is the opportunity cost of replacing the existing machine. The cash flows associated with the replacement decision are therefore:

Cash flow replacement decision

Year 0	Net cost	($ 3.5 m)
Year 1–5	Annual cash savings	($ 1 m)
Year 3	Opportunity cash flow	($ 300,000)
Year 5	Scrap value on new machine	$ 500,000

Conversion into cash

Improvements in energy efficiency may be related to improvements in product quality or delivery time. These improvements can often be converted into cash values. For example, a proposal may be for new machinery. This machinery is not only more energy efficient but it will also lead to improvement in product quality. If you do not include this benefit in the analysis, you may seriously underestimate the value of the project. For example, the quality improvements may lead to cost savings through the reduction in scrap and wastage, the amount of time spent on repairing or reworking defective returns and to inspect each product. As the quality improves, the company may expect to have less cash outflows from its warranty service since fewer products will need to be repaired within the warranty service period. The increase in quality may also lead to an increase in sales. You will need sufficient information to make informed judgments on how the increased quality will affect cash flows.

It is very important that you distinguish those improvements from the investments which are quantifiable from those which are difficult to quantify. The bank is interested in seeing those *costs and benefits which can be converted into cash*. However, you will need to make sure that you can show clearly how you derived these monetary values.

Strategic options

Investments of a strategic nature often offer hidden benefits beyond that found in their underlying cash flows. These hidden benefits may arise during the life of a project, but not be quantifiable, such as the greater production flexibility from the introduction of advanced manufacturing technology. Alternatively, the actual investment could open up the possibility of other wealth-creating opportunities. These opportunities could be called strategic options including:

- entry into new markets;

- developing follow-up products; and

- improving existing practices.

The introduction of new manufacturing technology or energy savings technology may provide the right opportunity to introduce new management practices such as just-in-time procedures. Investment in energy efficiency may also give rise to entry into other markets.

The true NPV is therefore the sum of the project NPV normally calculated and the value of strategic options.

Checklist of practical tips

- First, you need to decide what is the appropriate alternative to the investment project. Are there any opportunity costs which should be included in the analysis?

- Second, you may list all the tangible and intangible costs and benefits of the project that are *incremental* to existing expenditure. Can the intangible costs and benefits be *converted in to monetary values in a way that is acceptable to the bank?* You may need to focus on the incremental costs and benefits that are most relevant to the bank. Any other quantifiable benefits should be considered extra ammunition but not core to your central argument.

By way of review, the key points to calculating incremental cash flows are stated in the table below.

Key points to calculating incremental cash flows to investment decisions

- Include only future, incremental cash flows relating to the investment decision and its consequences. This implies that:

- only additional fixed overheads incurred are included;
- depreciation (a non-cash item) is excluded;
- sunk (or past) costs are not relevant;
- interest charges are financing (not investment) cash flows and therefore excluded;
- opportunity costs (eg the opportunity to rent or sell premises if the proposal is not acceptable) are included.

■ Profit is not so relevant as cash flow in decision analysis.

■ Replacement decision analysis examines the change in cash flows resulting from the decision to replace an existing asset with a new asset.

Commentary on Form

1 Operating profit

1.1 Total turnover

This includes any and all sales revenue connected to the project.

1.2 Turnover on investments

This includes any return from investments for funds on behalf of the project.

1.3 Raw material

This has been stated in Section 5 on transaction costs.

1.4 Other direct operating costs

These have also been stated in Section 5.

1.5 Gross profit

This is the addition of the turnover (lines 1.1 and 1.2) less the costs of raw material and other direct costs (lines 1.3 and 1.4).

1.6 Indirect costs

These are incremental costs associated with the project such as:

■ 1.6.1 Sales and marketing

■ 1.6.2 Utilities and maintenance

■ 1.6.3 Overheads

■ 1.6.4 Other

■ 1.6.5 Total Operating Expenses (excluding depreciation) This is the total of lines 1.6.1 to 1.6.4.

1.7 Operating profit (excluding depreciation)

This is gross profit (line 1.5) less total operating expenses (line 1.6.5).

2 Working capital

See the discussion above on working capital, p 143. Changes in working capital are taken account by the next three lines.

2.1 Decrease (increase) in stock

A decrease in stock (inventory) means that there is a net inflow of cash to the firm while an increase in stock is a net outflow of cash.

2.2 Decrease (increase) in debtors

A decrease in debtors (less number of outstanding debts owed to the firm) means a net inflow of cash to the firm while an increase in debtors is a net outflow of cash.

2.3 Increase (decrease) in creditors

An increase in creditors (a greater amount of debt to the firm) is a net outflow of cash while a decrease in creditors is a net inflow of cash.

3 Taxation

3.1 Taxes paid

See discussion above on taxation, p 144. The main point is that taxes appear in the cash flow statement when they are actually paid.

4 Servicing of finance

4.1 Free cash flow

This is the cash not retained and reinvested in the business. The free cash flow is the operating cash flow less tax paid and less capital expenditures. The capital expenditures should be clear from your analysis conducted in Section 5: Project costs and timetable.

4.2 Interest paid

This the interest paid on all long-term loans.

4.3 Bank fees paid

These are fees paid to the bank for obtaining the loan.

4.4 Net cash flow before financing

The net cash flow before financing is equal to the free cash flow less the total cost of servicing of finance (that is, the total of lines 4.1, 4.2 and 4.3).

5 Financing

5.1 Issue of ordinary share capital

Cash for equity stake in the firm.

5.2 Bank fees paid

These are payments on long-term loans to other banks.

5.3 Bank-long-term repayment

This the repayment on the project loan.

5.4   Long-term loan requirement

This should be equivalent to the capital expenditure on the project.

5.5   Short-term loan

This is any short-term loan obligation.

5.6   Net cash flow from financing

The net cash flow from financing is the net cash flow before financing less the amount paid for financing (ie all the expenses in lines 5.1 to 5.5).

6   Ratios

6.1   Gross profit margin

Total turnover (total revenues) less total direct operating costs divided by total turnover.

6.2   Net profit margin

Net profit before tax divided by total turnover.

6.3   Return on equity

Net profit before tax divided by shareholder's equity. (See balance sheet in Section 10: Appendix—Proforma Financial Statements.)

6.4   Current ratio

Current assets divided by current liabilities. (See balance sheet in Section 10 Appendix—Proforma Financial Statements.)

6.5   Acid test (quick ratio)

Current assets less stocks divided by current liabilities. This measures the ability of the firm to meet its short-term liabilities by generating cash flows from its most liquid assets.

6.6   Cash flow to debt service ratio

This is the free cash flow divided by the interest paid and the total long-term loan repayment. This measures the firm's ability to pay for its long-term loan out of the cash flow from the project.

SECTION 10

Introduction

The proforma financial statements consist of the Income Statement (Profit and Loss Account), the Balance Sheet, Cash Flow and Financial Ratios. Please note that the information provided in these statements may have already been stated in the Section 5: Project costs and timetable and in Section 9: Cash flow projections. In this commentary, a brief explanation of each of the items in the financial statements is given. For the sake of clarity, an example from a real-life project is presented at the end of this commentary so that the reader can see how the calculations of various items interrelate. (Please note that the name of the project and the actual numbers have been altered in order to preserve and protect the confidentiality of the parties concerned.) In general, there are three stages in preparing the proforma financial statements:

- Stage 1: Pre-finance In this stage, you present the financial condition of the company without any consideration of long-term finance.

- Stage 2: With finance In this stage, you show the financial condition of the company with finance.

- Stage 3: Differential between Stage 1 and Stage 2 Finally, in the last stage, you show the difference between the projections set out in Stage 1 and the projections in Stage 2.

Commentary on Form

The following is a commentary of the proforma financial statements in the Business Plan Form.

Forecasted income statement including bank loan (in thousand US$)

For items 1 to 13, please refer to the Commentary to Section 9 on operating profit, p 148:

1 **Turnover on fuel, operation and maintenance**

2 **Turnover on investments**

3 **Total turnover**

4 **Raw material**

5 **Other direct operating costs**

6 **Gross profit**

7 **Indirect costs**

8 **Sales & marketing**

9 **Utilities & maintenance**

10 **Overheads**

11 **Other**

12 **Total operating expenses (excluding depreciation)**

13 **Operating profit (excluding depreciation)**

14 **Depreciation**

This is an accounting measure of the declining value of an asset over the lifetime of the asset. For the use of depreciation in the calculation of cash flow, please see Chapter 7, Section 10, Table – Cash Flow from the forecasted income and balance sheet, p 113 et seq. Please note that depreciation must be 'neutralised' in the cash flow statement.

15 Operating profit

Operating profit is equal to the amount of operating profit excluding depreciation plus the amount of depreciation. This figure for operating profits is equal to line 1 of the forecasted cash flow below.

16 Interest expense

This is the interest expense on the loan sought.

17 Bank fees

These are fees to be paid to the bank.

18 Net profit before tax

Net profit before tax is equal to the operating profit less the interest expense and bank fees.

19 Taxation

This is the expected tax to be paid.

20 Net profit after tax

This is the net profit before tax less the taxation.

Forecasted balance sheet including bank loan (in thousand US$)

Introduction

The balance sheet is designed to illustrate a company's financial position (that is, the assets owned, shareholders' funds and liabilities owed) at a specific point in time. The balance sheet relationship between assets, shareholders' funds and liabilities can be expressed as:

$$assets = shareholder's\ funds + liabilities$$

Another way of saying the same thing is:

$$total\ assets = total\ capital + liabilities$$

In the format below, the long-term debt owed to the bank is clearly set out as part of the overall relationship:

$$total\ assets = shareholder's\ equity + long\text{-}term\ debt + current\ liabilities$$

Form

ASSETS

1 Tangible assets

The tangible assets are whatever 'you can kick'. In other words, they are physical items.

2 Accumulated depreciation

This the depreciation per year added consecutively for each year.

3 Net book value

This the value of the tangible assets less the accumulated depreciation.

4 Stocks

These are short-term items in inventory that are expected to be sold within a year.

5 Debtors

These are debtors to the firm which are expected to pay the firm within a year.

6 Cash

These are liquid assets that can be turned immediately into cash.

7 Current assets

The current assets are equal to the total of the stocks, debtors and cash together.

8 Total assets

The total assets are equal to the total of the net book value and the current assets.

LIABILITIES

9 Called-up share capital

This is the cash which shareholders have paid into the firm.

10 Profit and loss account

This is the amount of profits (or loss) which was not distributed as dividends.

11 Shareholders' equity

This is difference between the amount of the called-up share capital and the profit and loss account.

12 Long-term debt

This is the amount of payment on long-term debt.

13 Trade creditors

This is the short-term debt owed to suppliers and others who are expected to be paid within a year.

14 Short-term debt

These are debts due for payment within a year.

15 Current liabilities

This is the total of trade creditors and short-term debt.

16 Total liabilities

This is equal to the shareholder's equity plus the long-term debt and the current liabilities.

Forecasted cash flow including bank loan (in US$)

Please note that the definition of the following terms are found in the Commentary to Section 9: Cash flow projections.

1   Operating profits

2   Add back depreciation

3   Decrease (increase) in stock

4   Decreases (increase) in debtors

5   Increase (decrease) in creditors

6   Operating cash flow

7   Taxation paid

8   Capital expenditures

9   Free cash flow

10   Servicing of finance

11   Interest paid

12   Bank Fees paid

13   Dividends paid

14   Net cash flow before financing

15   Financing

16   Issue of ordinary share capital

17   Others long-term loan payment

18   Bank long-term repayment

19   Long-term loan requirement

20   Short-term loan

21   Net cash flow from financing

Forecasted ratios including bank loan (in US$)

Please refer to the definitions of the following ratios in the Commentary to Section 9: Cash flow projections:

■   gross profit margin;

■   net profit margin;

■   return on equity;

■   current ratio;

■   acid test (quick ratio);

- gearing;

- cash flow to debt service ratio.

8

Negotiating deal terms for transaction efficiency

LEARNING OBJECTIVES

After reading this chapter you will be able to understand the standard issues and basic tactics for negotiating project finance agreements, including:

- *Project risk insurance*
- *The essence of project financing*
- *Pre-development agreements*
- *Shareholder/sponsor agreements*
- *Sponsor support agreements*
- *Construction and equipment agreements*
- *Operating and maintenance agreements*
- *Fuel supply agreements*
- *Sales/offtake agreements*
- *Customer and supplier agreements*
- *Financing agreement*
- *Interim loan agreement*
- *Project loan agreements*
- *Security agreements*
- *Leasing agreements*
- *Legal opinions*
- *Guarantees and letters of credit*
- *Concession agreements*

8.1   INTRODUCTION

Project finance will continue to be a major factor in capital project financings for the foreseeable future. The demand is tremendous and it is worldwide. Foreign competitors often have more experience than US companies with the kinds of joint ventures being used and in doing business in the developing countries where demand for capital projects is the greatest. Because of the multiple parties and types of projects involved, and the dependence on numerous contracts to support each financing, complex risk allocations are key to a successful financing and careful draughtsmanship of documentation is an absolute necessity. Understanding the parameters of each project is crucial to the contractors and suppliers involved since they will be drawn into the risk allocations and may be 'partners' in the venture without any special return for their risk.

One of the main legal issues arising out of any project financing is 'frustration/force majeure'. Under English law the doctrine of frustration allows the parties to a contract to be discharged of all future obligations and in most cases for the loss in termination to be compensated where, without fault, either party becomes incapable of performing the obligation in the form that the contract contemplates.

Force majeure, a civil law concept, is less arbitrary and strict in that it relies upon four criteria to be fulfilled, namely the event or circumstance must:

- make performance of the obligations impossible;

- be irresistible;

- be external in the sense that no fault or negligence is attributable to the parties;

- be such that the party affected must have done everything to perform its obligations.

The precise terms of a force majeure clause will be the subject of much negotiation between the parties, however normal provisions would include dealing with acts of God, embargoes, natural disaster, etc. From a lender's perspective it would be prudent to adopt the *eiusdem generis* rule in interpreting the terms of the force majeure clause with the normal meaning of such words.

8.2   PROJECT RISK INSURANCE

Insurance can play a special role in project finance. While many of the risks such as the solvency of the project owner and other project participants and the adequacy of the cash flow projected to be generated by the project to service debt and other necessary costs are capable of financial analysis, other risks are not easily quantified. For example, risks of physical damage and third party liability may be significant. Typically, these types of fortuitous risk are dealt with under traditional insurance products, such as builders' risk and liability insurance policies.

A more unusual type of risk is the possibility of insufficient cash flow to meet debt service requirements and other costs because the project is not completed on time or to the specifications necessary to provide the required cash flow. Certain aspects of these risks can be addressed by delay in opening insurance (in the event of physical damage) and payment and performance bonds (in the event of contractor default).

However, even with these protections lenders are often left with the sometimes substantial risk of occurrences beyond the control of the project participants. For example, such diverse events as the discovery of an endangered species or an item of archaeological significance, or a change in emission control requirements can cause substantial delays in the completion of a project and/or reductions in a project's output that may translate into an adverse impact on the project.

An insurance product generally known as 'force majeure' insurance can address many of these risks. This insurance is usually obtained by the project owner to ensure its ability to meet its debt service obligations and other costs in the event of late completion, under-performance or permanent abandonment of the project following the occurrence of defined force majeure perils. These perils include physical events such as earthquake and severe weather, strikes affecting suppliers, changes in government regulations and, most importantly, 'any other cause beyond the control' of the owner and the other project participants. Although the underwriters of this insurance will typically exclude known perils, such as pending litigation or a known environmental remediation obligation, force majeure insurance can provide substantial protection to a project owner and its lenders. While certain US insurers offer cover of this type, the broadest form of such coverage has been available only from Lloyd's of London.

A related form of 'liquidated damages' insurance is available to contractors to cover risks they may have had to assume under the contract, including force majeure risks. Because it is insurance (ie risk transfer) and not a bond, the insurers would generally have no recourse to the contractor if they were to pay a claim. This insurance is designed to protect the contractor for its contractual liquidated damages liability to the project owner for late completion and/ or performance shortfall damages due to errors or omissions by the contractor and its sub-contractors. Although originally developed as a means of balance sheet management for contractors, liquidated damages insurance has increasingly been used in project financing as a means of securing payment of contractors' liquidated damages to project owners and their lenders, often in cases where force majeure risk has been transferred to the contractor under the construction agreement.

Examples of projects in which force majeure and liquidated damages insurance has been used include co-generation and other power facilities, composting facilities, office buildings, toll roads and bridges, subway systems and airport terminal buildings. These projects have generally been located in North America and Western Europe, but proposals are increasingly being received for projects in developing countries.

8.3 ESSENCE OF PROJECT FINANCING

The essence of any project financing is the apportionment of project risks amongst the participants in the project. The use of a complex matrix of contractual relations between the participants enables the implementation of this 'risk transfer' and commercial relationships.

Typically these agreements can be divided into five generic categories:

- feasibility/pre-development agreements;
- sponsor/shareholder documentation;
- construction agreements;
- operating agreements; and
- financing agreements.

Categorised in this way feasibility/pre-development agreements includes confidentiality and non-competition agreements and letters of intent. Sponsor/shareholder agreements though self-explanatory will centralise the relationships between such parties setting out any obligations and benefits of each party. Construction agreements include site agreements, engineering, equipment, construction and testing agreements. Operating agreements include customer and supplier agreements, management and technical service agreements, labour and employment agreements and other agreements that relate to the day-to-day operations of the project. Financing agreements include the loan and equity documentation and security agreements. In addition to these agreements, insurance coverage may be obtained to bridge any 'risk' gaps between the operations and financing elements of the proposed project.

This chapter is not intended to present a detailed discussion of each agreement nor does it intend to substitute professional legal advice, however, it will be useful to reflect briefly on the various categories of agreements used in a project financing and on the roles pertaining to such agreements.

8.4   PRE-DEVELOPMENT AGREEMENTS

At the feasibility stage of a project, the parties to the project 'idea' will become party to agreements relating to the undertaking of feasibility studies. These relationships typically fall below the requirements for a full shareholders agreement. For a limited period, the agreement will address issues such as proposed arrangements, terms of withdrawal of a party from the project, appointment of advisers, general cost sharing, confidentiality and non-competition clauses.

8.5   SHAREHOLDER/SPONSOR AGREEMENTS

8.5.1 Shareholder/joint venture agreements

Where the project is being undertaken through the use of a special purpose vehicle ('SPV') formed solely for the purpose of owning the project owned by two or more project parties, the shareholders to the SPV will regulate their relationship by entering into a shareholders agreement. Where the relationship between the parties is contemplated as a joint venture, this would be governed by a joint venture agreement.

Typically issues dealt with by a shareholders agreement include:

- the amount of, and the injection of, capital;

- funding of the project company;

- special voting requirements for particular matters;

- dispute resolution;

- dividend policy;

- management issues;

- disposal of shares and pre-emption rights; and

- termination provisions and distribution of assets.

Key lender issues

Key issues for the lenders will include:

- The identity of the shareholders, their experience and creditworthiness.

- Shareholders' commitments to management, resources and expertise. Lenders will want to see these issues clearly defined within the project documentation and the terms on which such commitments will be provided. In cases where lenders have separate concerns, a separate Management Agreement may be produced.

- Terms and conditions of equity investment. From the perspective of other lenders it is more prudent to obtain direct equity undertakings from the sponsors rather than rely upon an assignment of a security interest in the equity. The lender cannot claim for a loss in excess of that of the assignor by virtue of an assignment and it might well be the case that the lender's actual loss is considerably greater that that of the default. Set-offs or counterclaims could exist between the project company and the shareholders which would affect the shareholders' obligations and a further weakness is that an obligation to subscribe for equity in the project company will not survive the project company's liquidation, thus depriving the lenders of this source of income. Any claims by the lenders of breach of such equity commitments would be damages based which suffer from the usual common law rules as to causation, remoteness and mitigation. Therefore the lenders' perspective is for an equity commitment to be constructed as a financial guarantee or indemnity.

It will be the case in any shareholders agreement or joint venture agreement that any benefits derived from such an agreement will be subject to automatic assignment in favour of the lenders.

8.6   SPONSOR SUPPORT AGREEMENTS

A support agreement is usually entered into by the sponsor, project company and lender. It covers issues dealing with the level of commitments required by the lenders from the sponsor and project company. For example:

- requirements to provide management and technical assistance;

- requirements to provide further financing, whether through subscription for equity or through the use of debt financing;

- restrictions on the ability of the sponsor to dispose of their shares;

- completion guarantees or cost overrun guarantees;

- security requirements.

8.7   CONSTRUCTION AND EQUIPMENT AGREEMENTS

Although every part's goals are the same-the complete and timely constructing of the project-the relationships of the parties in a project financing are very different than in the traditional construction project setting. Rather than simply having an architect, designer, builder and owner with their separate and well understood roles, the typical project finance construction contract becomes an amalgam of often conflicting roles and relationships.

A bewildering variety of contracts have evolved which essentially contractualise forms of risk partnership. The most commonly used contracts, their terms and meanings, are: BOT (Build-

Operate-Transfer), BOOT (Build-Own-Operate-Transfer), BOO (Build-Own-Operate), BTO (Build-Transfer-Operate), BLT (Build-Lease-Transfer), LDO (Lease-Develop-Operate), EPC (Engineer, Procure, Construct) and Turnkey.

Each of the above contract types has its own unique requirements, however they have many terms in common. For example, the lender to the project is the controlling entity. This entity controls the receipt and disbursement of money and the enforcement of all the contract terms in all the contracts insofar as any perceived element of financial risk is involved. All other parties are subordinate to the lender and must ultimately acknowledge the demands of the lender. Where several sources of financing, with different levels of security, are involved, then this can become an issue.

In the international market, typically, projects are huge and the risks so immense that no single designer, construction contractor, equipment supplier, financier or owner is willing, or able, to assume the entire risk for that portion of the project. Accordingly, consortia are created at each level and the individual consortia participants may have quite different views of what is acceptable.

It is not at all unusual to have the lead construction contractor simultaneously being a member of a construction joint venture, a part of the owner consortium and perhaps of the lender group as well. Actual and potential conflicts of interest are endemic and negotiation of contract terms becomes an exercise in diplomacy as well as contract drafting. The situation is further complicated because international projects always include organisations from many different countries with a variety of legal systems.

Design and construction requirements are usually combined into a single contract. The construction contractor is fully responsible for both, thus virtually eliminating any rights it might otherwise have against either the designer or the owner for any alleged design defects. Major equipment contracts may be sub-contracted under the construction contract or may be entered into directly with the project owner. Where equipment is to be imported for the project, attractive export financing from the country of origin often dictates the source of major equipment packages. Local contractors for site, erection and similar work may be imposed on the contractor by the local politics of the project, in addition to the desire of the project owner and lenders to hold the construction contractor responsible for timely completion and performance of the entire project.

The merging of design and construction requirements and the demands of the lenders means the construction contractor becomes a guarantor of performance of the facility. It is generally the responsibility of the construction contractor to ensure that the project is completed on time and any performance tests satisfied. Failure to meet either of these would typically result in liquidated damages which are designed to protect lenders from potential cash shortfalls which would restrict completion being achieved at the design specification.

Where governmental ownership is involved most states and countries still have statutes that either prohibit, or create immense complexity for, this type of contracting. International, federal, state and local procurement requirements narrowly define public procurement and typically require different methods of procurement for design and construction. Anti-deficiency statutes and debt limitations may have an impact on such contracts. Advance payments, loans and pledges by governmental bodies to private entities are often prohibited. Civil service laws, prohibitions on transfers of public property to private organisations and delegation of governmental authority also create difficult conceptual problems that may require highly imaginative contract drafting.

As these contracts are finance driven the construction contracts tend to be drafted primarily from a finance perspective by lawyers without any real knowledge or appreciation of the construction process. Because the construction contractors are so anxious to obtain what they perceive as a major contract, normal business cautions and legal concerns are sometimes overridden for the overall deal. Accordingly, construction risks often arise in areas where they could have been avoided by more prudent draughtsmanship. Careful time and attention must be given to the draughting, the financier's views and requirements must be sought and understood early in the process and the construction contract will have to be carefully integrated into the overall loan and security documentation.

Clauses covering the following elements are of critical importance in construction contracts of this nature:

- design approvals;

- quality of construction;

- definition of completion;

- responsibility for time or cost overruns and disputes procedures;

- payment approvals and procedures;

- lender's right to inspect;

- consent of lender for changes to performance targets and underlying obligations;

- guarantee requirements from all parties;

- insurance and surety requirements;

- performance and completion tests and completion guarantees;

- defects liability periods;

- liquidated damages for defective performance or delay;

- method of compensation for changes and claims;

- termination;

- flow-down clauses from other documents;

- privity and third party beneficiary relationships, etc.

8.7.1 Standardisation of construction contracts

In an infrastructure project where the project lenders are taking all or part of the construction and completion risk the construction contract will be one of the key project documents. There are a number of standard form construction contracts in use, with perhaps the most common being the FIDIC model. The UK has a standard form and it is likely that parties would use this, ie the JCT model.

Typically construction contracts fall within two camps:

- 'Turnkey' contractsThis is where a single contractor assumes all risk of on time completion of a project. In a turnkey contract the project owner specifies overall performance and reliability standards for the plant and the turnkey contractor assumes full responsibility for design and engineering of the plant as well as selection of equipment and sub-contractors which will enable it to meet those general objectives. A project owner may include specifications, but with the caveat that they are only suggestions and the turnkey operator's responsibility to follow them is subject to the contractor finding them fully sufficient to meet overall performance and reliability objectives. The turnkey operator will generally be expected to guarantee overall performance of all components and sub-contractors. A turnkey contractor has more responsibility than an EPC contractor and greater liability if things go wrong, hence the reason that a turnkey contract costs more than an EPC contract.

- ■ EPC contractsThese are contracts to perform the engineering procurement and construction tasks so that a project is built according to specifications supplied by the owner and often using equipment specified or even designated by the project owner. An EPC contract sets construction deadlines and plant performance criteria but liability for failure does not fall so squarely upon the general contractor, since the general contractor did not design or select equipment or sub-contractors.

Lenders in either case will want protection for late completion and under-performance. Therefore a turnkey contract and a request that the sponsor assume the additional liabilities under an EPC contract is usually sought.

8.7.2 Price and payment clauses

Contractors usually prefer to be paid by stage payments. They also like to have some ability to vary the price if unforeseen circumstances or events affect assumptions on which the original price was quoted. Lenders, on the other hand, prefer as much certainty as possible about the price. Owing to cash flow requirements it is unrealistic for lump sum payments to be made, it is therefore more likely that stage payments would be made against certificates of work done, which would be issued by architects or engineers. Lenders will, however, stress that payments are subject to retentions, which are released for payment only upon satisfactory completion of all specified work and completion certificates issued in such respect.

8.7.3 Completion

Contracts usually include provisions for postponement of completion dates. Lenders will only allow such clauses in defined limited circumstances such as in force majeure situations. In circumstances where the lender permits default, they will expect the contractor to pay some form of liquidated damages for any delay, which at the minimum will cover interest payments of the loan, together with an uplift for delay in the project to cover increased operating costs for the delayed period.

Other issues that lenders will be concerned with include unforeseen ground risk, which will be the risk of the contractor. Contractors will be expected to warrant the quality and fitness for purpose of their work, a standard warranty from a UK lenders' perspective given the wording of the Sale of Goods Act 1979. Where the contract is a design and build, the design along with the construction would be warranted separately.

It must be remembered that any provision allowed in any one contract must be mirrored in all the other project documents to ensure that a breach of another contract does not occur on the occurrence of an event.

8.7.4 General sponsors' concerns

The most important conditions for a sponsor under a construction contract are time, cost and quality.

Time

The extension of time clause

The extension of time clause grants the contractor a benefit by extending the time stipulated in the contract for completion in certain circumstances which are beyond the control of either party. From a sponsor's viewpoint these circumstances should generally be as limited as possible. The rationale behind such a clause is the benefit to both sponsor and contractor in that contractual certainty is established.

The sponsor should ensure that it has the right to grant an extension of time clause. In the event that there is an absence of a suitable contractual relationship for extending time in common law jurisdictions courts will be minded to assess a reasonable completion date. A contractor is therefore estopped on insisting a strict completion date hence liquidated damages will not be payable.

Delayed progress

The programme will be more significant if it is a contract document rather than a document merely created by the contractor. In addition to the common law rights of termination in the event that delayed progress is so substantial that the sponsor is able to establish that the contractor cannot perform the contract in accordance with the contract terms, the sponsor should be aware what remedies they have for delayed progress. Such rights will probably be the ability to send a notice to the contractor, although in severe cases there may lie an automatic right of termination.

Progress certificate

The cost of completing details is most significant when considering a progress certificate, as this is one way of identifying cost overruns. Lenders will usually wish to appoint their own technical advisers to review the progress certificates which will be issued by independent consultants to the project.

In the event that entitlements are paid prior to materials being delivered, it is imperative to ensure that the contract requires goods to be insured, labelled and supported by sufficient documentation to establish title, ie the normal 'romalpa clause'!

Cost

Liquidated damages

This clause needs to be drafted in such way as to avoid it being construed as imposing a penalty and therefore void. The amount of liquidated damages specified should be a genuine pre-estimate of damage although it will usually not include an allowance for consequential loss. The total of the contract sum including variations is effectively the amount of money which the proprietor has invested in the project and on which, as a rule, the proprietor will receive no return until completion, therefore the day-to-day interest rates on the contract sum will be a good reflection of the true cost to the sponsor.

Delay costs

The delay costs clause is extremely important and will more often than not require amendment from the sponsor viewpoint. Here is an opportunity to limit the contractor's entitlement by using words such as 'costs incurred' or even the narrower 'extra costs necessarily incurred' as opposed to 'loss, expense or damage'. The entitlement to delay costs is in lieu of the common law right to sue for general damages for breach of contract, including possible heads of damage such as economic loss, loss of profits, indirect overheads, etc. Where there is a delay costs clause, a sponsor will not want to give the contractor delay costs for reasons other than the default of the sponsor.

The contractor will nonetheless be under a common law duty to mitigate the sponsor's loss and therefore must take all reasonable steps to minimise any potential delay.

Variation of valuations

The clause should be examined to see who ultimately decides the valuation of variations, and to what extent, and the specific rates or prices or other such devices that have been used to pre-stage the valuation on the variations.

Provisional sums

These are items that are impossible to cost accurately at the time of the contract. It is important to be aware of the extent to which any provisional sums may be within the contract. To this extent the sponsor must make itself aware of the nature of the contract, be it fixed price or cost plus.

Quality

Quality control

The contractual regime for quality control is of paramount importance, as this will be one of the contractual obligations upon which performance of the contractor will be assessed. It is important for the sponsor to identify a party who will ensure quality control by performing regular monitoring of the contractor or contractors.

Design brief

Where the contractual obligations upon the contractor include the design brief, the quality and extent of the product will depend considerably upon the design brief attached to the contract. Generally the sponsor is responsible for design information within the design brief and, as the contractor will place a significant degree of reliance upon such information, it is imperative for the sponsor to ensure the accuracy of such information.

In contracts where design obligations lie with the contractor, issues of liability concerning the following will be of concern:

- claims arising during the design period, following review by the sponsor, where the sponsor is dissatisfied with the contractor's design and the contractor asserts that the design is in accordance with the design brief;

- errors in the sponsor's design brief which become apparent during the design period.

It is therefore prudent that both sponsors and lenders perform independent verification of the information supplied in the design brief before contracting with a contractor to produce a design.

Warranties

A general warranty to the effect that the works will be delivered in accordance with the contract terms and documents, free of errors, omissions, defects or deficiencies, should be given by the contractor. The sponsor should ensure that the contractor assigns to him any corresponding warranties given by the sub-contractors which extend beyond such defects liability period given by the contractor.

In addition to warranties given to the sponsor, the lenders will seek collateral warranties from the contractor for the design and from the design team where the contractor is not responsible for the design.

Defects liability period

Express obligations are imposed on the contractor during the defect liabilities period. In particular, the sponsors need to consider carefully the procedures which apply if the contractor fails to rectify the defects within a reasonable time scale and, equally, whether the contractor is responsible under the contract for rectifying errors, defects, deficiencies and omissions after the defects liability period. It is also be necessary for the sponsor to investigate whether any provisions of liability exist under general law after the expiry of the period.

Termination

The contractor should only be able to terminate the contract for non-payment by the sponsor and only then following a substantial grace period. From the sponsor's perspective termination of the contractor's services should be possible on breaches of the contractor's obligations under the contract.

Limitation of liability

Contractors generally will not expect to be liable for consequential loss such as loss of profits. Their liability may be limited to the cost of rectifying the defects.

Insurance

Who is going to provide the insurance? It is usual for the sponsor to take out an all risks policy against the contractor rather than to rely solely upon the contractor's insurance policies. Equally, contractors will look for a waiver of subrogation rights for themselves and, where appropriate, their sub-contractors, preventing insurers from claiming indemnification amounts from them.

Dispute resolution

A preferable dispute resolution mechanism would be a combination of:

■ discussions between senior executives of the sponsor and contractor;

■ non-binding mediation;

■ arbitration or litigation in the courts.

8.7.5   Lenders' concerns

Direct agreements

Direct agreements allow the banks to preserve essential contracts with the project company on default by the project company. The contracts include the construction contracts, supply contracts, contracts for sale of the product, operating and maintenance contracts, lease of a project site, government concessions, etc. Without the rights of preservation, the project contractors would be able to strip the project company of the essential contracts on an event of default. From the lender's perspective it should be possible to preserve such contracts initially by bank guarantee or assignment of the benefit and ultimately hive down the contracts to a lender controlled entity, who in turn would be able to realise the value of such contracts on sale to a new project sponsor.

Issues relating to inhibition of enforcing security interest may rise in no English law based countries where fixed and floating charges may not be accepted. In such cases the issue of golden shares may be considered subject, of course, to insolvency provisions where such may be considered preferential treatment on insolvency. In practice lenders would not be willing to assume commercial contracts and hence direct agreements may be difficult to enforce.

Lenders will usually want a direct agreement with the contractor giving them certain protections, including:

■ rights to require the contract to be assigned to a nominee for, or purchaser from, the lenders where the lenders need to enforce against the sponsor; and

■ suspension of the contractor's right to terminate for default by the proprietor to give the lenders opportunity to remedy the default or replace the sponsor.

8.8   OPERATING AND MAINTENANCE AGREEMENTS

The operational phase only commences once construction has been completed. It is essential for the continued success of the project and for successful operation of the project that an experienced and skilful operator is selected.

The operating and maintenance agreement will attempt to ensure contractually that this criteria is met and continues to be so by the inclusion of provisions dealing with:

■ the allocation of operation and maintenance risk of the project to the operator;

■ ensuring that the project is operated in a manner which maximises the revenue earning capacity of the project;

■ ensuring that the facilities are operated and maintained at least at an agreed minimum level, if not at higher levels, and according to specifically defined budgets agreed with the project company and lenders.

Typically the forms of agreement take one of the following forms:

■ **Fixed price structure**   Where the operator is paid a fixed price for the operation of the project. Cost overruns are borne by the operator. Any cost savings are equally solely enjoyed by the operator.

■ **Cost plus structure**   A fixed fee plus the costs incurred by the contractor are paid, the fixed fee representing the profit for the operator. The project company assumes the risk of increased costs, however it retains the right to terminate any such contract at short notice.

■ **Incentive/penalty structure**   Operators' remuneration is usually subject to strict performance obligations. On achieving defined obligations, the operator will receive a bonus. A penalty will be suffered in the event that it is unable or fails to meet such defined obligations on time. In order to retain contractual equities, penalties and bonuses are subject to 'caps'. A lender will usually take the view that this alternative promotes efficiency through its incentivised structure and therefore is probably the most preferred option.

8.9 FUEL SUPPLY AGREEMENTS

Many projects rely upon essential supplies of natural resources and fuel such as coal, oil, gas, etc. Typically supply contracts of any form, but particularly a fuel supply agreement, will take one of two forms, namely:

- **Take-or-pay** Where the project company agrees to take delivery of an agreed volume of fuel at an agreed price over a specified period. In the event that the project company fails to take delivery it retains the obligation to pay for the agreed volume of fuel. It follows, therefore, that the supplier's obligation is to supply such agreed quantity at the agreed price within the specified period.

- **Sole supplier** The project company agrees to purchase its supply from one sole supplier, however, quantity, price and purchase periods will not be agreed until orders are placed. In this context, the fuel supplier is under no obligation to supply fuel production until an order is placed and a contractual relationship contemplated.

8.10 SALES/OFFTAKE AGREEMENTS

Where a project is dependent on guaranteed offtake for its products, agreements such as sales/ offtake agreements become of vital importance.

Long-term sales contracts provide for sales on arm's-length basis with a price calculated by reference to current market forces. The contract does not commit the purchaser to buy.

Two commonly used forms of offtake agreements are:

- **Pass through** Charges are calculated by reference to the costs incurred by the project company. These costs are passed through to the buyer which can include the whole or any part of the costs of purchasing fuel or other commodities required by the project, repayments of principal to project lenders, payments of interest, operating and maintenance costs, administrative costs, insurance costs and sponsor return on capital. Pass through contracts are typically used in power projects.

- **Take-or-pay** Similar to 'take-or-pay' contracts mentioned at 8.5.5 above. Often 'hell or high water' provisions will be included which will establish that the buyer must pay despite non-performance of the seller, which would normally be sufficient for frustration of the contract to be sought.

Enforceability of these contracts is of major concern to lenders in that there lies an inherent risk that such agreements may be deemed to be a penalty. These questions will be of importance in jurisdictions where sufficiency of consideration is an issue, unlike under English law.

8.11   CUSTOMER AND SUPPLIER AGREEMENTS

Many projects are dependent on one or two customers or on key raw materials that must be assured by long-term contracts in order for the project to be financed. This is typical of a power project. The value of these agreements depends on the financial and commercial stability of the supplier party, which in turn will depend on its market for the product and/or any underlying guarantees. In other words, even a strong, long-term power purchase agreement may not be enough to support a financing if the purchasing utility's market is uncertain or the utility itself has weak credit.

For example, although power is a critical need for a number of developing countries, the utilities may not be able to sell the additional power at rates sufficient to cover the project cost requirements. A power purchase agreement in that environment may be insufficient to support the financing which lacks, for example, a government or central bank guarantee for the take-or-pay obligations of the utility. In projects such as toll roads, there will be a number of customers, however, given the nature of the government concession agreement it may serve as the sole 'customer' agreement by giving the new toll road assurances as to the future of any competing road projects. The goal in both customer and supply contracts is to eliminate revenue and cost risks. It must be stressed that common sense should prevail and that all parties to a project financing must be wary of contracts too good to be true. A prime example of where this did not prevail is in the case of US co-generation producers whose contracts and prices were established in the 1980s and are today being fought vigorously by utility customers.

8.12 FINANCING AGREEMENTS

In most cases the loan agreement will take the form of a syndicated loan agreement entered into between the borrower, the project lenders and a facility agent activity for itself and the lenders. The agreement will regulate the relationship between the parties, the terms and conditions upon which a loan may be drawn down and what items such loans may be expended on and will contain clauses relating to representations, warranties, and covenants given by the borrower, along with defined events of default.

The terms and conditions of the basic loan or facility agreement will include:

- the amount and purpose of the finance;

- the interest rate and debt service/repayment profile;

- commissions and fees payable to the arrangers, the agent bank and the lending banks;

- conditions precedent to lending—legal opinions, board resolutions, copies of all project agreements, delivery of security documents, government approvals, waiver letters, experts' reports and financial statements;

- limitations on recourse to the borrower and/or other parties; dedicated applications of cash flows;

- protective clauses—tax gross-ups, increased costs indemnities, alternative interest rates, market disruption, supervening illegality, default interest, judgment currency and general indemnities;

- representations and warranties—as to corporate status and capacity, due execution documents, accuracy of all project and financial information, validity of obligations and ownership of project assets;

- project covenants—standard of workmanship; compliance with licences, laws and regulations; construction development and operation in accordance with development plan and feasibility study; maintenance of insurances; payment of taxes;

- coverage ratios and other financial covenants;

- restrictive covenants – borrowing restrictions, negative pledge, pari passu, restrictions on dividends and disposals of assets;

- events of default; acceleration procedures; enforcement of security;

- project completion, 'conversion' and abandonment tests;

- financial and project information, projections, reporting requirements and project supervision;

- mechanisms for withdrawal of monies from proceeds accounts, insurance accounts and other 'escrowed' accounts;

- agency provisions, payment mechanisms, interbank co-ordination and sharing receipts;

- assignment and transfer provisions; and

- dispute resolution – choice of law and forum, appointment of process agents.

Provisions dealing with the calculation and payment of interests will be similar to that usually found in a Eurocurrency loan documentation, save that in a project financing interest will be capitalised during the construction period or until the project revenues are generated. Repayment terms will vary from project to project and will often be linked to the receipt of project cash flows. The loan agreement will normally provide for the cash flows of all projects to flow through the project account which would be maintained by the agent bank and charged by way of a 'floating charge' to the syndicate banks.

8.13   INTERIM LOAN AGREEMENTS

Frequently the loan participants or other lenders agree to loan funds to the owner to enable it to make progress payments to the manufacturer during construction. Often this aspect of the transaction is reflected in a separate interim loan agreement among the owner and such lenders. Interest on the interim loan can be paid in instalments prior to the delivery date or in a single instalment on the delivery date, in either case from the funds paid by the lessee, or it can be capitalised and paid on maturity out of the proceeds of additional interim borrowings (the so-called roll-over device) or from the aggregate funds then obtained from the owner participants and the permanent lenders.

Interim lenders often acquire a security interest in the equipment under construction, but such security is substantially less valuable than a security interest in a finished product, since construction may never be completed or the final asset may fail to conform to specifications or legal requirements. Hence, in the absence of unconditional take-out commitments by the owner participants and the permanent lenders, repayment of the interim loans is usually assured in one of three ways:

- a direct guarantee by the project company;

- an indirect guarantee by the unconditional commitment to purchase the equipment on the maturity date, regardless of its condition, if other funds are not obtained, for a purchase price at least equal to the principal of and interest on the interim loans;

- or a guarantee by the manufacturer that the property will be completed to specification.

In the last case, either the manufacturer agrees to pay liquidated damages in an amount sufficient to repay the debt or the lenders rely on the value of the completed property being in excess of their loan amount.

8.14 PROJECT LOAN AGREEMENTS

In most project financing, the loan agreement is likely to be the key financing document. Almost certainly structured on a syndicated basis, there will be a number of key points for discussion between the parties.

The following are points which are likely to arise in most project financing and which will be important issues for both the lenders and the project company alike.

8.14.1 Warranties, covenants and events of default

In a project financing, the scope of the warranties, covenants and events of default will be expanded to cover the project, the project agreements, the security agreements and (usually) other principal project parties. Although it has already been noted that the remedies available to the lenders following a default may well be limited, the usual approach is for the lenders to demand extensive protection through warranties, covenants and events of default. The reason for this is more to do with the wish to be able to control matters should defaults occur than a desire to be able to accelerate and enforce the lenders' security for a seemingly minor default. That said, there is always a danger that if the warranties, covenants and events of default are too tightly drawn, minor delays or hiccups in the project can trigger a default, which may necessitate syndicate meetings, waivers and unnecessary (and expensive) aggravation to all concerned. There is a balance, therefore, to be struck between on the one hand giving the lenders a sufficient comfort level that, should things start to go seriously amiss with the project, they have the tools to take control (or at least to start issuing orders) while on the other hand avoiding the occurrence of default for minor and insignificant hiccups.

There is a very important point to bear in mind in the drafting of warranties, covenants and events of default, which relates to the recourse to the project company. It has already been noted that in most project financing recourse will be limited to the project assets and its cash flows. Where the project company is not a single purpose vehicle and therefore has other assets over and above the relevant project, or where the shareholders/sponsors have agreed to procure performance of the project company's covenants under the project loan agreement (except for the obligation to make payments of the project loan), it will be crucial for the project company and the shareholders/sponsors to decide whether an event or circumstance should be treated as a warranty, as a covenant or as an event of default. The reason is that, while the lenders will usually agree to limit their recourse on an enforcement to the project assets and its cash flows, they will usually not forgo any remedies (such as a claim in damages) which they may have in law against the project company and/or the shareholders/sponsors for breach of warranties and/or covenants.

This, therefore, gives the lenders the potential of a claim in damages against the project company and/or the shareholders/sponsors although, as has been noted above, a claim in damages is not the same as a claim for a recovery of a debt. Nevertheless, it is a valuable right and one which many lenders will not want to give up. On the other hand, the mere occurrence of an event of default is simply a trigger entitling the lenders to accelerate the project loan and enforce their security, it does not entitle the lenders to a damages claim. Borrowers and shareholders/sponsors will therefore prefer events to be treated as events of default, whereas lenders will prefer to characterise events as warranties and/or covenants.

An illustration of this point will help. In a concession-based financing, it is usual to see a warranty in the project loan agreement at the outset that the concession is in full force and effect. However, this is unlikely to be repeated because the termination of the concession will usually be something that is beyond the control of the project company. The project company will not want to warrant something over which it potentially has no control. The lenders will, however, require a covenant that the project company perform its obligations in accordance with the terms of the concession and does nothing of itself to precipitate a termination of the concession. This is perfectly reasonable from the point of view of the lenders since these are events within the control of the project company. Finally, the lenders will expect there to be an event of default should the concession be terminated for any reason. Structured in this manner, the borrower will be satisfied that a potential claim in damages against it will only arise in circumstances where it has breached an obligation and the lenders will be protected in any event should the concession be terminated.

Essentially, the distinction is one of fault versus no fault. If the event or circumstance is the fault of the project company, then the lenders will expect protection through warranties and covenants. If, on the other hand, an event or circumstance is not the direct fault of the project company (for instance, where expropriation or nationalisation of its assets arises), then the project company would not expect there to be any recourse against its non-project assets although, of course, the lenders will need to have the right to accelerate the project loan in these circumstances.

As noted earlier, however, this distinction is only really of significance where the project company is not a special purpose vehicle and therefore has assets other than the project in question which the lenders may seek to attach or appropriate in satisfaction of the project loan. It will also be of significance where the sponsors/shareholders have agreed with the lenders to procure performance of the project company's covenants. Where the project company has no assets apart from the project, then a claim in damages will give the lenders little comfort or recourse over and above that which they already have against the project company.

8.14.2 Project bank accounts

It has already been noted that one of the key features of project loan documentation will be the requirement that the project lenders control all of the project cash flows. This control is usually implemented through the requirement that the borrower (and other relevant project parties) opens a number of bank accounts with either the facility agent or another bank (the project accounts bank). These bank accounts will, of course, be charged in favour of the lenders as part of the overall security package.

At the very minimum there will be two such accounts. One account, the disbursement account, will be used in connection with draw-downs. All draw-downs under the project loan will be paid into the disbursement (or draw-down) account and the project company will be permitted to withdraw sums from that account, say, once a month against appropriate evidence that the payment in question is due. In the case of large items (for example, payments to suppliers or contractors), the account bank may be authorised to make the payment direct to the payee on behalf of the project company.

The second account, the proceeds (or project receipts) account, will be the account to which all sums payable to the project company in connection with the project will be credited.

These payments might include sales proceeds, insurance receipts, liquidated damages payable to the project company, sponsor payments, etc. The project company will be entitled to withdraw sums from the proceeds account in order to meet its operating costs, taxes, debt service and other payments which it is required to make in connection with the project. Often the proceeds account is split into a number of different accounts for different categories of receipts, where different conditions are to apply in each case. For example, insurance receipts may or may not be payable to the project company depending upon what type of claim they relate to.

These accounts will usually be interest-bearing and, sometimes, where there is a likelihood that sums will remain deposited in these accounts for longer periods, provision will be made for the investment of balances into low-risk investments (for instance government securities). Investments, however, will be controlled by the account bank and will themselves form part of the overall security package.

One of the key features of these provisions will be the establishment of a strict order of application (or payments waterfall, as it is often referred to), so that when the account bank receives payments it knows how to apply them. Therefore, if there are insufficient funds in the project accounts on any particular day, the account bank will know which payments it needs to make first. As might be expected, payment of the project company's operating costs will come fairly near the top of the payments cascade whereas payment of dividends and other distributions to shareholders will come fairly near the end. There can often be considerable debate between different classes of lenders as to the correct order of application amongst their respective loans. The common approach is that all interest is paid before principal and then all principal is paid pro rata unless one group of lenders is expressly subordinated.

8.14.3 Appointment of experts

One of the features of project financing is the extensive use by the lenders of experts. While the lenders themselves (or at least some of them) will profess expertise in the structuring of the financing package for a project, there are many technical areas associated with the project where the lenders will need the resources of external consultants and other experts. For example, in an oil and gas project, they will need to employ the services of external engineers who are able to advise them on the geology of the reservoir, the likely quality and quantity of the reserves, when mechanical completion has occurred, etc. Another example would be traffic forecasting experts for a road or tunnel project. Although some lenders will employ internal engineers to help them with such matters, most banks do not have this resource and in any event will want the protection of external consultants. In all these cases, the experts employed play a crucial role in advising the lenders since in most instances it is the data that they provide as forecasts which are fed into the banking cases for the project.

While these experts are retained by the lenders and are answerable to them, they are in fact paid for by the project company (or the sponsors). Many borrowers, not surprisingly, object to having to foot these bills, but in reality they have little choice since in most cases the lenders are not prepared to rely on the project company's or the sponsor's own analysis of the position or indeed the experts and consultants retained by them. Occasionally, if the project company or sponsor has retained a firm of international repute to advise it on a particular matter, the lenders may be prepared to accept their report, but almost certainly only on terms that they have seen, where they have approved the terms of reference for the appointment in the first place and where the report is expressly issued to them as well as the project company (thereby giving them a basis to sue should an action arise).

8.14.4 Information and access

The supply of reliable and accurate information in connection with a project is of crucial importance for the lenders and their advisers. Likewise, access to the project and its facilities will also be important for the lenders to be able to check regularly on progress and to monitor compliance with the terms of the documentation. The project loan agreement will contain detailed provisions on the type of information required and the frequency of delivery. The following are examples of the type of information usually required by lenders:

■ annual accounts and financial statements;

■ periodic (eg monthly) progress reports during project construction;

■ architects' certificates, etc accompanying draw-down requests, together with supporting invoices;

■ copies of material notices and communications received under all project agreements;

■ copies of communications from relevant authorities;

■ details of all disputes and claims in connection with the project;

■ periodic reports from experts;

■ copies of all insurance documentation and claims;

■ copies of all consents and permits relating to the project; and

■ certificate of compliance with cover ratios etc.

There is often a danger that the project company becomes overwhelmed with the information requirements from the lenders and that the lenders themselves get bombarded with excessive information, the majority of which they do not really need. There is a balance to be struck here and the parties need to take a sensible approach. As noted above, the lenders will want access to the project and the project facilities. They will also want their experts and consultants to be able to visit the project site from time to time in connection with the preparation of their reports. The project company should not object to this provided it receives appropriate notice and the experts comply with safety requirements and other reasonable stipulations imposed by the project company in relation to site visits. Confidentiality will usually be an issue and the experts will usually be requested by the project company to sign a confidentiality undertaking.

8.14.5 Cover ratios

One of the key features of project finance loan documentation is the use of cover ratios. Just as bankers will use financial ratios in unsecured lending in order to measure the financial health of a borrower from time to time, so the project lender will use cover ratios to assist it in evaluating the performance of the project both in the short term and over the life of the project. There are three main cover ratios used by project lenders:

■ **Annual Debt Service Cover Ratio**   This tests the ability of a project's cash flow to cover debt service in a particular year;

■ **Loan Life Cover Ratio and Project Life Cover Ratio**   These ratios test the ability of a project's cash flow over, respectively, the loan life and the project life to repay the loan.

Cover ratios such as these will be used for a variety of different purposes in the loan documentation—for example, it is likely that it will be a condition precedent to each draw-down that each of the agreed cover ratios will remain satisfied following such draw-down. If the cover ratio is not so satisfied, then the draw-down will not be permitted (although sometimes a partial draw-down may be permitted). The cover ratios may also be used as a tool in the pricing of the loan: thus, if the project is performing above expectations, the borrower might reasonably expect to pay a lower interest margin on the loan to reflect the fact that the lenders are assuming a lesser risk; conversely, if the project is performing less well, the lenders will expect a higher margin to reflect the increased risks they face. Another use of cover ratios will be in the event of default, where the lenders will set cover ratios, at a slightly lower level, which will trigger an event of default if they are breached. The levels at which the default cover ratios are set will obviously reflect a position where the lenders have real concerns about the ability of the project to generate sufficient cash flows to service principal and interest over the life of the loan. Other uses of the cover ratios might be in fixing minimum amounts of repayment instalments and in controlling the payment of dividends or other distributions to the shareholders.

The method of calculation of cover ratios is broadly the same from one project to another. The lender will construct a computer program (or software model), into which it will input all the projected costs which will be incurred by the project together with the project's forecast receipts. The lender will have to make certain assumptions as to future variables such as interest rates, inflation rates, foreign exchange rates and (unless a fixed price is agreed for products) product prices. The model will thereby contain all of the relevant financial information necessary for calculating the cover ratios, as well as other information concerning the project. The starting-point for the lenders will be a 'base-case' model, which will reflect the lenders' opening evaluation of the project at financial close. The base case will have been agreed with the borrower and its advisers and should show the cover ratios being satisfied throughout the life of the project. However, as we have seen, in constructing the base case, the lender has made a number of assumptions and it is axiomatic that the fundamentals of the project as well as the variables will change over the life of a project. The lender will, therefore, in addition to the base case, construct a variety of other cases (or sensitivities) to test the robustness of the project economics in various other situations. Thus, a lender might run sensitivity cases involving the following changes to base-case assumptions, with variables being changed singularly or in combination with each other:

■   a reduction in output levels;

■   product prices which increase more slowly than predicted in the base-case, remaining flat in real terms or declining;

■   capital cost overruns prior to project start-up;

■   delays to the start-up of the project;

■   increases in operating costs;

■   increases in interest rates; and/or

■   adverse fluctuations in exchange rates.

In running these sensitivities, the lender will be looking to see in which circumstances the cover ratios will not be met and how the lender can cover this risk. Ultimately, it may mean that the ratio of debt to equity in the project or some other aspect of the project's economics has to be adjusted in order to ensure that the cover ratios are satisfied.

It will be apparent that the assumptions used in these banking cases (as they are commonly referred to) are of considerable importance. For example, in an energy project, an energy company may take a very different view as to likely oil, gas or electricity prices and exchange or interest rates over a ten-year period from a lender. Indeed, even between different lenders there will be different views on such matters. Not surprisingly, lenders tend to take a more conservative approach to forecasting and, if they are too conservative, then this can make some projects unbankable. There is often, therefore, during negotiations on project loan documentation, considerable scope for discussion on how these assumptions are calculated and by which party. There is no hard-and-fast rule or right or wrong approach to this. Typically, however, a distinction will be made between financial assumptions (such as interest rates, exchange rates, discount rates and inflation) and technical assumptions (operating costs, capital costs, taxes, etc). It is likely that the lenders will want to fix the financial assumptions on the basis that these lie within their field of expertise. On the other hand, the banks may well concede that the technical assumptions should be matters that the borrower should be in a good position to estimate.

However, it is unlikely that the borrower will be allowed a completely free hand with all technical assumptions and the lenders will want to see these agreed with their own engineers. Sometimes, if no agreement on the technical assumptions can be reached, the banks will agree to submit the matter to an agreed third party expert, who will decide the matter on behalf of the lenders and the borrower. It is less likely that the banks would agree to the appointment of an expert to determine the financial assumptions, because we have already seen that they consider themselves expert on such matters in any event! From a borrower's perspective, therefore, it will be looking to try and establish as objective a standard as possible for the fixing of the financial assumptions.

Having agreed the assumptions to be used in the banking cases, the calculation of the cover ratios becomes a simple (but computer-based) arithmetical exercise. It is usually the case that a banking case will be run periodically (six monthly) throughout the life of the project, as well as at given points in time such as on draw-down.

One of the key features in the calculation of the loan life cover ratio and the project life cover ratio is the use of discounting. Because both of these cover ratios project forward and make assumptions as to future costs, receipts, etc, in order to arrive at a present day value of these sums for the purposes of establishing the cover ratios at a particular time it is necessary to discount items. The usual method of discounting (or establishing the net present value of future cash flows) is to split the relevant period into, say, six-monthly periods (perhaps coinciding with interest periods and/or repayment periods), calculate the project costs and receipts for each of these periods, aggregate them and then calculate their net present value at the agreed discount rate and their internal rate of return. The discount rate is usually fixed by reference to current interest rates. Having established the net present value of the project's cash flows, this is then divided by the projected loan values remaining outstanding at the time the calculation is carried out to give the cover ratios required.

Part of the methodology in using cover ratios will be to enable the lender to give itself sufficient comfort. Thus, for example, a lender may take the view that a reasonable safety margin in a given project would be a project loan of two-thirds of the net present value of forecast project cash flows. This produces a cover ratio of 1.5 to 1 (being the inverse of two thirds), which is not an untypical loan life cover ratio.

The principal difference between the calculation of the loan life cover ratio and the project life cover ratio lies in the calculation of the project's forecast receipts. No lender will construct a project loan on the basis that final repayment coincides with the end of a project's useful life. Instead, the lender will want to see that the loan is repaid some years before the end of the project's useful life. Therefore, in calculating the loan life cover ratio, the lender is looking at forecast project receipts over the life of the loan only, whereas with the project life cover ratio the lender is looking at the project's forecast receipts over the life of the project itself. This difference is illustrated in many oil and gas projects, where the typical approach of a lender is that it will not expect to lend against the field's 'reserve tail' (typically 25 per cent of the forecast reserves) since these are likely to be the most risky to extract in full and on time. In such a case, therefore, the lender has constructed two important safety barriers: in the first place, the lender will have fixed a cover ratio at a level that it feels comfortable with (in the above example, say, one-third), and in the second place the lender will have one against which it will lend (say, three-quarters of project receipts).

The calculation of the cover ratios is, therefore, a key feature of project loan documentation and one which requires considerable attention to detail in the loan documentation. It is one of the areas where it is essential for the legal advisers and the bankers to work especially closely.

8.14.6   Governing law and jurisdiction

The loan agreement for most internationally syndicated project financing will usually be governed by either the laws of England or New York. There are a number of reasons for this. Perhaps the most important reason is the feeling on the part of many banks that when lending internationally they prefer to see the laws of an independent country, such as England or the US, apply to the lending documents. This is not to say that the lenders distrust other laws. It is simply a question of being more comfortable with the degree of independence offered by the laws of a third country. It is also undoubtedly the case that where they are dealing with complex international financing lenders are also comfortable with the degree of knowledge and sophistication of the courts in England and the US. Not surprisingly, lawyers in those two jurisdictions as a result have managed to establish themselves as leading experts in documenting and negotiating international project financing. This is not to say that lenders will not consider using other laws to regulate their loans. However, there will usually have to be some compelling reasons to persuade the lenders to accept other laws.

The position is slightly different with respect to security documents. The proper law of a security agreement will depend to a large extent on the nature of the security interest and/ or the location of the asset in question being created. It is therefore not simply a question of the lenders selecting a law of their choice. It is far more a question of what is the appropriate way in which to take a security interest over a particular asset in a particular country. Thus, for example, there would be little point (and indeed it would be dangerous) in stipulating that English or New York law should apply to a mortgage over land in, say, Indonesia. In such a case, what is important is to ensure that the security interest over the land is valid and effective according to Indonesian law and other laws will simply not be relevant. Similarly, if the lenders are looking at taking security over monies in a bank account in France, then French law would be the proper law of the security and the security should be created in accordance with French law.

In most cases it will be obvious which is the proper law of the security interest but this will not always be the case and, where there is doubt, the parties will normally look at all the surrounding circumstances and see which law has the closest connection with the asset over which security is being taken or, perhaps, where enforcement is most likely. If all else fails, one might then look at the law governing the loan agreement and apply the same governing law. The whole area of choice of law and conflict of laws is a complex subject and outside the scope of this text.

When it comes to governing law for project documents the position is less straightforward. In most jurisdictions the parties to a commercial agreement will be entitled to select the governing law to apply to that commercial agreement subject to certain ground rules (such as public policy and non-evasion of mandatory laws of a country). Not surprisingly, lenders on international project financing would prefer to see English or New York law governing all the key project documents. This, however, is seldom achieved. For example, insisting that a power purchase agreement between a project company and a local state electricity company be governed by a law other than appropriate domestic law is always going to be an uphill struggle. Likewise, most concession agreements between a governmental entity and the concession company are governed by the laws of the host country. The grey area comes where there is a contract, such as a fuel supply agreement or offtake agreement, that is entered into between parties in different countries and therefore there is no compelling governing law. In these cases the lenders are likely to be more successful in stipulating that an independent law such as English or New York law should apply.

The question of jurisdiction is in most cases a less controversial issue. If the loan agreement is expressed to be governed by English or New York law then it will be a requirement of the loan agreement that the project company submits to the jurisdiction of the courts in those countries for the purposes of legal proceedings relating to the loan agreement. Having accepted that one of these laws will apply to the loan agreement there is usually no objection to a submission to jurisdiction. It is sometimes the case that if the project company has or is likely to have significant assets in another country, then the lenders will require a submission to the jurisdiction of that country in case it is necessary or expedient for the lenders to institute legal proceedings against the project company in that particular country. Most agreements will provide that the submission to a particular jurisdiction is made on a non-exclusive basis thereby allowing the lenders to bring proceedings in any other jurisdiction that may be appropriate or convenient at the time of enforcement.

Finally, if the project company is wholly or partly owned by a government or state entity then it is likely that the lenders will require that the project company waives any right of sovereign immunity that the project company may have in respect of any legal proceedings or enforcement action against it or any of its assets.

8.14.7   Key lender issues

Prior to the preparation of the term sheet for any project, lenders will review and conduct due diligence on each of the parties involved in the project. In particular the following issues will be at the forefront of the lenders' concerns:

- **The creditworthiness of the parties**   Do the parties have adequate financial resources to meet their obligations under the project documents? Where lenders are not satisfied, they are likely to seek guarantees or letters of credit from parent companies or other banks and financial institutions to provide support for such unsecured obligations.

- **The ability of the parties to deliver and perform the obligations under the project documents**   Ie do they have the specific management and technical resources, experience of similar projects or transactions, experience of the country, etc?

- **Any relationships the project company has with other project parties**   Lenders would require that such relationships be at arm's length, however, where such relationships are not at arm's length, undertakings and indemnities will be sought of the parties to the effect that any transactions between such parties will not be preferential in any respect.

- **The independence of project parties.**

- **Continuity**   Lenders will require restrictions on assignment of obligations under the project documents to other parties. Where assignments occur they may be considered events of default unless prior consent of the lenders is sought.

- **Technical advice** Where this is given by a party it should be covered by sufficient professional indemnity insurance.

- Each party contracting and party to the project documents should have the requisite authority to do sole be duly incorporated, etc, and such contracts must be valid, legal, binding and enforceable against the party and the lender. In order to ensure this, legal opinions of local counsel will be sought by the lenders and it will usually be a condition precedent to the project documents, in particular the credit agreement.

Typical issues of concern to lenders would also include:

- Are the lenders taking security over the project agreement – if so, can such an agreement be assigned or is consent of the counterparty required?

- Is the project company restricted from charging its assets in any way or form?

- What rights of termination are available to the counterparty for breach by the project company? In some cases the lenders will require a right to step in and cure such breach at the project company's expense rather than terminate the agreement.

- Do any licences or concessions exist?

- Are the agreements consistent in the exclusions and carve-outs relating to the project company and lender?

- Does the project agreement contain liquidated damages provisions? Are they set at a high enough level but so that they do not create a penalty granting of pre-emption rights.

- Does the agreement contain automatic set-off provisions?

- Are conditionalities making the effectiveness of the project agreement conditional upon certain other events occurring?

- Payment terms must be precisely defined, including express provisions dealing with withholding taxes.

- Bonding requirements should be stated.

- In joint venture agreements, where is security granted by the project company to be granted by the joint venture parties?

- The terms of any take-out provisions requiring assumption of obligations.

- In terms of financing documents lenders prefer the document to be governed either under English or New York law.

- Arbitration clauses are not popular with lenders.

8.15 SECURITY AGREEMENTS

The form of security agreement will depend upon the local jurisdiction and the nature of assets being secured in favour of the lenders themselves or the security trustee as agent for the Lenders. In common law jurisdictions such as the UK, taking security in relation to a project financing will take the form of various fixed and floating charges over, and an assignment of, all property, assets and rights of the project company. In jurisdictions based on civil law and other legal systems the position of security becomes more complex as separate agreements are required for different classes of assets.

In many project financings a syndicate of banks is formed in order to provide the project loan. The syndicate may from time to time alter, creating an issue regarding security. In such cases and in certain jurisdictions therefore security trusts are appropriate—the lenders are able to assign their rights and benefits and the use of a trustee ensures that the underlying security interests are not disturbed by virtue of the lenders' assignments.

The governing law for the security documents will depend on the location of the assets as enforcement and seizure will be in that specific jurisdiction.

8.15.1 Scope of security

Over what assets will the lenders seek security? If the lenders are lending to a special purpose vehicle and a universal security interest (such as a fixed and floating charge) over all the property and assets of the project company is permissible, then this approach is likely to be the most effective. Where the project company is not a special purpose vehicle or in those jurisdictions where universal security is not recognised, then it will be necessary for the lenders and their advisers to identify those assets over which they require security (and, indeed, over which it is possible to take security). In many jurisdictions, there will be different ways of taking security and different rules governing the taking of security over different classes of assets. For example, security over movable goods (such as goods and chattels) may require one type of security interest being taken, whereas security over intangible assets (such as receivables and other contractual rights) may require a different approach. In most jurisdictions security over land and real property rights involves the most formal procedures of all.

The key project assets over which the lenders will require security will include those set out immediately below.

8.15.2 Plant and machinery

The extent and significance of plant and machinery will obviously vary from project to project. For example, in a power project there is likely to be a considerable amount of fixed plant and machinery and the lenders will want to ensure that they have effective security interests over these assets. However, the extent to which it is possible to obtain a non-possessory security interest over chattels varies considerably according to the jurisdiction. In France, for example, a non-possessory pledge of machinery and equipment is possible (and is registrable), but only in favour of the person who loaned money to buy the equipment in the first place. Where plant and machinery has been supplied by third parties, it may be that in certain jurisdictions title to these assets is retained in whole or in part by the suppliers (under so-called retention of title clauses). Such devices are likely to frustrate the aims of lenders in taking effective security over the assets in question.

8.15.3 Real property

If the project company owns the land on which the project is being built or operated, then this should also form part of the lenders' security. In some BOT projects, the real property is only leased to the project company and it will be a matter of local law whether it is possible to take security over the lease in question. In any event it will be important for the lenders to know that, on an enforcement of this security, they have the right to enter the project company's property and take control of the property.

8.15.4   Construction agreement

In an infrastructure project, the construction agreement will be one of the key contracts during the construction period and as such will form an important part of the lenders' security. Quite apart from taking a security assignment over this agreement, the lenders are also likely to seek a direct agreement with the contractor. Where there is no turnkey contractor, the lenders are likely to have to take separate security interests over all of the construction-related agreements (or at least the most important ones) together with security over the project management agreements. This can be a cumbersome and difficult procedure. Further, the non-turnkey approach in construction projects gives rise to the risk that disputes arise between the different contractors over the scope of their respective responsibilities and liabilities, which is likely to cause delays and which could result in the project company being in default under other project documents. The result can be that significant gaps appear in the contract structure. It is for this reason that lenders prefer the turnkey model to project financing.

8.15.5   Performance bonds

If the contractor has been required to put up performance bonds frequently from a bank or insurance company in connection with the construction agreement, then the benefit of these will usually be assigned to the lenders. Such bonds will usually be written by the contractor's lenders and may amount to anything from 2 per cent to 20 per cent of the total contract price. The lenders will want to reserve for themselves the right to call these bonds and to direct that proceeds under them are paid direct to the lenders. It will also usually be a requirement of the lenders that such bonds are payable 'on demand' and are not subject to proof of default or breach by the contractor.

8.15.6   Other project agreements

The benefit of all other project agreements, including operating and maintenance agreements, offtake agreements, supply agreements, transportation agreements and tolling agreements, should also be assigned by way of security to the lenders. In the case of the most important of these other agreements, the lenders are also likely to require a direct agreement with the counterparty. In a perfect world, the lenders would aim to take security over all agreements entered into by the project company in connection with the project, but in some cases this may be too ambitious and the lenders may have to limit themselves to concentrating on the key project agreements. This is especially the case where universal security interests are not available. Further, in many jurisdictions it is necessary in order to perfect each security interest to serve notices of assignment on the counterparts to such contracts and undertake other formalities and this can prove cumbersome in those projects where there are a large number of project agreements.

8.15.7 Project insurances

In most projects, particularly infrastructure projects, insurance will be an important part of the lenders' overall security package. If a natural or other disaster occurs which, say, results in a total loss of the project or a key element of the project, then the only significant remaining asset that will be available to repay the lenders is likely to be proceeds of insurance taken out by the project company. The lenders, therefore, will want to be comfortable that the insurance cover will subsist at least for the life of their loans. They will also want to ensure that the policies are effectively assigned to them and that all proceeds are paid direct to them. As insurance in the context of project finance is a complete subject on its own, lenders will usually employ a firm of insurance advisers to provide specialist advice to them.

Lenders will also want to protect themselves against the risk that any insurance policy could be avoided by a non-disclosure on the part of the project company. If insurance companies are prepared to give a waiver, this issue can be dealt with by inserting a 'non-vitiation' clause into the policy. Alternatively, it may be possible to obtain mortgagee protection insurance (insuring against the risk of vitiation itself). Recently, it has become difficult to obtain either form of protection from the insurance market and this is an area that can prove contentious for lenders.

8.15.8 Bank accounts

Most project financing structures will envisage the close control of all the project cash flows operated through the facility agent, a security trustee or one of the other banks. In addition to ensuring that all project cash flows flow through these accounts, the lenders will also want to ensure that they have a valid security interest over these accounts so that at all times they can effectively control withdrawals and the use of the project cash flows. In many non-common law jurisdictions, the need to specify (with varying degrees of specificity) the identity of property being transferred means that granting security over a bank account is difficult. Further, in some civil law jurisdictions, it is only possible to perfect security over bank accounts in those cases where the bank holding the security has control over the account (in the sense that it can refuse to permit withdrawals from the account). Frequently, therefore, the project loan documentation will require project revenues to be paid into a jurisdiction where effective security over bank accounts can be obtained (often London or New York). The ability of the project company to withdraw moneys from these project accounts will be strictly monitored and regulated.

8.15.9 Products

Where the project produces products such as hydrocarbons or minerals, then wherever possible the lenders will seek to take security over these products. However, in many jurisdictions, title to hydrocarbons and minerals is vested in the Crown or national government until they are successfully extracted and, therefore, no security interest will be possible until the hydrocarbons have been extracted. For example, in the UK, North Sea oil in the ground does not belong to the oil companies but to the Crown so that the oil companies are merely granted the right to extract that oil and only upon extraction does the oil belong to the oil companies. Also, there may be further complications in certain jurisdictions where products are 'mixed', with the same product belonging to others. An example of this would be where oil or gas is transported through a common transportation system, making it impossible to identify individual ownership interests. In such cases, the best that the lenders can probably hope for is the right to take delivery of an agreed share of the products once they exit in the common transportation system.

8.15.10   Other project assets

Other relevant project assets will include all consents and permits, intellectual property rights (especially important in certain information technology projects), investments and rights under other contracts (for example, claims in damages), all of which are likely to be important to the lenders. If a hedging programme has been set up for the project, then the lenders will want to ensure that the benefit of this programme falls within the overall security package. Where universal security is not available, however, there can often be problems in identifying at the outset the extent of such other assets and which ones may be valuable. Extensive due diligence may be required to satisfy the lenders that there are no significant gaps in their security.

8.15.11   Third party security

So far we have looked at security provided by the project company itself. However, in many projects security and/or guarantees and/or support will be provided by third parties. Most commonly, this third party security will come from the shareholders of the project company and the project's sponsors, but sometimes other parties having a significant involvement or interest in the project may be called upon to provide guarantees or other support. The following types of third party support are frequently encountered in project financing.

8.15.12   Shares of special purpose vehicle

Security over shares in the project company can be especially valuable for project lenders where there are gaps in the security package given by the project company or where the local security laws do not allow for a comprehensive and effective security package to be taken. If the lenders have security over the project company's shares, then this will give them the option, at least, to sell the project company in its entirety rather than going through the perhaps painful and expensive route of security enforcement. Another added advantage of security over a project company's shares is that the lenders may be able to secure for themselves the right to remove directors of the project company and appoint substitutes (this may not always be possible, depending upon the jurisdiction concerned). In this connection, the lenders may in certain circumstances take a 'golden share' (or equivalent), which would give them the right to appoint a special director who has veto and other rights and is answerable to the lenders. Again, this can be a useful way of exercising control rights over a project where these cannot otherwise be achieved through the conventional security package.

However, in some jurisdictions it may not be possible for the lenders (as foreign persons) to have security over the shares of a local company, particularly in the case of projects in the public domain or in strategically important industries. It may be possible in these circumstances to circumvent such restrictions by ensuring that security over the project company's shares is taken by a local bank, which holds the security on trust for the lenders.

8.16 LEASING AGREEMENTS

8.16.1 Trust agreement

The trust agreement is a straightforward agreement between the owner and the trustee. A trust company or bank is appointed and agrees to hold the equipment and other assets in trust for the benefit of the owner participants and to perform such tasks as:

■ executing and delivering documents;

■ registering or documenting the equipment under appropriate laws;

■ receiving and disbursing funds in accordance with specified priorities;

■ receiving and forwarding notices.

The trust agreement will contain procedures for the removal or resignation of the trustee and will provide that the trustee is not relieved of its obligations until a successor trustee has been appointed by the owner participants or by a court. The standards for an entity to qualify as a successor trustee and the appointment of an individual or trustee to act in any jurisdiction in which the original trustee is unauthorised to act would also be stated.

The owner participants, in accordance with their respective interests in the trust, severally indemnify the trustee against all costs, expenses and liabilities it might incur as a consequence of its involvement in the transaction, except as the result of its own wilful misconduct or negligence. Trustees typically try to elevate the exception to wilful misconduct or gross negligence and often succeed. The owners usually argue that, while the trustee may be justified in insisting that it is not be liable to them for its actions short of gross negligence, it does not follow that they should indemnify the trustee for damages the trustee may inflict upon itself through simple negligence. The trustee is fully indemnified by the lessee, nevertheless, trustees insist on indemnities from their beneficiaries as well since the time when the indemnity is most important is when an event of default has occurred under the lease and frequently the lessee's indemnity is worthless at that time. Owner participants should assure that their indemnity of the trustee is no broader than the lessee's indemnity so that the owner participants will always have a claim against the lessee for any trustee indemnity paid by the owner participants.

The trustee usually makes no warranties or representations as to the condition of or title to the leased asset, except only that no unauthorised liens will attach to the asset from its own acts. It similarly has no duties to manage or maintain the properties constituting the trust estate except upon the proper instructions from the owner participants. The trustee has no duties to take any other affirmative acts unless explicitly set forth in the documents or unless an event of default under the lease has occurred and the owner participants have failed to give the trustee instructions.

All of the customary exculpatory clauses found in trust arrangements of any kind are usually found in the owner trust agreement, particularly since the trustees typically charge very low fees and consequently are desirous of taking no material risks. Normally very little time is spent negotiating the trust agreement because of its standardised, non-controversial nature.

A more difficult problem is whether the relationship between the beneficiaries and the trustee can be construed to create a principal–agent relationship for purposes of permitting liabilities incurred ostensibly in the name of the owner trustee to be imposed upon the owner participants. The relatively few cases and authorities that address the issue appear to turn upon the degree to which beneficiaries exert control over the activities of the trustee.

The less independent discretion the trustee is given, the more likely a court will be to view the trustee as the beneficiary's agent and deem its undertakings those of the beneficiaries. This is not to say that the trust itself is not a valid trust for most purposes if it otherwise complies with applicable law, but that the owner trustee will also be considered to be acting as the agent of the owner participants for certain purposes, as though the trust instrument expressly gave the trustee authority to bind the beneficiaries.

Commercial banks and other financial institutions serving as owner participants are generally reluctant to part with dominion over their investment. In fact, in many jurisdictions it is unlawful for banks to divest themselves of control over the disposition of their properties. In addition, institutions serving as owner trustees are unwilling to assume independent responsibility for management and disposition of the trust corpus. For these reasons, the typical owner trust agreement spells out in substantial detail the actions to be taken by the trustee to the fullest extent foreseeable and permits the trustee to refuse to take unspecified actions without additional directions from its beneficiaries. Virtually no independent discretion is given the trustee.

The liability risks arising from a trust being treated as an agency derive from four principal sources:

- results of actions taken by the trustee purporting to bind the owner;

- taxes imposed on the trust estate;

- the trustees' issuance of bonds or notes to the lenders; and

- tort claims arising out of the operation of the leased equipment.

The trust agreement will specifically negate the authority of the trustee independently to bind the owners and most trustees are selected for their proven responsibility. Moreover, since the institution acting as trustee generally assumes responsibility for discharging encumbrances placed upon the trust assets from causes unrelated to its ownership thereof (eg, claims against the equipment asserted by its general creditors, or resulting from unauthorised dealings with the trust estate), care should be taken to select a trustee whose corporate assets are adequate to support such an undertaking.

The trust estate itself could become subject to income taxes based upon its net income derived from the rentals. Some countries impose such liability (usually only if the trust constitutes a business trust). Taxation of the trust estate would probably place the debt borrowed to finance the equipment into default since generally little cash is produced by the rentals in excess of that necessary to service the debt, let alone to pay income taxes. To avoid any effort to assess deficiencies on the underlying beneficiaries, on the agency or some other theory, a series of covenants is usually provided in leveraged lease documents. These provide either that the lessee assumes all such taxes (including additional taxes payable as a result of such assumption) or that the owner participants assume such taxes to the extent that taxes levied upon the trust estate relieve them of income taxes they had otherwise anticipated in calculating their yields, with the lessee assuming the balance.

The trustees' issuance of the bonds or notes to the lenders must not bear recourse to the general assets of the owner participants. Theoretically, the accounting profession could apply an agency theory and treat the debt instruments, although nominally issued by the trustee, as the obligations of the beneficiaries. The problem is solved, however, by including express language in the debt instruments negating personal liability of the owner participants and having the lenders expressly agree pursuant to the terms of the indenture and the debt securities that they will not look to the independent assets of the owner participants even upon default.

Equity investors often assume that the trust will shelter them from any tortious liabilities, however, as a matter of public policy, the trusteeship may be ignored if major liability claims follow a catastrophe in the operation of the leased equipment and the trust estate and the lessee are judgment proof. For this reason owner participants always insist upon the protection of liability insurance and indemnities from financially responsible persons.

In transactions involving more than a single owner participant, ease of administration dictates the use of a common trustee to collect and disburse rentals (subject to the prior right of the lenders), to execute and deliver various documents, including the lease, and to perform the miscellany of administrative chores that fall upon the lessor. It is also easier for an equity investor subsequently to transfer its interest in a trust than in the property itself, as financing statements, mortgages and other governmental filings and permits would normally not need to be amended.

Since it is universally the custom not to reflect non-recourse indebtedness issued in the name of a trustee upon the balance sheet of the beneficiaries, the risk of such consequences is generally averted by use of the trust. In the face of an argument posed by holders of prior indebtedness issued by an owner participant, however, a court theoretically might find that the trustee had made the borrowing as a mere agent of the owner and thus construe the indebtedness as having been incurred directly by the owner, as principal, in violation of negative financial covenants. Those engaged in leasing, however, usually expressly exclude from the financial covenants given to real lenders any non-recourse debt incurred in a leveraged lease.

There are some very definite advantages to an owner trust. Non-resident owners of leased property located in some states may be able to avoid formal qualification requirements if legal title is taken in the name of an entity already qualified to conduct a trust business there. Commercial banks under the laws of some states are not permitted to issue certain securities without prior approval from applicable regulatory authorities. It is generally believed that the necessity for obtaining such approval can be avoided if the security is nominally issued by a trustee.

Lenders and lessees in leveraged leases often insist that owners use a trust as a shield against the consequences of the owner participant's bankruptcy in the belief that, because the owner trust is engaged only in the single lease transaction, it is far less likely to become bankrupt without a lessee default than is an owner participant engaged in other business activities. If a lessor does become bankrupt, the trustee in bankruptcy for the lessor has the power to assume, assign or reject a lease. If the trustee does reject the lease, however, the lessee can be dispossessed against its will only with respect to personal property.

It is reasonably clear that a lender's security interest in leased property and the lease itself (if perfected prior to the filing of a bankruptcy petition against the lessor) will be recognised over claims of the lessor's trustee in bankruptcy. However, the lender will not be free to exercise its right to repossess the property or, perhaps, capture the rental flows to the exclusion of the lessor because of the automatic stay against such actions, although secured persons can challenge such a stay.

In addition, the bankrupt lessor would have the right to continue to use the leased asset, the lease cash flow, or both although the secured party is entitled to adequate protection with respect to such use. The latter, constituting cash collateral, can only be used by the bankrupt if the secured party consents or the court, after notice and hearing, so orders.

It is, of course, essential from the lender's point of view that, if a trust is to be used as a shield against the consequences of an owner participant's bankruptcy, the trust be made irrevocable. Otherwise, the owner's trustee in bankruptcy could simply exercise the power of revocation, put title to the asset directly in the bankrupt owner participant and possibly defeat, or at least delay, the lender's efforts to foreclose under its previously perfected security interest. It should be noted, however, that even an irrevocable trust could probably be penetrated by the bankruptcy trustee of its single settler-beneficiary on general equity principles or under specific statutes, but such a result most likely would not obtain if the bankrupt held a non-controlling interest among several beneficiaries.

8.16.2 Indenture of trust

A separate trust indenture is entered into between the owner trustee and the indenture trustee, under which the former assigns to the latter, as security for repayment of the debt and discharge of its other obligations, all of its rights in the leased asset, the lease, including its rights to receive rent and other payments owing by the lessee thereunder (subject to any negotiated exceptions) and any guarantee or other credit enhancement agreements (with corresponding exceptions). In the absence of an indenture trustee, an ordinary security agreement serves in place of the indenture.

Because of the argument that an assignment of a right to receive money not yet payable (stipulated loss or optional termination payments, for example) cannot legally be effective until the payment obligation has matured, language is added that a present assignment is intended and that the owner trustee agrees to execute and deliver additional instruments in the future effecting an assignment at that time of such rights as requested by the indenture trustee.

In order to perfect the liens granted by the indenture, it is almost always necessary to take further steps, usually by recording or filing certain documents.

Beyond creating the security, the principal purposes of the indenture are:

- to set forth the form of the debt instruments and to spell out the administrative details with respect to the outstanding debt (such as maintenance of a register and replacing lost or stolen instruments) ;

- to provide for the priorities under which proceeds will be distributed among the various parties;

- to prevent alterations to or waivers of the other documents, since the lenders are parties only to the participation agreement;

- to establish defaults under the debt instruments; and

- to establish the rights, obligations and exculpations of the indenture trustee just as the trust agreement does for the owner trustee.

The indenture is normally completely non-recourse to the owner trustee and owner participants except for their obligations to remove liens and other encumbrances on the collateral that do not relate to their interest in the leased asset (since the lessee always agrees to remove all liens that do relate to the leased asset specifically) or their obligation to pay income taxes.

It is important from the owner's viewpoint that the only events of indenture default that do not also constitute a lease default be entirely within the control of the owners or their trustee. In addition, if the lessee is given a grace period for payment of rent under the lease, it is essential that a grace period of at least equal duration be provided in the indenture for payment of principal and interest on the debt, again to avoid an indenture default in the absence of a lease default under circumstances beyond the owner's control. Otherwise, innocent owners could find themselves in default under the indenture and dispossessed of their residual interests in the property while the lessee remains in full possession. For example, non-receipt by the lenders of payment on the debt should not constitute an indenture default if the lessee has made timely rental payment but the funds have not found their way into the lender's hands because of the indenture trustee's negligence, or because a tax claim intervened upon the general assets of a special-purpose corporation positioned between the lenders and the owner trustee for the lenders convenience.

8.16.3   Purchase agreement assignment

The lessee usually comes into a leveraged lease financing already obligated to purchase the asset under an existing construction or purchase contract. In contemplation of a lease financing, the lessee enters into an assignment of the purchase or construction agreement, assigning to the owner trustee all rights against the supplier (the right to receive delivery, obtain title and pursue breaches of warranties), but not obligations (including payment obligations). The owner trustee agrees to pay for the asset only if it receives adequate funds.

The supplier executes a consent to the assignment, under which it agrees to continue looking exclusively to the lessee and under no circumstances to the owner participants or their trustee, for discharge of the purchaser's obligations.

Occasionally the owner trustee enters into an acquisition agreement directly with the vendor, as in railroad transactions, using the conditional sale agreement. Such an agreement must be accompanied by an unconditional assumption by the lessee (or some party other than the owner participants and lenders) of all of the owner trustee's obligations, to which the vendor agrees to look exclusively, or by an acknowledgment that the vendor will not look beyond the trust estate for payment.

The owner trustee also enters into the construction agreement directly when construction financing is being provided by the equity, the permanent lenders, interim lenders or a combination thereof. Lessees use this structure when they do not want to be the direct obligor on the debt for regulatory reasons (as is often the case with utilities) or when parts of the asset to be leased will go into service at different times and one overall financing package is desired for simplicity.

8.16.4   Tax indemnification agreement

Perhaps the most arcane of the documents, but one that is often basic to the transaction, is the tax indemnification agreement, which provides for the circumstances under which the lessee will protect the owner participant against the failure of the tax assumptions on which the pricing of the transaction has been based. The tax indemnity provisions are typically, although not invariably, the subject of a separate agreement between the owner participant and the lessee. There is some truth in the observation that this is largely in order to permit the tax lawyers to negotiate the agreement over tax points without impeding the course of the parallel negotiations taking place between the other participants in the documentation (and vice versa), but there are frequently other reasons as well. It is a convenient way to keep tax indemnity matters isolated from the rights of, and restrictions imposed by, the lenders with respect to the other documents and apart from any documents which may be required to be publicly filed or otherwise disclosed. It permits amendments to be made by the only parties with an interest in the matters which are the subject of the agreement without having to have even the formal involvement of others, such as the owner trustee.

The subject matter of the tax indemnification agreement is the allocation of the risk of loss of tax benefits taken into account by the owner participant in pricing the transaction. It usually does not cover indemnification for other taxes (such as property taxes, sales and use taxes and state income taxes, which are not taken into account in pricing) that may be imposed on the lessee, the property, the lessor or another party to the transaction. Such taxes are usually the subject of the general tax indemnity, which is normally contained in the lease or the participation agreement.

The tax indemnification agreement is typically broken down into at least six basic sections.

The first substantive section sets forth the assumptions regarding the income tax benefits anticipated by the owner participant on the basis of which the rents provided in the lease have been set. This is not an operative section, in that the lessee usually has no responsibility for the accuracy of these assumptions except as provided in other sections of the agreement. Nevertheless, it is important for two reasons. If a circumstance arises as a result of which an indemnity is payable, this section provides part of the basis on which the amount of the indemnity will be calculated. Moreover, the negotiation of this section frequently brings to light areas of possible misunderstanding between the owner participant and the lessee that might not otherwise come to the surface if the agreement focused solely on operative provisions.

The second basic provision, of particular interest to both parties, sets forth a series of representations, warranties and covenants of the lessee, the inaccuracy or breach of which will be a trigger giving rise to an indemnity payment to the owner participant if it suffers a consequent loss of tax benefit. The lessee often is required to bear some of the tax risks that are inherent in the transaction without regard to fault and it is through specific representations and undertakings contained in this section of the tax indemnification agreement that the scope of that obligation is defined.

Generalisations regarding the content and scope of the representations section of a typical tax indemnity agreement are particularly unreliable because the section is so heavily negotiated. At a minimum the lessee must make factual representations regarding the qualification of the property for the anticipated tax benefits: for example, if it is intended that the owner participant will be entitled to investment credit, the lessee will represent facts supporting the conclusions that the property is of a type that qualifies, that it has not been placed in service at a time or in a manner that would limit the credit and, if the credit is available only by reason of the application of a statutory transitional rule, that the conditions of the rule are satisfied. If the availability of anticipated depreciation deductions depends on how or by whom the property is used, the lessee will represent and covenant that the use of the property does and will meet acceptable standards. Similarly, the lessee may be required to make factual representations bearing on the true lease analysis. The principle underlying this type of representation is that the lessee should have responsibility for the correctness of those facts that are within its knowledge or control, particularly where the owner participant does not have equal access to the relevant facts.

However, the lessee's representations frequently extend beyond factual matters to legal conclusions based on those facts. For example, it may be unclear under applicable legal authority whether a given set of facts regarding the start-up and testing of property suffices to cause it to have been placed in service for tax purposes; this is a mixed question of fact and law as to which the lessee may be in no better position than the lessor to predict how the taxation authority or a court would decide the issue. As another example, it may be a relatively pure question of law whether a particular item of property is or is not a structural component of a building, a determination relevant to the items qualification for investment credit and accelerated depreciation; in this case again it is arguable that the owner participant and its tax adviser are as capable of evaluating the risk of an adverse determination on the issue as the lessee. Nevertheless, more often than not the lessee will, through its representations, bear the risk on this type of issue. In practice, subject to numerous exceptions, the lessee tends to bear the risk of an adverse determination, factual or legal, regarding the qualification of the property for anticipated tax benefits, while leaving to the owner participant the risk that the structure of the transaction is legally ineffective to invest it with tax ownership. Again, however, this latter observation is frequently inaccurate: for example, where the lease structure contains features that draw the true lease determination into question, particularly where such features are novel, the lessee may be required to bear the tax risk associated with those features as a condition to obtaining the benefits that their assumed permissibility entails. Ultimately, the bargaining positions of the parties determine how the tax risks of the transaction will be allocated and the representations section of the tax indemnification agreement reflects the bargain.

The third basic section of the tax indemnification agreement describes those causative events that, if they produce a specified adverse tax consequence for the owner participant, will give rise to a lessee obligation to provide indemnification. As already discussed, the inaccuracy or breach of a lessee representation or undertaking constitutes one such trigger. The other typical triggers are acts and omissions of the lessee (or other persons having possession or use of the property or otherwise on the lessee's side of the transaction) and casualty events. As to the acts or omissions trigger, the issue sometimes arises as to whether the lessee should have a tax indemnity obligation with respect to acts that it is required or, in a further variation of the issue, expressly permitted to perform under the lease or other operative documents. The lessee may understandably feel that it is unfair for the owner participant on the one hand to require the lessee to do something that it would prefer not to be obligated to do and on the other to be responsible for the tax consequences of doing so. The issue is rarely as simple, in fairness or in detail, as the preceding sentence might suggest. Still, it is not uncommon to find required, and sometimes permitted, acts excluded from the tax indemnity trigger.

The other issue with which the trigger section is concerned is the circumstances under which the owner will be deemed to have suffered a tax loss. Clearly, if the taxing authorities assert additional tax liability against the owner participant that event should, subject to the contest provisions described below, give rise to the indemnification obligation. Frequently, however, the owner participant will want the right not even to claim it on its tax return and still be entitled to indemnification, if it believes it is clear that an anticipated tax benefit has become unavailable,. The lessee, on the other hand, will require some protection, usually an opinion of counsel at a minimum, as a condition to the owner participant's right not to claim the benefit (or to volunteer an indemnifiable detriment) on its return. One reason is that if the owner participant can subject the lessee to an indemnification obligation without a challenge by the taxing authorities, the lessee may have no effective right to obtain a judicial or administrative determination as to the merits of the tax issue presented by the owner participant's determination. Another is that the lessee wants the assurance when it enters into the transaction that it is not walking into an automatic indemnification situation. To deal with this latter concern, agreements that allow the owner participant to claim an indemnity based on an opinion of counsel frequently require that the opinion be based on a change in law or facts from those that existed on the closing date, so that the owner participant, whether or not it has received an approving opinion of counsel in connection with the closing of the transaction, is precluded from claiming tax indemnification by reasons of circumstances known to both parties at closing, absent a challenge from the taxing authorities.

The fourth substantive section of the agreement deals with the computation of the indemnity amount. The purpose of the indemnity payment(s) is to keep the owner participant whole, ie to put it in the same position as it would have enjoyed if the indemnified event had not occurred. However, accomplishing this result is not as simple a matter as might first appear. The first problem is to ascertain whether and to what extent the indemnifiable event has harmed the owner participant. If, for example, for the taxable period in which the tax loss occurs the owner participant is for reasons unrelated to the transaction in a loss or excess credit position, it is arguable that it has not been hurt by the tax problem with the lease transaction and is not entitled, at least currently, to indemnification from the lessee. As another example, if tax rates have changed from those taken into account by the owner participant in pricing the transaction, its injury from the indemnified event may be less or more than that it would have experienced if rates had not changed. Typically, the amount of the loss is determined on the assumption that the owner participant has adequate income and tax liability to experience the full impact of the indemnified event and the further assumption that the applicable tax rates for measuring the harm are those in effect (or scheduled) at the time the transaction is closed.

The last issue usually raised by this section of the tax indemnification agreement is whether the indemnity is to be paid in a lump sum or over time. Here, the basic alternatives are a rolling indemnity, a lump sum indemnity or a rental adjustment. Under a rolling indemnity the lessee pays an amount with respect to each taxable period that, after gross-up, will reimburse the owner participant for the additional tax liability it has for that period on account of the indemnified event. If, as is the case with most indemnified events, it results in later years in a tax benefit for the owner participant that it would not have otherwise received, a properly structured rolling indemnity will impose a reverse indemnity obligation on the owner participant to pay to the lessee the amount of that benefit (together with an additional amount reflecting the tax benefit to the owner participant of the payment, sometimes referred to inelegantly as a gross-down). The lump sum indemnity takes a different approach: upon the occurrence of an indemnified event and the lessee's responsibility therefor, all the tax consequences stemming from that event, negative and positive, are predicted and taken into account in deriving a lump sum amount that will keep the owner participant whole on a present value basis. This approach has the advantage of enabling the parties, upon the occurrence of the indemnified event, to settle up and not thereafter have to deal further with the consequences of the event. A disadvantage to this type of indemnity is that it may pose a cash flow problem for the lessee. To meet this problem, a third approach is sometimes adopted pursuant to which the same assumptions and calculations are made as those in determining a lump sum indemnity, but with the objective of producing an amount, generally level, payable by the lessee over the remaining term of the lease. This method of determining the indemnity is sometimes referred to as a rental adjustment approach, but in a leveraged lease it may be either difficult or undesirable actually to adjust the rents payable under the lease (which may be payable to an indenture trustee or otherwise involve the lenders); in transactions where this is a significant consideration, the tax indemnification usually provides for separate payments that the lessee may think of as, but that are not actually, adjustments to rent.

Whatever assumptions and approach may be adopted for the calculation of the amount and payment of the indemnity, both the owner participant and the lessee will want to know that the process produces the right number, a consideration that is addressed in a verification provision. The computation involves matters that may be confidential to the owner participant, eg its actual tax position or the particular method and programme by which it computes its return from the transaction, which it does not wish to disclose to the lessee. Frequently, the agreement will require verification to be done by the owner participant's independent auditors or some other independent party that will be provided with the confidential information.

The fifth major section of the tax indemnification agreement sets forth a list of excluded events, circumstances under which an indemnity will not be payable. These circumstances typically include the failure of the owner participant to have sufficient taxable income or tax liability to benefit from the assumed tax benefits (although such a failure is not taken into account in computing the amount of an indemnity payment due as a result of a trigger event unless that is otherwise the agreement), its failure properly to claim an assumed tax benefit, the occurrence of an event giving rise to a lessee obligation to pay termination value or stipulated loss value, at least to the extent that such values properly take into account the tax consequences of the event, and other circumstances relating to the status of the owner participant, and changes in law except to the extent otherwise agreed. As a matter of logic it may be questioned whether these circumstances need to be mentioned in an acts, omissions and misrepresentations indemnity; however, just as the owner participant is concerned that the circumstances under which it *is* entitled to indemnity be clearly spelled out, so the lessee is concerned that the events for which it is *not* responsible be made clear.

The last basic section in the tax indemnification agreement sets forth conditions and procedures under which the lessee may cause the owner participant to contest a loss of tax benefit or other indemnifiable tax consequence asserted by the tax authorities. Here the negotiations centre on the circumstances under which the owner participant will be obligated to contest a tax loss, who controls the litigation and the extent to which the lessee will be entitled to participate, in what forum it will be pursued, who will bear the expense of the contest and whether and how it may be settled. Invariably the lessee pays the costs of the contest (and frequently is required to provide security in advance therefor) and, given that it—rather than the owner participant—bears the burden if the contest is unsuccessful, it generally demands the right of control to the greatest extent possible. From the owner participant's viewpoint, however, because the issue involved in the lease transaction generally arises in connection with an examination and possible challenge to its entire tax return, it must have the right to choose the forum and usually demands the right to control all aspects of the contest, subject only to an agreement not to settle an issue adverse to the lessee's interest without either obtaining its consent, preserving the right to contest the issue in another forum or releasing the lessee from liability with respect to the issue. Beyond this, the lessee is usually successful in negotiating the right to be kept informed and consulted regarding the conduct of the contest, but the details of the agreement on this point are often the subject of extensive and heated negotiations.

In the event that circumstances occur as a result of which an indemnity is payable, it is generally appropriate that the stipulated loss values and termination values be recalculated. This is frequently provided for in the tax indemnification agreement but, for such a provision to be effective, particularly in a transaction involving lenders (which are not parties to the tax indemnification agreement), it is necessary to have a corresponding provision in the lease.

8.16.5   Participation agreement

All parties to the transaction (except the supplier) execute a participation or financing agreement, particularly if commitments from the owners and lenders are obtained in advance of equipment acquisition. Under the agreement:

■   each owner participant agrees to make its investment;

■   each lender agrees to make its loan;

■   the owner trustee agrees to purchase and lease the equipment; and

■   the lessee agrees to hire the equipment.

The other documents generally appear as exhibits to the participation agreement to establish the form in which they will be executed.

When setting up the sale to the owner trustee and the lease to the lessee, the parties must always investigate whether such transfer will be respected. Most lessors and lenders insist in all transactions that an obvious notice identifying the owner and any security interest holder be permanently affixed to the equipment, if practical, in the hope that a court will disallow claims asserted by someone who could have learned about prior interests by simple inspection of the property.

The absence of title recordation systems for most types of personal property is particularly troublesome in sale-leaseback transactions. Because physical possession of property sold and immediately leased back by the seller does not change, there is concern that a third party, relying upon prior knowledge that the seller-lessee once held good title to the property, might advance valuable consideration thinking that it is receiving valid title to, or some interest in, the property. As an innocent purchaser for value and without actual knowledge of the prior sale, it might successfully enforce its claim against the lessor.

One of the principal purposes of the participation agreement is to set forth the various conditions precedent to each party's obligations. Typically these include:

- the continued truth of warranties and representations;

- delivery of counsel opinions;

- receipt of a favourable opinion from tax counsel and, occasionally, a satisfactory ruling from the relevant tax authority;

- issuance of necessary governmental approvals or licences;

- production of corporate certificates, certified resolutions and organic documents; and

- accomplishment of available actions to secure the interests of the parties, such as registration of the leased property, perfection of mortgages or security interests and completion of surveys or appraisals.

An important condition in every participation agreement is the production of proof that the insurance required by the lease is in effect. Many transactions are closed on the basis of the standard one-page printed certificate signed by an insurance broker, which states only the names of the insured, the type and amount of coverage and one or two other items. In transactions where the lessee credit is less than ideal and insurance is important, the parties are well advised to review the entire policy. It is a common occurrence for the detailed insurance provisions in the lease not to be reflected in the policy. Not infrequently insurance brokers will even opine that the policy complies with the lease when it does not. There is unfortunately no substitute for carefully reading the usually lengthy and confusing policy itself.

The participation agreement is also the place where the parties must solve the common problem of an uncertain purchase price. This can arise because of uncertainty as to transaction costs (such as legal fees), an ongoing dispute with the manufacturer or an incomplete leased asset. The problem can be solved in several ways. The equity and debt investors can agree to future closings as the additional costs are known. As all parties dislike a multiplicity of small closings, this option is frequently avoided in such cases. The equity and debt investors can alternatively fund a portion of their investments in escrow, which will be used to pay costs when they are known. This option results in the possibility of an additional closing or of a partial refund, if the escrow is too small or too large. Earnings from investment of the escrow are typically for the benefit of the lessee, who also must compensate the escrow for any investment losses suffered, since the lessee typically pays rent on the entire amount expended by the investors. The complexity of this option usually results in its being utilised only when a substantial sum is involved. When the uncertain portion of the purchase price is small, particularly when it is limited to transaction costs, the equity investors often agree to pay all of such sum in order to keep the funding simple. The problem with this last option is that the lack of leverage makes the financing of such sum entirely at the equity investor's yield more expensive to the lessee, since in all such cases the equity investor will require an adjustment to rent in order to compensate the equity investor for this additional expenditure. The final option is for the lessor to purchase the leased asset at an estimated price, with the lessee being obligated to make up any shortfall and retain any overage.

As mentioned above, the lessor is frequently obligated to pay all legal fees and other closing costs (other than those incurred by the lessee) including investment banking fees. This obligation is normally in the participation agreement. All participants should be careful, however, to be sure that someone creditworthy (usually the lessee) has agreed to pay such fees and costs if the transaction does not close and the participation agreement is not signed. Often this obligation is in the equity and debt commitment letters. Note, however, that these documents frequently state that they do not create a binding agreement and are subject to many conditions. An exception to the non-binding nature of such letters should always be made for the lessee's obligation to pay transaction costs if the closing never occurs.

8.17 LEGAL OPINIONS

A few words are in order regarding legal opinions at closings. They normally cover all the same issues that would be covered in any financing:

■   the legal status, power and authority of the parties to perform their respective obligations under the project agreements or credit and security documents;

■   good standing, authority, the binding effect, due execution, delivery and enforceability of the documentation;

■   the ownership and good title to the project assets;

■   the need to obtain and comply with licences, concessions and other regulatory measures;

■   the existence of any exchange controls, witholding taxes or other duties, eg stamp duties;

■   the enforceability of gross-up clauses, default interest provisions and other indemnities;

■   the pari-passu status of the borrower's obligations and local rules giving preferred status to certain creditors;

■   the likelihood of local courts awarding judgment in foreign currency;

■   the validity of the choice of law and forum for dispute resolution and the enforceability of foreign judgments and arbitration awards;

■   the existence and extent of any immunities from suit or attachment of assets;

■   pending litigation, perfection of liens, etc.

Of equal interest, however, and somewhat unique to lease financings are certain of the exceptions in the opinions. In addition to the usual exceptions of bankruptcy and general equitable principles to enforceability, many counsel also require an exception stating that certain of the remedies in the lease and the indenture may not be enforceable, but that taken as a whole the remedies will permit the lessor or indenture trustee to achieve the practical realisation of the benefits intended to be provided thereby. This exception is necessary. because remedies usually are written to be cumulative and broad and include liquidated damage and self-help provisions and the lessee usually waives any statutory or common law protections available to debtors, such as a requirement that the lessor mitigate damages. The parties realise that these provisions may not be enforceable, but assume there is little harm in drafting broadly. If a remedies section is too overreaching, of course, the entire section or agreement might be struck down by a court for unconscionability. The necessity for such broad remedies in the lease is created in part by the absence of any coherent body of law applicable to leases of personality.

8.18 GUARANTEES AND LETTERS OF CREDIT

Even though the lessee and its affiliates may not guarantee the debt without precluding a favourable tax ruling, other types of guarantees are often employed. The broadest guarantee is that often given by a parent or affiliate of the lessee, which itself agrees to perform all the lessee obligations to the extent that the lessee fails to do so for any reason.

A narrower type of guarantee, typified by commercial bank letters of credit, applies only to the payment of all or a portion of rent, termination value and stipulated loss value and does not cover additional payment obligations incurred by the lessee, such as those under indemnification provisions. The value of a guarantee is often obtained through hell-or-high water provisions of an assigned sublease, a keep-well agreement from a lessee affiliate, or a take-or-pay agreement, each of which is designed to produce a stream of cash flow from a creditworthy source.

Although the credit support of greatest concern is always that related to the lessee's obligations, owner participants also often have to supply guarantees. In some transactions there are affirmative ongoing equity obligations (such as deferred equity payments), but usually the guarantee is just to assure that a lien (or bankruptcy proceeding) does not interfere with the cash flow to the lenders or the quiet enjoyment of the lessee.

Two questions often arise with respect to separate guarantees of the lessee's obligations under the lease and other documents. First, does such a guarantee remain enforceable even if the primary obligations of the lessee are discharged in bankruptcy? Second, do the rules regarding mitigation of damages that generally apply to lessors under leases in default also apply to beneficiaries of separate guarantees relating to such leases?

A guarantee by a solvent person of all of the lessee's rental obligations under the lease which contains language to the effect that the guarantee creates a separate, distinct and independent obligation of the guarantor which cannot be diminished, reduced, discharged, or offset by reason of any limitation or defence available to the lessee, or of any reorganisation or discharge of its debts or obligations, is clearly enforceable without regard to the foregoing limitation, however, the result is likely to be different if the guarantor is also in bankruptcy.

Under common law, a lessor will normally be compelled to mitigate the damages it seeks from a defaulting lessee, when the lease has not been assumed or assigned by the trustee, by re-leasing or selling the leased property after repossession. If the lessor has failed to do so, the courts will generally calculate damages by subtracting from the remaining unpaid rentals (assuming the limitations discussed above concerning recovery for accelerated rent under real property leases are inapplicable) an amount equal to the fair market or fair rental value of the leased equipment. Does the guarantor of such lease obligations have a corresponding right to reduction of its obligations under the guarantee?

For purposes of bankruptcy law it is often asserted that a guarantor cannot be held to greater damages than the prime obligor, but under general contract law a guarantee that creates an independent undertaking of the guarantor to pay a sum measured on its own terms without regard to any other limitations probably will be enforced without reduction.

Many transactions today utilise a letter of credit to support some or all of the borrower's obligations. There are three basic types: those that secure obligations to equity and debt, those that secure only obligations to the debt and those that secure only obligations to the equity. The first type is issued by the borrower's bank with the borrowers as account party and the lessor as beneficiary. The letter of credit is then usually assigned in its entirety to the indenture trustee. If the letter of credit secures only stipulated loss value, the drawing procedure is straightforward in that the indenture trustee would draw the full amount, utilise as much as necessary to pay principal and interest on the debt and remit the balance to the borrowers. The fun starts if the letter of credit secures all the borrower's obligations. Does the indenture trustee control all draws? What if the only default is a failure to pay an indemnity to the borrowers? If the borrower can draw for indemnities, what if its draws reduce the letter of credit below an amount equal to outstanding principal and interest on the debt? The parties must draft an intricate set of priorities to cover these and other scenarios.

When the letter of credit secures only amounts owed to the equity, none of these complications arises and there is little to negotiate relating to the letter of credit once its economic conditions are set.

Two other interesting issues arise in deals with letters of credit. The first relates to the rights of the letter of credit issuer upon a drawing: there is value to the issuer in being able to step into the shoes of the beneficiary to the extent of its drawing. Thus, if the letter of credit is drawn by the debt, the issuer would be assigned pro tanto the notes by the lenders and would thus obtain a first lien on the leased property. The equity can be expected to object to this arrangement since there will always be an unpaid lender foreclosing on the property in the case of a default, thereby depriving the owner participants of their residual, causing tax recapture and making it more difficult for the owner participants to recover sums owed to them for which the letter of credit is insufficient. One possible compromise is for the letter of credit issuer to obtain these rights but be obligated to first use the proceeds of any foreclosure to pay sums owed to the owner participants, to then reimburse itself for its payments and expenses and finally to pay any balance to the owner participants as their residual.

When the letter of credit secures only amounts owed to the equity, a right of substitution for the equity's position is less controversial, although the equity will still be concerned that it does not lose its residual.

8.19   CONCESSION AGREEMENTS

In BOT projects the concession agreement will be the key project document as it is the document which will vest in the project company the right to explore, exploit, develop or operate the concession or other relevant rights to the project. In a BOT project it will invariably be the case that the project vehicle will be granted a concession by the host government with respect to the project. The concession agreement, often comprising a build-operate-transfer obligation, is popular in countries where political or budgetary constraints prevent governments from developing essential and increasing expensive infrastructure in the public sector. Typically a concession agreement will offer the host government advantages which include:

■   minimising the impact of the project on its capital budget;

■   introducing increased efficiency into the project;

■   encouraging foreign investment and the introduction of new technology.

The BOT structure ends with the transfer back of the project to the relevant state authority at some future date. This results in normal cases with the state acquiring an operational project, although in most cases the transfer is not effected during the economic life of the project.

The terms of a typical concession agreement include:

■   the grant of a concession for a designated period of time;

■   the duties and obligations imposed on the project company with respect to the project and the concession;

- certain undertakings given by the concession grantor, eg as to non-competition and taxation;
- payment of concession fees;
- default and forfeiture terms;
- assignments and transfers;
- termination events and hand-over provisions.

Example 8.1

A brief summary of three different project financings done over a 12-month period illustrate the breadth of different agreements and structures that may be used:

	Project 1	**Project 2**	**Project 3**
Purpose	Paper recycling	Construction materials	Power
Location	US	E Europe	Asia
Ownership	Partnership	Local joint venture corporation	Local joint venture corporation
Lenders	Institutional (tax exempt mutual funds)	Multinational lenders; Local development banks; Export credit facilities for equipment	Multinational lenders; Commercial banks; Export credit facilities for equipment; Rule 144A debt
Equity investors	Project sponsors	Project sponsors plus certain lenders	Project sponsors plus passive investors and suppliers
Security	Mortgage and equipment liens; Assignment of customer contract and technology licence	Off-shore escrow; Mortgage and equipment liens when laws confirm enforceability; Limited take or pay agreement	Power purchase agreement; Fuel supply agreements; Mortgage and equipment liens; Off-shore escrow
Project sponsor guarantees	None	Limited completion and currency exchange guarantees	Limited completion guarantees
Type of debt	Tax exempt industrial development bonds	Fixed and floating rate loans, but all pari passu	Various types of debt, but all pari passu

Project lenders will be concerned in addition to the foregoing to ensure that the concession grantor cannot unilaterally vary or terminate the terms of the concession, that the concession is assignable and that the concession grantor assume the risk for any delays in the project arising as a result of change or law of force majeure.

Project 1 used tax exempt debt and had only one class of debt holders with identical rights and terms. A trust indenture governed the mechanics for construction cost payments and other uses of proceeds, the enforcement of covenants and defined defaults. The security included a mortgage and equipment lien on the project. As tax exempt debt the bonds were exempt from registration under the Securities Act of 1933 and accordingly were freely transferable by the bond purchaser. An investment banker placed the bonds with the purchasers.

Since tax exempt bonds bear lower interest rates than taxable debt, they are commonly used for many types of US projects. The Internal Revenue Code of 1986 ('Code') provides that interest on bonds of a state or political subdivision is not taxable, but limits this to certain kinds of borrowing. Among the permitted kinds borrowing are those for publicly owned and operated projects (such as a state turnpike system). Where private ownership is involved, as it was in project 1, projects which meet the requirements for 'exempt facility bonds' may be financed with tax exempt bonds. Where a project is publicly owned, but managed by a private company, it can only use tax exempt bonds if (a) it meets the 'exempt facility bonds' test, or (b) the management agreement meets strict Code requirements on the duration and fee paid under the management agreement.

Section 142(a) of the Code sets forth the basic definition of the term 'exempt facility bond'. Included within the definition are bonds issued to provide any of the following types of facilities: airports, docks and wharves, mass commuting facilities, facilities for the furnishing of water and sewage facilities, solid waste disposal facilities, qualified residential rental projects, facilities for the local furnishing of electric energy or gas, local district heating or cooling facilities, qualified hazardous waste facilities and high speed intercity rail facilities. Each type of facility is subject to detailed definitions and rules set forth in the Code and regulations.

If a project qualifies, the bonds are issued by a state or local agency and the proceeds are made available to the project owner under a loan or instalment sale agreement. Issuing 'exempt facility bonds' requires local and state approvals, including an allocation from the state for the amount of the financing from a limited amount made available to the state each year. Neither the state nor local agency issuing the bonds will have any responsibility to pay off the bonds—this remains the obligation of the project itself. Where the project is publicly owned and operated (such as a state turnpike or city water system), there is no allocation required.

Project 2 had several unique aspects. First, because there were only a limited number of customers, the project revenues depended on the general market for the construction materials instead of a long-term customer contract. Second, because the country involved was one where mortgages on real property were new and untested, lenders could not rely on a mortgage for security. Third, there were both currency exchange and valuation risks. The result was to use a dollar denominated offshore escrow as collateral. Take-or-pay agreements with certain offshore sponsors to cover escrow requirements were put in place to cover the possibility that local sales could not be converted to sufficient dollars to cover debt service.

Project 3 had the advantage of a power purchase agreement with government backing. The project sponsors had to provide limited project completion guarantees (in addition to their basic equity investments), but no ongoing guarantees after completion were required. In both projects 2 and 3 a local sponsor/investor was involved. Because of the huge debt financing for project 3, there were four groups of lenders—multinationals, commercial banks, a Rule 144A debt placement with US institutional investors and export credit facilities for the equipment suppliers.

In all three, there were common agreements among all lenders as to disbursement of loans, defaults, consents and enforcement of collateral and sharing of proceeds of collateral. In projects 2 and 3 there were government approvals for offshore escrows and conversion of the local currency to dollars to cover debt service costs.

As noted, the three projects run the gamut of the types of investment used. Project 1 was US tax exempt debt. Project 2 had both debt and equity investments with equity subject to a put to the project sponsors and also a call (repurchase right) at a predetermined price formula. Project 3 had all types of taxable debt, including Rule 144A debt, which is debt placed with institutional investors under Rule 144A of the SEC. Under Rule 144A the debt is transferable without a lengthy holding period.

In all three projects financial covenants were imposed on the project owner, but they were less rigorous in project 1 because of the strong security offered by the mortgage. Typical financial covenants would be a limit on debt as a percentage of equity (debt equity ratio), a limit on debt in terms of cash flow available to pay debt (coverage ratio), a minimum working capital requirement, a debt to net tangible assets test, restrictions on future borrowings, restrictions on investments and payments of dividends and restrictions on creating liens or encumbrances on property. Some of the financial tests are only applicable where new debt is created, others may be applied on an annual or more frequent basis and the failure to meet the ratio may be a default.

In US projects that are owned by government entities, mortgages on the project are rarely used because many state constitutions prohibit giving liens on government property. Instead, a pledge of the project revenues is given, together with covenants requiring the project owner to increase rates and charges to meet various rate covenants. In both public and privately owned US projects, the project revenues may flow through a trustee for lenders who disburse revenues in a fixed order of priority (usually, first to pay operating costs, then to debt service, replenishment of reserve funds and last to the project owner). In international projects, particularly where currency exchange is an issue, sufficient project revenues are diverted to offshore escrow accounts to cover debt service and reserve requirements in the currency of the key lender.

Governing law and dispute resolution provisions in the different documents present an issue on all projects, but particularly on international projects. It will benefit all parties if each contract contains similar provisions regarding where and how disputes are to be resolved. Consolidation provisions may be written into arbitration clauses allowing for the adjudication of common disputes among several parties in a single, cost-effective proceeding. Although lengthy court proceedings do not favour the person waiting to be paid, many lenders nevertheless prefer court proceedings over arbitration for loan agreement disputes. Careful negotiation of these clauses and consistency among all the contracts is very important in the event the parties are unable to resolve their problems without use of a dispute resolution mechanism.

Finally, co-ordination among lenders is an important issue to be addressed in project financing. As noted above, projects 2 and 3 both involved multiple lenders, each group with its own set of loan documents. Although their rights to collateral and security were pari passu (meaning they all had equal rights to collateral), the exercise of rights by different lenders had to be addressed. For example, the export credit facility lender might want to stop advancing funds for the project even though another lender wished to continue advancing funds. Unless all advances are made as scheduled the entire project will be jeopardised. Who decides if the conditions for advances have been met? Lender consents during the operations present similar problems, as do defaults and what actions can and should be taken by lenders. These issues are all the subject of intense negotiations among the different lenders and the project owner and must be resolved in ways that protect the lenders as well as the project owner from a recalcitrant or arbitrary lender.

FORM: DUE DILIGENCE REPORTS

In addition to feasibility studies a thorough due diligence exercise needs to be undertaken on the lines of investigating the following:

1   Corporate documents

- Minutes and Protocols of meetings held since incorporation of the boards of directors, committees of the boards of directors and stockholders of the company and any subsidiaries. Any relevant information disseminated in connection with such meetings should be included.

- A corporate structure and organisation chart, including:

    - the identification of all subsidiaries and summary description of their businesses (including the place of incorporation or association and the principal place of business);

    - the location in corporate structure of major assets and liabilities; and

    - a list of directors and officers and management organisation chart dated as of recent date.

- A list of any names under which the company has done business over the last five years.

- Stock ledger and evidence, including letters from auditors, of full payment for and non-accessibility of issued and outstanding stock of the company and its subsidiaries, names of all record and beneficial stockholders and any other records of stock issuances by the company and its subsidiaries.

- A list of all jurisdictions in which the company and its subsidiaries are qualified to do business and evidence of such qualification.

- A list of all partnerships, joint ventures and other businesses in which the company owns an equity interest and copies of the relevant documents.

- Copies of any agreements, arrangements or understandings (including proxies, voting trusts and other voting or stockholder agreements) relating to the ownership, voting, sale or issuance of securities of the company or its subsidiaries.

- All agreements under which any person has registration rights, pre-emptive rights, or any rights of first refusal for securities of the company or its subsidiaries, a joint venture, a partnership or other entity in which the company or any subsidiary has an interest.

- Stock option plans, forms of stock option agreements and a list of option holders.

- All agreements, memoranda, registration statements, prospectuses, information statements, disclosure documents or offering circulars relating to sales of securities of the company or its subsidiaries, copies of correspondence with investors and copies of any written proposals for the acquisition securities of the company or its subsidiaries.

■ Annual reports, interim reports and other communications with stockholders of the company.

■ Officer and director questionnaires dated as of recent date for the contemplated offering.

2 Credit and related documents

■ A schedule of all outstanding debt issues and securities and the current outstanding amounts thereof, including outstanding warrants or option agreements to purchase stock.

■ All indentures, agreements, bank lines of credit (whether or not drawn upon) or other instruments evidencing debt obligations of the company and its subsidiaries and all amendments, consents and waivers thereto.

■ The latest current compliance certificates as to covenants or restrictions thereunder and any material correspondence relating to all indentures, bank lines of credit (whether or not drawn upon), agreements or other instruments evidencing debt obligations and all amendments thereto.

■ All documents relating to short-term credit lines, commercial paper programmes and master note borrowings.

■ Any and all documents and agreements evidencing other material financing arrangements such as sale and leaseback arrangements, capitalised leases and instalment purchases.

■ A schedule of all material guarantees, indemnifications or loans made or entered into by the company or its subsidiaries, as well as underlying documentation.

■ A schedule of all inter-company indebtedness, guarantees, etc, as well as underlying documents.

■ A schedule of all mortgages, liens and security interests, as well as underlying documentation (including information relating to relevant filings).

■ All documents circulated to lenders and prospective lenders for the purposes of syndication.

■ All documents pertaining to any bankruptcy, involuntary liquidation, creditors administrative or analogous proceeding to which the company or any subsidiary have been subject.

■ All other agreements or documents evidencing or relating to borrowings and financing to which the company or any subsidiary is a party, including any reimbursement agreements, repurchase agreements, sale and leaseback arrangements, capitalised and operating leases, instalment purchases and equipment leases (other than those referred to in item 5 hereof).

3 Litigation

■ A summary and status report of all non-routine and significant routine litigation, administrative proceedings, investigations or inquiries threatened or pending and a list of all such litigations settled.

- All litigation letters from the company's outside legal counsel to the company's independent auditors.

- Litigation files, including pleadings, opinions of counsel, correspondence and analysis of material litigation status.

- Correspondence and documents relating to material contingent liabilities.

- All consent decrees, judgments, injunctions, other decrees or orders, settlement agreements and other agreements presently applicable to the company, its subsidiaries or any of its officers, directors, key employees or controlling stockholders.

- Correspondence during the last five years dealing with actual or alleged infringement (either by the company, its subsidiaries or another party) of patents, trademarks or copyrights and misuse of trade secrets.

- Waivers or agreements cancelling claims or rights of substantial value, other than in the ordinary course of business.

- All reports, notices or correspondence concerning any violation or infringement of government regulations by the company or its subsidiaries including, but not limited to, the areas of securities regulation, equal employment opportunity, occupational safety and health, environmental protection, energy, transportation and antitrust.

- The company's Code of Ethics or Conduct and Compliance Procedures Manual and any related employee certification manuals.

4 Insurance coverage

- A schedule of insurance policies, including policies covering real or personal property, workers' compensation and life insurance policies owned by the company or its subsidiaries.

- A summary of all claims made under the company's insurance policies during the last five years.

- Correspondence with insurance companies regarding reservation of liability or rights.

- Director and officer indemnification agreements.

5 Material contracts

- All agreements entered into or proposed to be entered into by the company or its subsidiaries or relating to a material acquisition or disposition of assets or stock or a merger, reorganisation or consolidation, or any of the foregoing entered into at any time pursuant to which the company or its subsidiaries remains liable.

- Any agreements between or among the company, its subsidiaries or its affiliates, including management agreements.

- All material royalty, licensing, marketing, sales, sales agent, sales representative, dealer, distributor, consignment, pricing, franchise and participation agreements.

- All joint venture, R&D and similar agreements.

- Form purchase, sale, distribution, etc, contracts.

- A list of the ten largest customers and suppliers of the company and copies of agreements relating thereto.

- All leases of any substantial amount of personal property to which the company or its subsidiaries are a party, either as lessor or lessee.

- All contracts entered into outside the ordinary course of business of the company or its subsidiaries.

- Any other material contracts and agreements involving the company and its subsidiaries not otherwise covered by the foregoing items including, but not limited to, interconnection agreements, service contracts, equipment supply contracts, systems contracts, installation contracts, long-term supply contracts, purchase and requirements contracts, government contracts and sub-contracts, commission and agency agreements and agreements with customers.

- A list of customers or suppliers involved in bankruptcy proceedings or that could otherwise be considered credit risks.

6 Employee matters

- The most recent copies of all employment, consulting and compensation contracts, agreements, arrangements, plans and programmes (eg bonus, incentive, compensation, severance, stock option, deferred compensation, capital accumulation) and qualified plans and programmes (eg pension, profit-sharing, stock bonus) entered into, contributed to, or maintained by the company or its subsidiaries, including the following related documents as applicable and all amendments thereto:

  - trust agreements, insurance contracts or other funding vehicles;

  - summary plan descriptions;

  - investment management agreements;

  - annual reports including, in the case of pension plans, certified actuarial reports;

  - valuations of plan assets;

  - employee data;

  - information relating to any litigation, proceeding, prohibited transaction or other unusual event relating to any plan, programme or arrangement described above; and

  - historical cost figures under any such plan, programme or arrangement described above.

- A list of executive employees with a breakdown of compensation, severance and other benefits.

- Collective bargaining agreements (specifically identify when each is due for negotiation) and a history of labour disputes and grievances.

- Information concerning the number of employees, turnover and anticipated hiring needs.

- A schedule setting forth the names of the company's officers, directors and other key employees and the names of any officers, directors and key employees who have recently resigned or been terminated.

- Non-competition, secrecy, confidentiality and non-disclosure agreements with employees and third parties.

- A schedule of all transactions involving the company or its subsidiaries and

    - any officer or director of the company, or

    - any affiliate of the company as well as underlying documentation.

- All documents pertaining to any accounts receivable from, accounts payable to or any guarantee agreements with, or which benefit, any director, officer or owner of more than 5 per cent of the equity securities of the company.

- Copies of all personnel policies, personnel manuals and employee handbooks and other employee communications relating to benefits.

- Copies of any cost studies relating to retiree benefits (eg any study estimating the recent value of retiree medical benefits).

- Workers' compensation data (current accounting practice, current insurance rates, past cost history).

- Indemnification arrangements with officers and directors of the company and its subsidiaries.

7   Patents, trademarks, etc

- A list of all patents, copyrights, trademarks, service marks, royalty agreements, licences and trade names and other intellectual property owned or used by the company or its subsidiaries together with all agreements pertaining thereto and a schedule of any confidentiality agreements.

- A description of all claims by or against the company or its subsidiaries relating to the validity or ownership of intellectual property.

8   Tax documents

- Copies of all tax returns (including schedules and exhibits) filed by the company and its subsidiaries for the latest closed and all open years.

- Any strategic plans and forecasts of the company or any of its subsidiaries relating to its tax status and other tax matters.

- Documents and data relating to the following:

    - the company's consolidated year-end accruals, reserves and provisions;

    - copies of any prior federal, state or foreign revenue agent's reports on the company and its subsidiaries and any outstanding protests, petitions or deficiency assessments;

    - accounting methods and procedures used by the company and its subsidiaries and any recent changes thereto;

    - any unusual tax planning practices or transactions of the company and its subsidiaries;

    - amount, origin and status of any net operating losses or credit carry-forwards of the company and its subsidiaries; information on any changes in stock ownership to date which might affect such items; and

    - any relevant tax elections.

- The tax basis and fair market value of the stock of all subsidiaries, major assets, asset categories and business segments.

- Tax audits and results thereof.

- Tax-sharing arrangements and related documents.

9   Real estate

- A listing of all properties owned by the company or its subsidiaries and all material properties leased by the company or its subsidiaries and showing the following information relating to each such property:

  - location (including street address and jurisdiction in which such property is located);

  - size of the land and building in which the facility is located;

  - fee or leasehold ownership and percentage of ownership interest of the company; and

  - if leased, the economic terms, including:

  - rent (fixed, percentage or other);

  - renewal options;

  - assignability;

  - financing provisions;

  - financial maintenance covenants; and

  - any other covenants, conditions or other terms related to or affected by a transfer of the property;

  - if partially owned, the form of partial ownership.

- All material deeds, mortgages, title reports and policies, and all material leases and related agreements concerning all real property owned or occupied by the company or its subsidiaries.

- All material leases (including capitalised leases) and mortgages to which the company or its subsidiaries are a party.

10   Plants, equipment and inventory

- A list of material machinery, equipment, furniture, fixtures and inventory.

- A list of material machinery, equipment or inventory in possession of any third parties.

- A list of all liens, encumbrances and security interests.

- Copies of all security agreements and financing statements.

- Copies of all material equipment leases.

11   Governmental

- A summary of any governmental permits or licences held or applied for by the company and its subsidiaries.

- A description of all filings, reports, registration statements, correspondence, complaints, consent decrees, determinations, orders, etc, relating to governmental agencies during the last five years.

- Copies of all Russian Central Bank licences required in connection with the operation of the Company's business.

- Copies of all anti-monopoly approvals by the Russian Anti-Monopoly Committee.

12 Financial statements and accounting

- Accountants reports and correspondence for the past five years. Management letters to the company and its subsidiaries and responses.

- Audited financial statements, interim unaudited financial statements and consolidating financial statements for the company for the past five years.

- Audit committee reports for the last five years to the Board of Directors of the company or its subsidiaries.

- Internal financial plans, budgets and projections.

13 Other

- Details of any internal or independent valuations of the assets and businesses of the company and its subsidiaries.

- Any document not covered above restricting the sale or transfer of any of the material assets or stock of the company or its subsidiaries.

- Any restrictions on the company or its subsidiaries carrying on its business anywhere in the world.

- Any document not covered above which would require a consent upon, or which would be triggered or otherwise affected by, a merger or change of control of the company or its subsidiaries.

- Description of any special relationships between directors, officers, managers or employees and customers and suppliers that could affect future sales or purchases.

- All recent analyses of the company or its industries prepared by investment bankers, investment analysts, engineers, management consultants, accountants or others including marketing studies, credit reports and other types of reports, financial or otherwise.

- All material press releases, articles and brochures issued by the company or others concerning the company or any of its products, services or any material events involving the foregoing.

- Any other documents or information which the company believes are material with respect to any portion of its business or which should be considered and reviewed in order adequately to disclose the company's business and financial condition.

- Any other documents or information which support statements made by the company in its Offering Memorandum relating to market size, relative market position, competitors, growth and other business or industry matters.

- Copies of advertising materials and breakdown of advertising expenses.

- Remuneration of officers and directors for the past three years.
- Customer complaints.

Checklist: Project documents

Underlying project documents might include:

- Concession agreements, government licences, royalty agreements.
- Documents of title to land, including the obtaining of necessary surface and sub-sea rights.
- Joint venture agreement between project sponsors.
- Shareholders' agreement.
- Constitutive documents of a project company.
- Project management agreement and technical consultancy contracts.
- Construction contract and sub-contracts.
- Contractors' and sub-contractors' performance bonds and advance payment guarantees.
- Other guarantees, eg of obligations under sales contracts.
- Project insurances.
- Supply contracts-whether on normal commercial terms or supply-or-pay or tolling agreements.
- Sales contracts-again, whether on commercial terms or under offtake, take-or-pay or take-and-pay arrangements.
- Throughput agreements.
- Technology/operating licences.
- Planning and environmental consents.
- Utility supply agreements-electricity, gas, water.
- Refining agreements (where additional refining is required to put the production into saleable condition), the transportation contracts.
- Other financing documents of the project sponsors.

9

Special issues for BOT and PFI transactions

LEARNING OBJECTIVES

After reading this chapter you will be able to understand the major issues concerning BOT and PFI transactions, including:

*   *Sponsor issues*

*   *Concession grantor's issues*

*   *Project company's obligations*

*   *Guarantees*

*   *Warranties and indemnities*

9.1 INTRODUCTION

This chapter examines the structure of BOT and PFI transactions.

9.2 LEGAL ISSUES RELATING TO BOT PROJECTS

BOT investors are critically concerned with a number of aspects of country and political risks. The role of governments either in creating or reducing risks can be central.

Typically a government grants a concession to a concession company under which the company has the right to build and operate a facility. The concession company will usually borrow from banks in order to finance the construction of the facility and the loans are repaid from tariffs paid by the government or consumers during the life span of the concession.

Banks expect to share some of the completion risk and some operational risk, however, they will require some form of protection against political risk. Where the governing law for the concession is acceptable, there may be some degree of leverage in reducing the political risk.

9.2.1 Sponsor issues

Key points arising in the negotiation of the concession agreement include:

- the control of the government agency over the design and carrying out of the project and in particular ensuring that it exercises promptly and fairly any discretion to approve design or other matters;

- ensuring the appropriate legislative framework and obtaining any licences, exemptions or assurances required as to the effect of local legislation;

- the definition of force majeure events and events entitling the government to terminate the concession and any step-in rights required by funders;

- stand-by financing in the event of serious adverse foreign exchange movements.

The key features are, therefore, the grant of a concession, the assumption of responsibility by the promoter (or sponsor) for the construction, operation and financing of the project and the retransfer at the end of the concession period of the project assets to the grantor of the concession. A very common variant of the BOT model is the BOO (build-own-operate) project which is structured on similar lines to a BOT project but without retransfer of project assets at the end of the concession period. The concession agreement will, therefore, be the key project document and as such is likely to be examined with considerable care by the project lenders.

From the concession grantor's point of view, a BOT or similar project has a number of advantages. The principal ones are:

- it offers a form of off-balance sheet financing because the lending in relation to the project will be undertaken by the project company;

- because the concession grantor (usually a government or government agency) will not have to borrow in order to develop the project, this will have a favourable impact on any constraints on public borrowing and will potentially free up funds for other priority projects;

- it enables the concession grantor to transfer risks for construction, finance and operation of the facility to the private sector; and

- it is a way of attracting and utilising foreign investment and technology.

Under the concession arrangements, the project company will usually own and operate the project for the duration of the concession. The revenue produced by the project will be used by the project company to repay the project loans, operate the concession and recover the investment of the sponsors plus a profit margin. Overall, the structure is similar to much other project financing in that the project loans will usually be provided direct to the project company (which is likely to be a subsidiary of the sponsors based in the host country) and the lenders will take security over (principally) the project company's rights under the concession agreement, together with any other available project assets.

The principal terms of a concession agreement for a typical BOT project are set out below.

9.2.2 Concession grantor's obligations

The concession grantor's obligations are likely to include:

- granting to the project company an exclusive licence to build and operate the project for the stipulated concession period;

- acquiring the project site and transferring it to the project company;

- making and obtaining required compulsory purchase orders for land;

- providing required consents and licences;

- making an environmental assessment;

- passing enabling legislation if required;

- constructing connecting services including roads;

- granting, where applicable, tax concessions or holidays;

- (possibly) providing raw materials and purchasing the offtake;

- (possibly) an agreement to compensate the project company against certain risks, such as uninsurable force majeure risks and change in law risks; and

- granting to the project company the right to termination of the concession (with compensation) following default by the concession grantor.

9.2.3   Project company's obligations

The project company is likely to have obligations as follows:

- to acquire the project site from the concession grantor; to finance, construct, operate and maintain the project to the contract specification, which may be variable by the concession grantor either with or without compensation; to comply with certain standards of construction work and to permit the concession grantor access to the site for progress checks and monitoring; to complete the project by the specified date and to provide performance guarantees or bonds;

- to comply with all applicable legislation and if the concession grantor (being a state entity) introduces new legislation which increases the cost to the project company of carrying out the project, then the concession agreement may include compensation terms for the project company;

- where appropriate, to enter into sales or other offtake contracts in respect of the project's products;

- to permit the concession grantor to terminate the concession upon default by the project company; to train staff of the concession grantor prior to retransfer; and

- (possibly) to transfer the project assets to the concession grantor at the expiration of the concession.

Where the concession is in respect of a public transport facility, the concession may well provide for control of the level of charges, permitted adjustments and the duration of the period when charges can be levied. In return for any restrictions on charges, the concession grantor may agree to pay a subsidy or guarantee a minimum level of demand.

In the event of a default by the project company of any of the terms of the concession, or the occurrence of some other event which makes it unlikely that the project will be completed, the concession grantor will wish to have the ability to terminate the concession and/or take over the project company in order to complete the project itself. Of course, the project lenders will be concerned about any rights which the concession grantor has to terminate the concession agreement or to alter any of the terms of the concession agreement in a way that is likely to impact on their financing arrangements. They are also likely to want the ability to step in themselves and take over the project company's rights under the concession agreement in certain circumstances.

9.2.4 Forward-purchase model

Under this structure, sometimes known as an 'advance payment facility', the project lender will make an advance payment for the purchase of products generated by the project, which will then be deliverable to the lender following completion of the project. The project company will utilise the proceeds of the advance payment towards financing the construction and development of the project. On delivery of the products following completion, the lenders will either sell the products on the market itself or to the project company (or a related company of the project company) and it will use the proceeds to 'repay' itself.

Alternatively, the project company may sell the products as sales agent for the lender. Some structures entitle the project company to make cash payment to the lender in lieu of delivering products. A common feature of most structures, however, will be a requirement for an indemnity by the lenders for any loss or liability that the lender may suffer or incur as a consequence of taking title to the products in question.

Sometimes a more complicated structure is used whereby another company, jointly owned by the lenders, acts as a vehicle through whom the funding is passed. In such a case, this vehicle will assign the benefit of the forward-purchase agreement and any related agreements to the lenders by way of security. The introduction of this further stage is usually designed to remove the lenders from the commercial arrangements relating to the sale of products, often for regulatory reasons, but sometimes because the lenders will not want to take title to the products.

This type of structure has frequently been used as a way of circumventing borrowing restrictions. The argument is that a structure such as this does not amount to a borrowing, nor would it infringe negative pledges and similar covenants. Whether or not this in fact achieves the intended objective will depend on the legal and accounting rules in the relevant country, but certainly the trend in the accountancy world these days is to look at the substance of the structure rather than accept the strict application of the documents. Another reason for using the structure might be in circumstances where it is not possible for the lender to obtain a perfected security interest in the assets being financed and the lender is not prepared to finance the project on an unsecured basis. The forward-purchase type of arrangement, if it is legally effective, will give the lender title to the project assets, which is at least the equivalent of (and probably better than) security over those assets.

Lenders participating in such transactions will obviously be concerned to ensure that, if a financing vehicle is not used, they are entitled under banking regulations applicable to them to participate in such 'trading' activities. They will also be concerned that, in the case of certain types of assets such as oil and related products, they are not exposing themselves to any liabilities (for instance pollution) that may arise through ownership (however briefly) of those assets. The existence of an indemnity from the project company will give some comfort on this issue, although the lender will still be assuming an additional credit risk (in respect of the project company) for any amount that might be payable under this indemnity.

A similar structure is the 'production payment' model frequently used in the US to achieve significant tax advantages. Under this structure, the lender (or a vehicle established by them) acquires a production (ie ownership) interest in a project. The lender will then be entitled to an agreed share of the project's production proportionate to the production payment that the lender has acquired. The structure usually obliges the project company to repurchase the products delivered to the lenders or to sell the products as agent for the lenders. The interest acquired by the lender can either be an interest in the project itself (that is a right to, say, the agreed proportion of oil and gas or minerals that are produced) or an interest in the proceeds of sale of the products.

The essential difference between the forward-purchase structure and the production payment structure is that in a forward-purchase transaction there is merely a contract to deliver and take the products as and when produced whereas in a production payment transaction there is a conveyance or sale of the products (or the proceeds of sale of the products) in exchange for the purchase price.

Both of these structures were used on occasions in the very early days of financing in the North Sea but have not been seen in the North Sea since. They are, however, still popular for certain types of projects (eg minerals).

9.2.5 Completion guarantees

In the absence of a turnkey (or equivalent) construction contract with a construction company of suitable credit standing, which provides for an acceptable level of liquidated damages in the event of delayed completion, the lenders may not be prepared to assume the construction/ completion risk on the project and they may seek a guarantee from the shareholders/sponsors to the effect that the project will achieve completion by a stated date.

A definition of completion will need to be agreed and it will usually be a requirement of the lenders that completion is verified by an independent engineer acting for the lenders. A completion test will usually incorporate three general criteria:

- confirmation that the project is physically complete and that it has been built to the plans and specifications;

- a demonstration of installed technology;

- demonstration that the project can be expected to operate reliably as represented by the project company over the term of the loan.

As a completion guarantee from the shareholders/sponsors will necessarily involve the lenders in taking a credit risk on the shareholders/ sponsors, the lenders will be concerned as to the credit standing of the completion guarantor and will need to be satisfied that it is of sufficient financial standing so as to be able to meet its maximum potential liabilities under the guarantee (which may be very significant, should the project run into serious difficulties). Accordingly, one might expect to see extensive covenants and warranties asked from the completion guarantor. Should the completion guarantor lack the necessary financial standing, then it may be that the lenders will demand back-up support, either in terms of a counter-guarantee from another group company or perhaps even a letter of credit or guarantee from its bankers.

One significant problem with completion guarantees (and similar instruments) is that, under common law principles, the principal remedy for breach lies in damages for breach of contract. This is significantly weaker than, say, a financial guarantee, as the lenders will not only have to prove causation and that their loss was reasonably foreseeable, but will also be required to mitigate their loss.

9.2.6 Concession agreement/licence (or equivalent)

In a concession-based (or build-own-transfer) project, this will usually be the key element of any security structure as it will be through this document that the project company (and therefore the lenders) acquire the rights to build, use and operate, as appropriate, the project. Without effective security over the concession agreement, the value of security over any property or fixed plant and machinery is likely to be very limited. In some jurisdictions where security assignments are not recognised, if the lenders are to create an effective security package it will be crucial for the lenders and their advisers to attempt to construct equivalent contractual rights with the concession grantor and the project company. The end result may be to achieve substantially similar protection through a combination of a negative pledge, other covenants and a direct agreement with the concession grantor (see below), or alternatively, in some jurisdictions it may be possible to take an absolute assignment of the concession agreement subject to some form of conditionality (eg such as the occurrence of an event of default).

Another issue that frequently arises in the case of enforcement of security over concession agreements is the identity of any assignee. In many cases local laws may prohibit foreign entities owning the concession in question. Even where this is not the case, it is likely that the concession grantor will reserve the right to approve any assignee, which is likely in practice to seriously weaken the position of the lenders.

9.2.7 Cost overrun guarantee

This is a close relative of the completion guarantee and often goes hand in hand with it. As its title suggests, it is a commitment by a third party that, should the costs of achieving completion of the project exceed the agreed project budget, the cost overrun guarantor will meet the shortfall. Sometimes the cost overrun guarantor is required to meet cost overruns as and when they occur (that is, measured against the ongoing project budget), whereas in other cases it is only required to pay up once loan funds have been exhausted. In either case, the lenders are again taking a credit risk on the cost overrun guarantor and therefore the same considerations that applied to the completion guarantor also apply to the cost overrun guarantor.

Sponsors will often try to limit their obligations to covering cost overruns and even then only up to an agreed maximum, as this is a more limited degree of support than entering into a full-blown completion guarantee, where it is almost impossible to quantify the potential maximum liability. Whether or not the lenders are prepared to accept this reduced degree of support in any particular case will depend on a number of factors, not least the availability of technical assistance and experienced personnel to enable the project company to achieve completion.

9.2.8 Management agreements

These are agreements which provide for the project company to have available to it the necessary technical assistance, employees and management to embark on and complete the project. Usually these services will be provided by one or more of the sponsors. Lenders will usually want the commitment to provide these services clearly defined so that, should problems arise, the lenders will be able to look to the responsible party. Further, the lenders would expect to have an assignment of the benefit of any management agreement, enabling them to sue the sponsors direct should the sponsors not fulfil this contractual commitment to the project company.

9.2.9   Equity contribution agreements

These are agreements entered into by the shareholders or sponsors of the project company under which they commit, in certain circumstances or alternatively at specified times (with the agreement of the lenders), to inject further equity into a project company. Lenders will not always insist that shareholders or sponsors subscribe for all their equity at the outset of the project, but may, depending on the credit standing of the shareholder or sponsors, permit shareholders or sponsors to make equity injections during the construction period. One of the problems with such agreements is that if the project company is wound up before a call is made on a shareholder or sponsors, then clearly a shareholder cannot subscribe for further shares in the project company. Ideally, therefore, there should be contracts entered into by the shareholders or sponsors with the lenders (or their agent) direct and they should contain a direct covenant to pay (or, perhaps, guarantee) in favour of the lenders (or their agent). This will not, however, always be acceptable to the shareholders or sponsors.

These agreements are sometimes referred to as 'cash deficiency agreements' and may give the shareholder or sponsor the option of subscribing for further equity or making loans to the project company. If the shareholder or sponsor is to be permitted to make loans to the project company, then these must be fully subordinated to the project loans and (preferably) unsecured. It would usually be the case that no interest would be payable on these loans until the project loans have been repaid in full or, perhaps, in circumstances where the project is meeting minimum cover ratios.

9.2.10   Collateral warranties

These are agreements entered into between the lenders and key individuals or firms providing advice and services to the project company. Most typically, these will be obtained from professional firms of architects, surveyors and engineers retained by the project company to advise it in connection with the project. The purpose of collateral warranties is to extend to the lenders the duty of care which the professional firm owes to the project company. Without this, the lenders may not have an enforceable right of recovery against a professional person to cover losses sustained by the lenders through the acts or omissions of the professional; they are, in effect, intended to confer the right for the lenders to sue the professionals directly. A related point for lenders to note in connection with collateral warranties is the right for lenders to be able to assign these collateral warranties in connection with any subsequent sale by the lenders following an enforcement, since subsequent purchasers will want to have the benefit of these rights against the professionals.

If these collateral warranties can be obtained from the professional team, then the lenders will usually go one step further and demand that they are made aware of the professional negligence insurance taken out by the professionals, which will have to be at a level acceptable to the lenders and maintained at that acceptable level (but obviously subject to availability).

Collateral warranties are not always sought by lenders, frequently due to the difficulty of obtaining them from professionals. Many professional bodies have now produced their own standard form letters and negotiating against these forms can be difficult and not very rewarding as the professionals have in many cases settled their respective forms with their insurers and, therefore, are most reluctant to change them. Faced with such difficulties, and where the lenders are taking security over all of the project company's assets (including, therefore, the rights to sue third parties), some lenders will seek to rely instead on inheriting rights of the project company against the professionals on an enforcement of the security.

9.2.11   Direct agreements

Direct agreements are a particularly important feature of most of those projects where the project company enters into important commercial agreements with third parties and, in practice, that means most projects. Their purpose is to protect the lenders against the loss of their investment if the project company defaults under one of the key contracts it has entered into (typically the concession agreement, main construction contract, long-term supply contract and any long-term offtake contract) such that termination of that contract is threatened. They are a relatively recent development of the last 12 or so years, although requiring third parties that have contractual relations with the project company to give undertakings direct to the lenders is nothing new: in the early oil and gas financing in the North Sea during the 1970s it was quite common to seek certain assurances from the other joint-venture parties in any particular licence area. The way in which these agreements developed is that, as part of the process of perfecting their security interest over the joint operating agreement amongst the participants in a particular licence area, the lenders would serve notice on either the operator of the field or each of the joint venturers, notifying them of the lenders' security interest and asking the operator to notify the lenders of any defaults etc before exercising any rights they may have to forfeit all or part of the interest of a defaulting participant.

As projects have become more complex, lenders and their advisers have focused more and more on the contractual relations between the project company and other third parties, particularly in those jurisdictions where it is not possible to take effective security over the whole of the project company's assets or where the lenders did not have the right to appoint a receiver over the project assets. These agreements have now almost taken on a life of their own and can be extremely complicated and difficult to negotiate. Typically, they will cover the following key points:

- Notice of the lenders' security will be given to the third party and, where required, consent given to the security by the third party.

- The third party will be required to notify the lenders (or their agent) of any default by the project company under the relevant project agreement.

- Upon such a default, the third party will be required to suspend any right it has to terminate the project agreement for a minimum period of, say, 28 days (suspension period).

- During this suspension period, the lenders have the right either to cure the default in question or to take over the rights of the project company by 'stepping in' to the project contract. Frequently, lenders will seek to place a maximum ceiling on their liabilities under the project contract.

- As an alternative to stepping in themselves, most direct agreements will afford the lenders the option of stepping in through another vehicle, often a lender-controlled company (the reason being that the lenders would prefer to distance themselves from a direct contractual relationship with the third party). However, it is likely that the third party would require the lenders to guarantee the step-in vehicle's liabilities under the project contract.

- The lenders would then be given the right to step out at any time should they not want to continue with their involvement in the project contract although, subject to performing all their obligations under the project contract during the step-in period after the lenders have stepped out, they would not incur any new liabilities in respect of the project contract.

- The lenders would also be given a further right of step-in upon the occurrence of a project loan agreement even of default independently of the third party's rights to terminate the project contract. (This is often referred to as the 'acceleration step-in'.)

- The third party would be asked to agree to waive rights of set-off or counterclaim against the project company which are not directly related to the project agreement in question.

■   In addition, other protections, such as convenants not to amend the project contract nor, where appropriate, to make payments of any sums due to the project company direct to the lenders or their agent, would be included where appropriate.

One can see from the scope of these undertakings sought from third parties that they can impose not insignificant obligations and liabilities on the third parties and direct agreements can frequently consume disproportionate amounts of time and effort during the negotiating of the project loan documentation. This is particularly the case where the third party and the project contract in question is only a small part of the overall contractual framework for a project. Many third parties are extremely reluctant to expose themselves to obligations of this type towards the lenders. One way of overcoming this, which is becoming more of an accepted practice, particularly in projects where there is a tender process, is the requirement for a direct agreement to be made a part of the tender documentation and perhaps even for a form of agreement to be included in the tender documentation. In this way, the project company has the comfort of knowing that the successful tenderer has committed itself to entering into the direct agreement required by its lenders.

Direct agreements can be extremely useful security tools in those jurisdictions where it is not possible to take effective security over all the project's assets.

9.2.12   Host government support

In some projects, particularly those in developing countries, lenders will often seek an additional layer of comfort from the host government. This may be part of the desire on the part of the lenders to reduce the political risk associated with the project, or it may be a desire on their part to secure particular contractual commitments in relation to certain aspects of the project. Many host governments will object to having to enter into contractual commitments with lenders (particularly foreign lenders) which are providing finance for a project, particularly where one of the desires of the host government is to pass on responsibility for the financing and implementation of the project to the private sector. Whether or not the lenders in a given project are able to obtain such support from the host government will depend on the relative bargaining strengths of the parties involved and (to a large extent) on whether similar projects have been successfully completed in the host country. For example, in the early days of North Sea oil and gas financing, certain undertakings were sought and obtained from the UK government with a view to assuring the private sector that the government would not exercise its powers arbitrarily or in a manner which could prejudice the financing arrangements. Over the years, as lenders have become more comfortable with the technology and risks associated with financing such projects in the North Sea, the UK government has substantially cut back on the scope of this support.

Where this support is obtained, it may extend to the following:

■   agreement that there will be no change of law that will have a material adverse effect on the project (for example, the introduction of new laws which require changes to the specifications of the project) – this is the non-discrimination principle;

■   a guarantee of the availability of foreign exchange to the project company in order to enable it to service its debt to the project lenders, particularly important where the project's income is in the local currency and the project debt is in another currency;

■   no expropriation/nationalisation without full compensation (including, at a minimum, the repayment of the project loans and related costs);

■   undertakings as to levels of taxation applicable to the project company and the project (again, the principle of non-discrimination);

- undertakings concerning non-imposition (or exclusion from) exchange controls; and

- guarantees that all consents and permits will be granted to the project company in order to enable it to complete and operate the project (subject, of course, to the project company complying with its obligations under the concession agreement or other appropriate agreement).

Often, the most sensitive area is taxation, where most governments will object strenuously to having their hands tied as to future taxation policies. Similarly, governments do not as a rule like to be told that they cannot change laws. One compromise that is often acceptable is that the host government will agree to such constraints on its powers on a non-discriminatory basis, in other words it will not, in exercising its taxation or legislative powers, discriminate against the project and/or the project company on an individual basis.

9.2.13 Comfort letters

Strictly speaking a comfort letter is a letter acknowledging a moral but not a legally enforceable obligation. However, there is no standard text for a comfort letter and at one end of the spectrum they confer no legally enforceable rights whereas at the other end of the spectrum they can confer legally enforceable rights.

Comfort letters generally arise in a project financing when lenders or other project participants wish to obtain a guarantee or other legally binding commitment from either a host government or the shareholder(s) of the project company or any of the other project parties but are unable to obtain this. There may be any number of reasons why a host government or shareholder will not want to give a guarantee or other legally binding commitment. For example, they may be restricted by banking covenants in other loan documentation, or they may need to obtain exchange control or other government consents, or they may be restricted by the terms of their statutes from giving such guarantee or other legally binding commitments, or they may wish to keep the guarantee or other legally binding commitments off their balance sheet, or they may simply not be prepared for sound commercial reasons to give a legally binding commitment of the type requested.

If the lenders are unsuccessful in persuading the project party to issue a guarantee or other legally binding commitment, then they may succeed with a comfort letter. As noted above, there are, essentially, two types of comfort letter. The first type of comfort letter will be phrased in fairly clear and unambiguous terms and will contain obligations that are enforceable in the courts. For example, and assuming that the essential elements of the formation of contract exist (such as consideration and an intention to create legal relations), the following are obligations that are capable of being enforced:

- '. . . so long as the project company is indebted to you under the project loan agreement we will not sell or dispose of or create any encumbrance over, any of our shares in the project company';

- '. . . it is our policy to ensure that [the project company] and our other subsidiaries are at all times in a position to meet their [financial] obligations'.

If, however, the second obligation had been phrased in terms of '. . . it is our current policy to ensure . . .' then the position would be quite different and, indeed, the English Court of Appeal in *Kleinwort Benson v Malaysian Mining Corpn Berhad* ([1988] 1 WLR 799) held that, although the comfort letter in question (which was in these terms) evidenced an intention to create contractual relations, the content of the comfort letter (and in particular the statement as to current policy) did not amount to a promise as to future conduct. This case clearly illustrates that the parties wishing to rely on comfort letters in legal proceedings are faced with two hurdles, namely (a) to prove that there is a contractual intention, and (b) to prove that the nature of the promise in the comfort letter is such that it can give grounds for a breach. The bank in the *Kleinwort Benson* case fell at the second hurdle as the court found that the terms of the letter were merely a statement of present fact and were not sufficient to amount to a promise regarding future conduct.

While the *Kleinwort Benson* case represents the current position on comfort letters under English law, it is not necessarily the case that this line of reasoning would be followed in other jurisdictions. For example, the Australian courts have criticised the decision of the Court of Appeal in this case and have suggested that it is inappropriate in the context of a comfort letter to subject it to minute textual analysis. Instead, it is suggested that more attention is paid to the circumstances surrounding the giving of the letter of comfort. Other jurisdictions may take a similar approach to the interpretation of comfort letters.

One of the problems with comfort letters is that, due to their essentially concessionary nature, they often quite deliberately contains unclear or ambiguous wording in an attempt to keep both parties happy. This can, and frequently does, lead to problems later on when events occur that cause the bank or other project party to seek to rely on the statement given in the comfort letter. Many comfort letters end up being a mixture of obligations, some of which are clearly unenforceable and some of which may be enforceable. Inevitably, there is a dilemma for the parties in agreeing the terms of a comfort letter. If the terms are too precise and clear then they run the risk of giving rise to the same problems that the rejected guarantee gave rise to. If, on the other hand, the terms are ambiguous and unclear, then they almost certainly will only constitute a moral obligation at best. What is clear, however, is that both parties should take legal advice to ensure that they understand the legal implications in the relevant jurisdiction of the terms of the comfort letter.

9.2.14 Governing law

As has been noted earlier, the issue of which governing law should govern a particular project agreement can be a controversial issue. Lenders, understandably, prefer to see an independent law, such as English or New York, applied to project agreements (especially loan documents), not only because of the neutrality issue, but also because it is felt that these legal systems are better equipped to deal with disputes concerning sophisticated project structures and documentation. However, although in many jurisdictions parties are free to choose the law that is to govern a particular contract, in the case of security documents it is crucial that the security interest in question over the project assets is properly and effectively documented according to the project asset's 'governing law', which, in very broad terms, is as follows:

Type of asset	Country of governing law
Land and buildings	Country in which they are located
Registered assets: eg registered vessels, shares, patents	Country of registration
Physical chattels and also negotiable instruments	Country where they are physically located on the date of mortgage
Benefit of a contract, including receivables	Country where the governing law of contract applies

9.2.15 Insurance protection for lenders

In order to cover themselves effectively against as many of the risks mentioned in Chapter 6, Legal considerations to project finance, as possible, the lenders will look to take the action set out immediately below and will usually require that each of the elements is in place.

Insurance advisers

In most large projects, the lenders will appoint a firm of internationally recognised insurance brokers to act for them in providing specialist advice on the scope and level of insurances applicable for the project. A detailed insurances memorandum will be entered into between the lenders and the project company (or whoever is responsible for undertaking the insurances for the project), which will spell out the minimum insurance obligations at all stages of the project.

Security assignment

As part of the security package, the lenders would expect to receive an assignment by way of security of the all right, title and interest of the borrower to all project insurances or, where the insurances are arranged by the contractor or another party, then a security assignment from this party. Notice of this assignment will be given to the insurers in the usual manner.

Loss payable clauses

A 'loss payable' clause will be endorsed onto each of the policies. This clause will stipulate that the proceeds of any claim (usually above a certain minimum threshold) are to be paid to (or to the order of) the lenders. Because of the uncertainty as to the exact legal characterisation of loss payable clauses, they are rarely relied upon without a formal security assignment.

Co-insurance

It is possible under English law to insure in the names of both the project company and the lenders or, alternatively, to note the lender as a co-insured on the policy. This has the advantage that protection for some of the previously mentioned risks falls away. For example, if there has been a breach of warranty by the project company, it is unlikely that the lenders will be aware of such breach; in these circumstances, the insurers should have no ground to resist a lender's claim. Because the lender's insurable interest is expressed as a separate interest to that of the project company's, it is thought that under English common law principles a policy should not be tainted with any non-disclosure or misrepresentation by the project company with respect to the policy. However, where so much may turn on the policy validity most lenders are reluctant to rely simply on the common law, since it could always be argued that where only one party arranges the insurances that party is in effect acting as agent for the other party and that, accordingly, each party is affected by non-disclosure or misrepresentation. It is therefore safer to combine a co-insurance provision with an express endorsement on the policy whereby the insurer acknowledges that non-disclosure or misrepresentation by one party should not affect the other.

Broker's undertaking

This is an undertaking delivered by the broker (of the project company) to the lenders regarding the insurances and forms an essential part of the overall security package for lenders. The terms are a matter of negotiation between the broker and the lenders, however, standard forms have been produced for these undertakings in the market. Typically, the following undertakings would be asked of the brokers:

■ to have on each and every insurance policy agreed endorsements together with a copy of the notices(s) of assignment to the insurer signed by an authorised signatory of the project company and acknowledged by the insurers;

■ to pay to the facility agent without any set-off or deduction of any kind for any reason any and all proceeds from the insurances received by them from the insurers (except as might be otherwise permitted in the relevant loss payable and notice of cancellation clauses);

■ to advise the facility agent;

– at least 30 days (or such lesser period, if any, as may be specified from time to time in the case of war risks and kindred perils) before

• cancellation of any of the insurances is to take effect, and

• any alteration to termination or expiry of any of the insurances is to take effect;

– of any default in the payment of any premium for any of the insurances prior to any cancellation or lapse of cover which may then arise;

– at least 30 days prior to the expiry of the insurances if they have not received renewal instructions from the project company and/or any jointly insured parties or the agents of any such party and, if they receive instructions to renew, to advise the facility agent as soon as reasonably practicable of the details thereof; and

– of any act or omission or of any event of which they have knowledge and which might invalidate or render unenforceable in whole or in part any of the insurances as soon as reasonably practicable on becoming aware of the same;

■ to disclose to the insurers any fact, change of circumstance or occurrence material to the risks insured against under the insurance promptly when they become aware of such fact, change of circumstance or occurrence;

■ to treat as confidential all information marked as or otherwise stated to be confidential and supplied to them by any person for the purposes of disclosure to the insurers under the insurances and not to disclose, without the written consent of that person, such information to any third party other than the insurers under the insurances in satisfaction of their undertaking in the previous paragraph;

■ to hold the insurance slips or contracts, the policies and any renewals thereof or any new or substitute policies (in the case of new or substitute policies, issued only with the facility agent's consent), to the order of the facility agent;

■ to notify the facility agent at least 30 days or such lesser period as shall be practicable prior to ceasing to act as brokers to the project company or, if impracticable, promptly following their ceasing so to act; and

■ to use all reasonable endeavours to ensure that if any of the insurances are on a claims made basis that such policies of such insurances are endorsed to provide cover for at least eight years after the expiry or cancellation of such policies or that alternative arrangements are made in order to achieve an equivalent result.

9.2.16 Completion issues

In many projects, particularly infrastructure projects, one of the key milestones will be when the project achieves 'completion'. This will mark the end of the development and construction phase of the project and the start of the operational phase. The significance of this milestone is that one of the key risks, namely construction risks, will be substantially reduced once completion has occurred. In recognition of this reduction in risk it is often the case that the interest rate will be reduced following completion (assuming everything else is going to plan).

This milestone also marks the time when the project should be moving into its income generating phase and therefore the repayment schedule will usually be triggered by the occurrence of completion.

The completion test for most infrastructure projects will usually comprise at least three elements:

- the completion of the infrastructure in accordance with the design specifications (sometimes referred to as mechanical or plant completion);

- evidence that the technology works; and

- the satisfaction of a number of performance related tests to establish that the equipment or plant operates at, or in excess of, its design capacity levels.

It will also usually be stipulated that completion will not occur unless or until the project company has furnished evidence that all consents and authorisations for the equipment or plant to enter into commercial projection have been granted.

One of the key issues concerning the completion test will be the actual manner in which the completion test is treated as being satisfied. The lenders will usually seek to stipulate that completion will only be treated as having occurred when the lenders' engineer is satisfied that the various elements of the completion test have been met and he has issued a certificate to the lenders to this effect. The project company, on the other hand, will seek to impose the influence of its engineer in determining the completion test. Given the significance of this milestone for the lenders it is not usually acceptable to them to allow control of this milestone to be left with the project company and its engineers. One compromise that is often agreed is that the two engineers will meet to determine whether the completion test has been satisfied and if they agree it has been satisfied then the lenders' engineer will issue the completion certificate. With this compromise the lenders' engineer is still left in control of the process but what is removed is any discretionary or subjective element.

9.3 PFI: IMPORTANT TERMS

9.3.1 Contract duration

The proper duration of a PFI contract is an issue of some importance. Too long a period could be challenged by the European Commission on the basis that competition has been restricted. However, long periods may be justified on the basis that this facilitates the best financing arrangements, for instance financing payments may be lower if the contract lasts at least as long as the life of the longest available debt finance. Tenderers would be concerned to make a return on their investment by the end of the project and to be put in a position where they can retender the project at the end of the concession period. Many contracts provide for break clauses, giving the contractor or the government the right to terminate the contract, either so as to incentivise the contractor or after a certain period of time, eg after the expiry of the debt associated with the contract.

In some projects, the government body has asked tenders to submit bids in respect of different contract durations so as to enable it to consider various options as to the optimum time of the contract.

9.3.2 Contract price

Complete non-performance is often quite a remote risk. However, since the government authority is often under a public duty to provide the services or the works which are the subject matter of the PE contract, it is concerned to ensure that the contractor performs its duty properly. Persistent minor failures are perceived as a bigger problem than significant failures. The solution is to link performance to payment, for example by providing incentives for good performance and penalties for poor performance. Most PE contracts split payment into two parts: an availability or usage payment and a performance-related payment. This will be structured in a way to suit the particular project.

Hospital and prison projects are often linked to availability so that penalty points are incurred if a particular part of the facilities is not available. Performance-related payment can be structured so that performance is assumed to be 100 per cent unless the government body issues a fault notice in the delivery of any of the services. An appropriate dispute resolution mechanism should be included.

In the roads sector, payment for operating and management is also split into two parts. The first component is linked to the usage of the road in the form of a shadow toll. The formula is kilometres of road length multiplied by the volume of traffic every year. There is no payment over a certain volume. The second component is a performance-related adjustment in terms of which the amount payable is reduced depending on the amount of lane closure charges (the level of the charge depends on the time it occurs, the number of hours it is closed for and the normal volume of traffic for that particular road) and safety performance systems (the cost of personal injury accidents prevented by the safety improvement). Again, a penalty point system is used.

These contracts commonly stipulate all the breaches which could attract a penalty point in an annex and the maximum number of points that can be awarded for a particular breach. The government agency's representative can decide whether or not to award points and the number of points to be awarded, subject to the maximum. For example, a recent water and sewage project contract stipulated that performance events considered minor enough by the government authority could be waived.

In some such projects, the government authority has been given the option to terminate the contract if the contractor reached a certain level of penalty points for three years in a row. As an alternative, the government agency could be given the right to step up the level of monitoring once the contractor reached a particular number of points and to recover the costs of such increased monitoring from the contractor. Yet another technique is to provide for warning notices to be served once a particular number of points have been accumulated or once a particularly serious breach occurs (for instance, a breach of safety provisions) and for termination once a certain number of warning notices have been served. In addition, the parties can provide for the government agency to have a right to step in and remedy a defect which is the subject of a warning notice if the contractor does not do so within a specified period of time.

Payments for over-congested roads have now been linked to availability rather than usage. Usage cannot increase any more, so the contractor would always be able to achieve the maximum usage level. Instead, payments are adjusted according to availability criteria. Payment for constructing the roads has also been constructed in such a way as to incentivise the constructor to comply with contractual requirements. For example, once a particular amount of building work is complete, the levels of payments will be stepped up significantly. These incentives may be accompanied by huge disincentives if the contractor fails to meet the construction programme.

The price of certain PFI projects may have to be structured in such a way as to take account of the regulatory regime which governs those particular types of contracts. For example, in the water industry in the UK, the public provider is under an obligation to comply with the Water Regulator's price fixing and the private contractor's tender price has to be structured in such a way as to enable the project to comply with the Regulator's requirements.

When a contract continues over a long period of time, the government body will be concerned that the money it pays for the services compares favourably with the market rates. For example, a recent NHS project provides for market testing and benchmarking to assess ongoing value for money. Market testing is the retendering of the project after contract award. If it transpires that the price being paid is uncompetitive, the contractor may be obliged to change its sub-contractors. Benchmarking is the requirement to rebid every five years at competitive market rates, which may mean that the fixed price will be adjusted. If no price can be agreed upon after benchmarking, the contractor may be compelled to market test.

9.3.3 Performance regime

Most of the PFI contracts in the UK incorporated detailed specifications setting out the required performance standards. They may describe what method should be adopted to achieve a particular result (called input specification) and/or the service level that has to be achieved (output specification). These requirements may in turn be divided into 'core' and 'illustrative' requirements. The core requirements would be the characteristics which the government agency regards as essential and for which an alternative would not be acceptable, for example, in the case of roads projects the requirement to provide a safe road. The illustrative requirements would be a benchmark for tenderers in respect of which there would be room for negotiation. Illustrative requirements would become fixed at the time of the contract signing.

An over-emphasis on input requirements makes the specifications very detailed and leaves little room for innovation, whereas an over-emphasis on output requirements asks tenderers to do more work themselves. Which approach should be adopted will depend on the tenderers' appetite for risk on new technologies and the ability of the government agency to analyse and compare the different types of tenders effectively.

One method of giving the contractor comfort that it will be able to meet the output requirements is the Design and Certification Procedure set out in the Model DBFO contract in the UK's roads projects. Certification can be used at various stages of the project: before the works have started (to ensure that conditions precedent have been met), for complex elements of the works, to confirm compliance after completion of a particular phase, for material changes and where the governmental authority's statutory functions would be affected (eg if roads have to be closed). These certificates should be drawn up by professionals according to professional standards and the professionals should assume the risk of professional liability.

9.3.4 Performance guarantees

Performance guarantees have been less common in UK PFI projects than in private sector construction projects. In roads projects, performance bonds have to be put in place for the early years of the contract when the cost of retendering and rectifying the consequences of the breach would exceed the positive value of the works completed to date. The bond would be released upon the issue of a final permit to use, or upon the contractor having made a particular level of investment or on completion of a particular phase of works.

Alternatively, it may make sense to require a performance bond or performance guarantee in the middle of a project, so that where the works completed were small compared with the extent of the maintenance required at a later stage, the contract could require a performance bond or guarantee to be put in place in (say) year 20.

9.3.5 Warranties and indemnities

There is no discernible trend in the lists of warranties and indemnities included in UK PFI contracts. Government agencies will be concerned to extract maximum comfort from the contractor and ensure as wide a scope as possible for the exclusion clauses applicable to itself (subject to the requirements of law as to reasonableness, etc).

9.3.6 Change mechanisms

PFI contracts are long-term contracts which provide for continuing performance by one party to another who is in the public sector and who has to fulfil certain public duties. In contracts of this length, it is advisable to provide for mechanisms to deal with change over time. There may be changes in the law, changes in regulation and market movements that increase costs to the contractor. The nature of the project will determine the level of market risk taken on by the contractor. There is generally very little risk in hospital projects, but a greater level of risk in IT or telecommunications projects, where technology and an increase in competition are more likely to drive down costs. Contract provisions should stipulate clearly the list of events which will trigger a request for a change, a related procedure and a dispute resolution mechanism. The clauses should be such that the risk matrix is not altered radically so as to affect the project's bankability. The change provisions should be scrutinised by the funders.

In the roads projects in the UK, variations to the specification of the contract, additional works, changes in law which do not result in a right to terminate and changes in user paid tolls are defined as 'eligible changes' which trigger a 'general change procedure'. The procedures require the parties to calculate the impact of the change on the costs of the project and usually involve amendments to the financial model. It is in the interests of the government party to narrow the changes in law provisions to legislative changes (in secondary and primary legislation and in EU directives). It is generally thought to be too onerous to include changes in law resulting from changes in case law.

9.3.7 Delays

Most PFI contracts make detailed provision for delay. Without such provision, common law damages (which may be inappropriate in that they do not reflect the parties' respective assumption of risk correctly) will apply. Delays can be either party's fault or can be the result of something not within their control, eg force majeure. From a contractor's point of view, a delay on the part of the government agency, for instance a failure to provide site access on time, is extremely expensive if the contract price is payable by reference to performance achievements. Accordingly, many tenderers have insisted on compensation for delay being built into each contract. Although some events are within the project company's control, such as cost overruns and inadequacy of design, others are not, and it is here that the contractor and the government agency will have to work out which will bear responsibility for a particular risk. In the case of force majeure, the contract may provide for an extension of the contract period and eventually termination with compensation.

9.3.8 Remedies

It is generally in the public sector's interests not to impose penalties for defaults in a heavy-handed manner. Accordingly, PFI contracts in the UK have usually contained some form of flexibility, allowing for agreements to continue even if an event of default happens which is serious enough to warrant termination. Apart from the right to step in contained in the direct agreement (mentioned above), the Model DBFO contract contains, for example, the remedy of payment suspension, appropriation of retention account sums, suspension of part of the functions and termination at various stages. These remedies can be used individually or in combination and provide the government agency with considerable scope in deciding how to deal with events of default. They are discussed further as follows:

■   **Payment suspension**   Payment suspension is the most effective remedy. It has an immediate financial impact on the contractor, it means that the banks will bring considerable pressure to bear on the contractor and it need not be directly correlated with the extent of the default. The main disadvantage is that without cash the number of defaults is likely to increase. A solution is to provide credit to the contractor for work done during the period of suspension of payments. The contract can also provide for the retention account, set up to hold moneys as security for performance of the hand-back obligations, to be applied towards outstanding liabilities following an event of default. This method of dealing with an event of default has been less controversial than payment retention.

■   **Performance suspension**   Suspension of part of the contractor's functions is a variant of the step-in provisions found in direct agreements. This remedy entitles the government agency to perform part of the contractor's functions itself or to get others to do it and is essential where the government authority has a statutory obligation to carry out the service. Government agencies have been concerned not to have to prove a link between the particular default and the step-in it proposes to perform – such a burden may have delayed its ability to step in to such an extent that the right becomes valueless. However, this is an extreme remedy to be exercised only when necessary.

■   **Termination**   As in standard loan documentation, insolvency, non-permitted change in control, material disposals, failure to satisfy conditions precedent, repudiatory breaches and non-payment within the agreed grace period all give rise to an immediate right to terminate the agreement. Remediable breaches become subject to an immediate right of termination if not remedied within a specified period. Such an event can occur before or after the commencement date, ie the date on which all conditions are satisfied. The Model DBFO contract provides for pre-commencement costs to be paid if termination happens before commencement. Those costs are limited and include the cost of preparatory work, eg investigations and surveys, liabilities in respect of costs consequent upon the termination, financing charges other than principal or default interest and swap termination amounts.

If termination happens after the commencement date, compensation will be paid in respect of the financing and other liabilities and the 'equity' or project value. The financing costs commonly cover principal (unlike pre-commencement termination), interest, breakage costs and swap termination and the government agency may successfully negotiate a cap to these liabilities (in case the finance arrangements are amended later on and the risk on termination is different from what was previously expected). Under 'other liabilities' would be grouped liability arising from exposure to third parties associated with the project and from the termination. The government department will be concerned to define what 'associated with the project' means and include a shopping list of liabilities not covered, eg borrowing not applied in the project, liability in respect of loss of profit for work not executed and the contractor's tax liabilities.

The Model DBFO contract provides that 'equity' or project value compensation is only available if the termination does not occur because of force majeure. If the contractor is not a listed company, compensation will consist of a lump sum payment based on the fair market value of the ordinary shares. Special provision may be made for other types of security, such as preference shares. If the company is listed, the assessment of compensation involves a complex calculation representing the drop in value of the shares as a result of the default. This aspect of the compensation provisions has been criticised on the basis that it over-compensates the contractor who has not completed the project at the time of termination. Two alternative ways in which to structure this compensation would be to refer to the actual costs incurred or to future payments under the contract.

9.3.9 Subcontractors

Government agencies have been concerned to ensure that the sub-contractors comply with the provisions of their contracts with the contractor. Accordingly, the Model DBFO contract requires the contractor to procure that its sub-contractors implement effective quality management systems and perform their obligations. The insolvency of a sub-contractor or the disposal of most of its assets, where this would have a material effect on the ability of the contractor to perform, is an event of default in most PFI contracts.

9.3.10 Transfer of interests in land

The property issues in a PFI project need to be considered carefully at the outset. What right will the contractor have in the completed road or building? The contractor could be a mere licensee (ie no interest in land is passed), or a lessee or a freehold owner. The lessee structure would also include an underlease to the government agency or department. This is because there would be joint occupation of the asset, for example in the case of a school, where the school would carry on educational functions and the concession company would be responsible for the maintenance and upkeep of the building it constructed. The lease would provide for an automatic termination on the termination of the concession agreement.

The licence structure is most commonly chosen in the case of road projects. It is not possible to create a property interest, because common law rights over highways are for the public to pass and repass.

The disadvantage of the lessee structure is that there is uncertainty as to the position of the tenant. Under the Landlord and Tenant Act 1954, the tenant would after a period of time be a protected tenant (whatever the position of the landlord), but government bodies often do not have the authority to grant leases over their property. One solution is to apply for a court order that the Landlord and Tenant Act does not apply. In addition, the government body should be granted an underlease of the whole property so that they always have access to all areas (even those operated by the contractors, eg in the case of hospitals, non-clinical areas such as the shop and car park) so as to ensure that the granting of the lease is not ultra vires in that it restricts their access to the property. The concession company would then be appointed as managing agent of those non-clinical areas, a provision that would probably not fall foul of ultra vires requirements.

The problem with the freehold route is how to ensure that the asset or assets come back into government hands at the end of the concession period or if the company defaults. The solution most commonly adopted is to give the public sector an option over the property. This has to be carefully drafted to avoid problems with the perpetuity rule arising. The other disadvantage of becoming a freeholder from the contractor's point of view is that it then takes on the risk of environmental liabilities. If the arm of government involved is a local authority, it must additionally show that it has obtained the best price available for the land (Local Government Act 1972 s 123).

9.3.11 Problems associated with local government PFI

Local government PFI has not taken off to the same extent as PFI for other projects. The main reason for this is the unacceptable legal risk associated with these projects. It was not clear that local authorities had the power to enter into some of the contracts typically encountered in a PFI transaction. The protections of the Companies Act 1985 s 35 are not available. As statutory bodies, they could only do such things as were expressly or impliedly authorised by Parliament, including functions ancillary to their main function (s 111 of the Local Government Act 1972). These fears were augmented when the Court of Appeal decided that Credit Suisse could not recover £17m of loans made to Allerdale and Waltham Forest councils, because the two authorities acted outside their powers in guaranteeing the loans to the contractors.

These concerns were partially addressed in the Local Authorities (Contracts) Bill, which was expected to come into force in the autumn of 1999. Local authorities were empowered to certify that the contracts they enter into come within their powers, but that does not make the transaction immune from attack by way of judicial or audit review. In the case of such a successful challenge, the 'discharge terms' of the contract shall remain enforceable. It is up to the parties to draft the discharge terms in such a way as to account for the risk that the contract will be declared void for lack of authority which is the same as the risk that the local authority has issued the certificate incorrectly.

In addition, funding from central government could initially only be obtained on specific request. Automatic funding is now available, provided that the contract structure test in the Local Authority (Capital Finance) Regulations has been satisfied.

Index

Index

Documentation—*contd*
  credit, 201
  due diligence, 200-207
  employees, 203-204
  equipment, 205
  feasibility studies. *See* FEASIBILITY
      STUDIES
  financial statements, 206
  governing law, 177-178, 199, 218
  government, 205-206
  guarantees, 195-196
  insurance coverage, 202
  intellectual property, 204
  inventory, 205
  legal opinions, 194
  letter of information, 61
  letters of credit, 195-196
  litigation, 201-202
  participation agreement, 192-194
  patents, 204
  plant, 205
  project,
      bank accounts, 172-173
  purchase agreement assignment, 188
  real estate, 205
  signing, 61
  tax indemnification agreement, 188-192
  trademarks, 204
  trust, 184-187
      indenture of, 187-188
  types of, 200-207
Due diligence
  accounting, 206
  checklist, 207
  contracts, material, 202-203
  corporate documents, 200-201
  credit, 201
  documents, 200-207
  employee matters, 203-204
  equipment, 205
  financial statements, 206
  general, 206-207
  governmental, 205-206
  insurance, 202
  intellectual property, 204
  inventory, 205
  litigation, 201-202
  patents, 204
  plant, 205
  real estate, 205
  reports, 200-207
  tax documents, 204-205
  trademarks, 204

Economics. See INVESTMENT APPRAISAL
Emerging markets
  financing, 2
  restructuring risk, 2
Energy
  bankable proposal form, 128
  economically recoverable reserves, 22-23

Energy—*contd*
  economically recoverable reserves—*contd*
    extent of, 63
  efficiency,
    costs of, calculating, 33-36
    investment appraisal, 51-53
  risk,
    input, 18
    market, 20-21
    offtake, 21
    production, 22-23
    reserve, 22-23
    sales, 21
    supply, 18
  take-or-pay contract, 22, 168
Environmental
  bankable proposal form, 128
  costs checklist, 20
  improvements, 128
  legislation, compliance with, 66
  risks, 19-20
Equipment
  contract, 160-167
Equity investors
  role of, 7
Experts
  appointment of, 173
  payment of, 173
Export credit agencies
  role of, 8

Facility agent
  role of, 6
Feasibility studies
  added value potential, 66
  contents, 63-67
  costs,
    calculation of, 31-36
    construction, 64
    development, 64
    projection of, 66
    site, 64
  country risks insurance, 67
  currency controls, 66-67
  due diligence. *See* DUE DILIGENCE
  environmental legislation, 66
  foreign exchange,
    barriers, 65
    controls, 66-67
  government permits, 65-66
  import barriers, 65
  insurance, 67
  major issues, 63-67
  markets, accessibility of, 65
  operating licences, 65-66
  passenger flows, 64
  permits, 65-66
  pre-development agreements, 159
  raw material supplies, 65
  reserves, 63
  returns, projection of, 66